Ethics and Process
in
The Narrative Study
of Lives

Volume 4

The Narrative Study of Lives

The purpose of this Series is to publish studies of actual lives in progress, studies that use qualitative methods of investigation within a theoretical context drawn from psychology or other disciplines. The aim is to promote the study of lives and life history as a means of examining, illuminating, and spurring theoretical understanding. *The Narrative Study of Lives* will encourage longitudinal and retrospective in-depth studies of individual life narratives as well as theoretical consideration of innovative methodological approaches to this work.

Guidelines for authors:

The editors invite submissions of original manuscripts of up to 35 typed pages in the areas described above. As a publication of an interdisciplinary nature, we welcome authors from all disciplines concerned with narratives, psychobiography, and life-history. In matters of style, we encourage any creative format that best presents the work. Long quotations in the protagonists' voices are desirable as well as discussion of the author's place in the study.

References and footnotes should follow the guidelines of the *Publication Manual of the American Psychological Association* (4th ed.). A separate title page should include the chapter title and the author's name, affiliation, and address. Please type the entire manuscript, including footnotes and references, double-spaced, and submit three copies to:

Ruthellen Josselson, Ph.D., Co-Editor
The Narrative Study of Lives
Department of Psychology
Towson State University
Towson, MD 21204

Ethics and Process
Volume 4
of
THE NARRATIVE STUDY OF LIVES

Ethics and Process
▪ *in* ▪
The Narrative Study
of Lives

Ruthellen Josselson
editor

The Narrative Study of Lives ▪ Volume 4

SAGE Publications
International Educational and Professional Publisher
Thousand Oaks London New Delhi

For information address:

SAGE Publications, Inc.
2455 Teller Road
Thousand Oaks, California 91320
E-mail: order@sagepub.com

SAGE Publications Ltd.
6 Bonhill Street
London EC2A 4PU
United Kingdom

SAGE Publications India Pvt. Ltd.
M-32 Market
Greater Kailash I
New Delhi 110 048 India

Printed in the United States of America

Library of Congress Cataloging-in-Publication Data

ISBN 0-7619-0236-8 (cloth); ISBN 0-7619-0237-6 (paper)

ISSN 1072-2777

This book is printed on acid-free paper.

96 97 98 99 10 9 8 7 6 5 4 3 2 1

Contents

Introduction

*I*n her analysis of the ethical dilemmas of journalism, Janet Malcolm (1990) begins with the following shocking and candid observation:

> Every journalist who is not too stupid or too full of himself to notice what is going on knows that what he does is morally indefensible. . . . The catastrophe suffered by the subject is no simple matter of an unflattering likeness or a misrepresentation of his views; what pains him, what rankles and sometimes drives him to extremes of vengefulness, is the deception that has been practiced on him. On reading the article or book in question, he has to face the fact that the journalist—who seemed so friendly and sympathetic, so keen to understand him fully, so remarkably attuned to his vision of things—never had the slightest intention of collaborating with him on his story but always intended to write a story of his own. The disparity between what seems to be the intention of an interview as it is taking place and what it actually turns out to have been in aid of always comes as a shock to the subject. (p. 3)

As a narrative researcher, I must ask—can the same be said of the work we do? For we, too, collect interviews for the purpose of shaping them into our own story about them. What are the ethics we can hold to in order to morally defend our work? And how can we take account of the fact that our work will have effects beyond our intentions in doing it?

When we listen to another's story, our intention is to bring our own interpretation to the material. Even if we ask our participants to corroborate our interpretation, it is still our interpretive framework that structures understanding. As with any work, each observer interprets from his or her own meaning-making horizon. This is the essence of a reflexive hermeneutic stance. But only rarely do we write lives in a way that fully recognizes our role as inventors of the questions we pose, shapers of the contexts we study, and coparticipants in our interviews and in their interpretation (Fine, 1995). The mores of publication in most social science journals still require the observer to remain in the shadows. Although our work may be born on hermeneutic soil, it may yet be understood by our participants as well as our readers on positivistic ground, as though we are defining a preexisting reality in some so-called objective sense—which is, after all, the dominant epistemology of the 20th century. Our participants may regard us as trying to be objective when, in fact, we purport to do no such thing.

Phillip Steedman (1991) makes the point that if Puccini were to come back to life and protest current interpretations of *Tosca,* Steedman would reply to him, "Tormented shade, you plainly know a lot about *Tosca* but what we have is libretto and score; your *unique* role was in creating the work but now you, like us, are one of its interpreters" (p. 59).

In narrative work, we are engaged in an interpretive enterprise in every phase of the work. We recognize that there is no observer-free science and that accounts of objects are never independent of the observer (Denzin & Lincoln, 1994; Gergen & Gergen, 1991). But in that we are making use of real people to inform us and in that we are writing about real people to demonstrate our understandings, how can we take an ethical position in regard to both our participants and our science at the same time?

There are no easy answers to these questions. Merely waving flags about confidentiality and anonymity is a superficial, unthoughtful response. And the concept of *informed consent* is a bit oxymoronic, given that participants can, at the outset, have only the vaguest idea of what they might be consenting to. Doing this work, then, requires that we find a way to encompass contradictions and make our peace with them.

One inherent and indelible contrast between us and our participants is that although we interrogate their specificity in quest of what may be generalizable, their interest remains lodged in understanding their own uniqueness (Hermans & Bonarius, 1991). We write, as scholars, *for* our peers *about* our participants. But our participants remain free to read what we have written about them—to react and to make use of it for their own purposes. In addition, our knowing or writing about our participants' lives may expose them to consequences that neither we nor they could have foreseen.

Our narrative about doing narrative research must recognize its dangers and its pitfalls; our search must be for a way to contain this awareness rather than to silence it. Mishler (1990) suggests that we rely on Kuhn's prescription of *exemplars* for working toward new paradigms of inquiry:

> Those of us engaged in inquiry-guided and interpretive
> forms of research have the task of articulating and clarifying
> the features and methods of our studies, of showing how the
> work is done . . . so that together we can develop a community
> with shared exemplars through which we confirm and
> validate our collective work. (p. 423)

This volume is an effort to offer examples of the ideological, moral, emotional, and practical complexities that attend the doing of narrative research.

This is, and is intended to be, a daring volume. I have invited those who expose others' lives to expose themselves—the process of their work and their thoughts and feelings, their anxieties and concerns while doing it. I have asked them to say in print what is usually said only in private if it is said at all, whispered behind the hand, in Gwen Etter-Lewis's image.

First, I want to thank the contributors to this volume for their candor and courage in taking up this task. These senior researchers (from psychology, sociology, anthropology, psychoanalysis, philosophy, and oral history, from the United States, Israel, Canada, England, and the Netherlands) are here willing to reveal the struggles and worries that accompany them on their journeys into narrative representation. As a result, this volume attempts to be a real conversation about the doing of narrative research. The contributors have written in response to my invitation to speak from their own experience, to tell about the ethical and procedural dilemmas they have faced and how they have come to terms with them and to share what has been unexpected or troubling in their work. I hoped, in putting together this volume, to get beyond the usual ethical pieties and idealized procedures to the gritty realities that form both the challenge and the torment of working in a narrative framework.

Although I think all of the contributors adhere in the abstract to common values, they are not of the same mind when it comes to making tangible choices about procedure or even in how they reason about their work. This is a strength of this volume: Rather than camouflaging difference in lofty phrases, concrete divergences are apparent as these researchers tell how they think about—and do—their work. Especially on the problematic issue of who owns or controls the narrative, and what happens to it after the interview, researchers arrive at very different positions.

The first chapter is by David Bakan who, in many ways, provided the impetus for doing this volume. When we (Amia Lieblich, who is on leave for this issue, and I) first invited him to be on the editorial board of *The Narrative Study of Lives,* he raised a question about whether this work could ever be fully ethical in that it risked exposing sensitive aspects of real people's lives. In his contribution, he elaborates his concerns and sketches a way of thinking about and writing through a distinction between *literal* truth and *real* truth.

But we do write about literal others. We work with core aspects of people—data that are alive rather than inert. The next series of chapters in Part I are experiential accounts of narrative researchers who tell the stories of their struggles in doing this. These narratives are often intense and moving; all illuminate some of the dilemmas of trying to turn people's life stories into "science."

Dan Bar-On reveals his personal struggle as an Israeli Jew to bring himself to the study of children of Nazi perpetrators and documents his emotional journey over the course of his research, showing how the work affected him as well as those he interviewed.

Terri Apter, Susan Chase, and I are concerned with how what we write might be read by those we have written about. Terri Apter, in a soul-searching chapter, unmasks what she believes is the inherent cruelty in psychological research, including research that is based on narrative approaches. When we write about people who have offered us finely tuned, carefully balanced stories of themselves, both the context and proportion are lost. As a result, the written narrative is no longer emotionally true. Yet in the end, there is no escape from the fact that the psychologist controls the final product. Sharing these worries, I write about what I have learned from reinterviewing participants about how they have been affected by my writing about them. I try to understand the difficulties in raising these questions, and I locate the distress in the narcissistic tensions aroused by this kind of work.

Susan Chase, recognizing the personal vulnerability of participants in interview studies, writes about how she nevertheless claims her authority as an interpreter of the narratives she collects. Participants may not be conscious of social forces that operate in and through them, social forces that become apparent only when narratives are juxtaposed—and deciphering these is the task she authorizes herself to pursue. In her chapter, she maps the different layers of analysis that attend this work.

Pirkko Graves reflects on her concerns as she prepares a psycho-analytic case report for publication. In her contribution, she makes, among others, the important point that what we write about someone may be an aspect of themselves that, although conscious at the time they revealed it to us, may be re-repressed and no longer available or real to them by the time it sees print. Whereas what is written is static, life is always in process.

Gail Agronick and Ravenna Helson present an empirical, question-naire-based follow-up study of the effects of being written about that demonstrates that different people react differently to this experience. Indeed, it seems that those most intent on their own personal growth are the ones who take our observations most seriously.

Part II highlights how narrative researchers bring themselves to the inquiry, how they understand what they are doing, and how they position themselves vis-à-vis the participant. Mel Miller argues that dialogue is a form of ethics. Thus the "I-thou" exchange of narrative research is not only ethical but life enhancing for both the participant and the researcher. In his chapter, he offers examples of the change that has occurred in himself and his participants and wonders about the boundary between this work and psychotherapy.

Richard Ochberg reflects on the way in which his process of interpreting an interview centers on posing a question about the material that the interviewee may never ask. His orientation to interpretation is to focus on what is not being said. His position (and his purpose in doing his work) stands in opposition to that of Gwendolyn Etter-Lewis, writing from the point of view of an oral historian, who argues that a narrative and its interpretation belongs to the narrator. She writes about the particular challenges of collecting life histories from older African American women.

Part III details the aftereffects of the research on the researcher. Yoram Bilu writes a riveting account of how his ethnographic work was appropriated in ways he could never have imagined. A kind of postmodern detective story in form, his chapter shows that ethnographic work is often so much more than we think it is.

Amia Lieblich takes us behind the scenes of her narrative-based inquiry into a community. She narrates the twists and turns of her relationship with the people she studied and shows how this became a relationship without end.

Then I have included, in Part IV, the work of four doctoral students or recent PhD's, all in different fields, who write about what they are learning about doing narrative research. They write about the dilemmas they have faced from the threshold of a field that offers no clear guidelines in the literature that might have prepared them for what they would face. These contributors bring fresh eyes, the thrill of discovery, and a dash of idealism to their efforts to find a way to use narrative to explore the questions that interest them. Scott Webster, from the field of history, describes how he has found solutions to the problems inherent in interviewing the famous and almost famous. June Price, in nursing, describes the ethical and legal tangles she encountered in trying to interview mothers who have abused their children. In an evocative and amusingly written story, anthropology student Emanuela Guano describes how she learned that the anthropological interview is not necessarily what the textbooks say or the researcher intends. Last, Edna Lomsky-Feder, in sociology and anthropology, writes about the learning process she went through as a woman trying to interview Israeli combat veterans.

This volume concludes by moving onto more conceptual ground in Part V. George Rosenwald offers a provocative, integrative piece that critiques the ethics of "the mainstream" and argues for the inherent ethicality of a holistic approach to the study of lives. The hopefulness of his position serves, to my mind, as balm to some of the enigmas and entanglements the other authors lay bare.

Finally, Guy Widdershoven and Marie-Josée Smits, both ethicists, develop the intriguing idea that beyond the fact that narrative needs an ethics, ethics needs narrative. Their work helped me to understand that this volume is an effort to develop a narrative of the ethics of narrative.

As an editor, I am delighted with this volume. These are new, creative pieces that wade into uncharted waters. They are narratives about narrative, and they are written with the immediacy of experience. They read like the adventure stories they are.

I have encouraged these authors not to "conclude" things. The aim of this volume is to share and to instruct with the power of personal example. We hope to keep this dialogue open in future volumes.

RUTHELLEN JOSSELSON

References

Denzin, N., & Lincoln, Y. (1994). *Handbook of qualitative research*. Thousand Oaks: Sage.

Fine, M. (1995). *Disruptive voices*. Ann Arbor: University of Michigan Press.

Gergen, K., & Gergen, M. (1991). From theory to reflexivity in research practice. In F. Steir (Ed.), *Research and reflexivity*. London: Sage.

Hermans, H. J. M., & Bonarius, H. (1991). The person as co-investigator in personality research. *European Journal of Personality, 5*, 199-216.

Malcolm, J. (1990). *The journalist and the murderer*. New York: Knopf.

Mishler, E. (1990). Validation in inquiry-guided research: The role of exemplars in narrative studies. *Harvard Educational Review, 60*, 415-442.

Steedman, P. H. (1991). On the relations between seeing, interpreting and knowing. In F. Steir (Ed.), *Research and reflexivity*. London: Sage.

PART I

❦ 1 ❦

Some Reflections About Narrative
Research and Hurt and Harm

David Bakan

*W*hen Professors Josselson and Lieblich wrote to me about their proposed journal of the narrative study of lives, I replied with a misgiving. That misgiving is that narrative research, based on the real lives of people made public, converts what is private into public; can violate privacy; and can cause mental, legal, social, and financial hurt and harm.

The question came to my attention very forcibly some years ago when a young undergraduate student, who had transferred from another university, came to my office overwrought by humiliation and outrage. He waved a book on personality written by a professor whose class he had once been in at another university. I knew that professor personally. As part of the class work, the students had been required to participate in a study being conducted by that professor. The student was presented in the pages of the book as a "case" to make some point. The account contained some very personal information. The student was also deeply offended by the way he was characterized and typed in the presentation in the text. The identity of the student was thinly disguised. For the sake of the record, I would add that I arranged for a contact between that professor and the student, and the professor apologized and sought to make amends.

In my mind, as I read it, the presentation of the case contributed positively to the book. At the same time, I could not overlook the possibility of hurt and harm associated with this kind of reporting.

I have thought about this a lot, about such hurt and harm associated with psychological research. In my mind, I have fancied several scenarios, including legal ones. For example, suppose one's life story were in some published source. Suppose that one were involved in some kind of legal action in which character was important. Might such an account become evidentiary? Might not the author of such an account be compelled to testify? Even if there were a privilege with respect to clinical psychology—which some have called for—would it, or should it, extend to research psychology?

There is an issue here with respect to the value of the progress of science and the rights of persons who might allow their lives to be open for investigation for the sake of science.

Let me offer some considerations about the science of psychology.

Overall behavioristic, statistical and experimental research, the dominant form of psychological research in the academy in the past century, is mostly harmless. Sometimes, when I lecture on the history of psychology, I express gratitude on behalf of society at large to John B. Watson for his behaviorism, notwithstanding all of my criticisms of it. There are two things to be grateful for.

First, by denying the existence or significance of human mentation, there was never any danger of discovering or revealing it. In this way, the region of ultimate privacy of the human being, having been declared off-limits scientifically, was protected against that science.

Second, Watson led those who followed him to believe that they were promoting the ability to predict and control human behavior. The truth is that behaviorism, notwithstanding the fantasies and fictions of B. F. Skinner, could never rise to power, as it were, to truly predict and control human behavior. For one cannot predict and control human behavior without taking the role of human mentation in conduct into account. Behaviorism was the great red herring, sending the wicked who would predict and control the behavior of others for their own benefit on a path that could not bring them to their goal.

It is a similar case with statistics. By taking a measurement on a person, surrendering the personal identification in the process of entering that measurement into an aggregate, one may win some research advance without identifying the contributors. I had the privilege of having had several conversations with Alfred Kinsey in which he strongly emphasized the way in which his methods guaranteed the confidentiality of all those who provided him with information concerning their sexual activities. One of his main purposes in gathering large samples was to conceal the identity of the persons who contributed their sex histories to him.

And the experiment: The experiment in psychology aimed to identify the invariable. It thus ignored the unique and variable, which characterize the narrative. The narrative contributes to knowledge not so much by identifying the invariable as by increasing our collective knowledge of human experience—and especially by indicating its possibilities.

So what does one do? The most significant truths about human beings inhere in the stories of their lives. Yet they need protection for making their stories available to others.

I have no doubt that the hope of humanity has to rest with the power of human beings and that power is necessarily enhanced by advances in knowledge. One should not become an enemy of knowledge because one recognizes danger in it. On the contrary, knowledge is the only reliable way to counter the hurt and harm that can come from knowledge.

I do have this misgiving. But a misgiving is not an objection. It is, rather, a problem, a problem that needs to be dealt with.

I do not pretend to solve the problem. Toward the end of finding solutions to the problem, however, I find myself taking note of two great contributors to the history of psychology, James and Freud, and the way in which they coped with the very same problem.

William James's (1902/1985) *The Varieties of Religious Experience* is, in my opinion, one of the great works in the history of psychology. The fundamental data for that book were provided by the narratives of religious experience that James found among the books in the library. He collected lengthy passages of narrative, studied them carefully, and provided a series of extraordinary observations and reflections in connection with them. It is a model of the use of narrative material in the field of psychology.

And all of the narrative material that he used was already public. There was no danger of any compromising publication. I suspect that the library contains great narrative ore for much more psychological mining.

Freud dealt with this problem in several ways. He used a considerable amount of information from himself. He variously attempted to conceal the identity of his cases. He wrote of fictional figures, such as Oedipus and Hamlet, and figures who were dead, such as Woodrow Wilson, Michelangelo, Moses, and Leonardo.

I would like to take this occasion to express a thought that comes strongly to my mind every time I consider Freud's (1910/1961) writing on Leonardo. Whether that which occurs to me is indeed true cannot be determined. However, I hope that what I have to say might be of value whether what I propose is true or not.

Some historians with whom I have spoken are extraordinarily reluctant to consider Freud's essay on Leonardo as a serious historical study. It is far-fetched even for one who might be sympathetic or even deeply involved in psychoanalytic thought. As a study of the psychology of Leonardo, it is not at all convincing. But the discussion of the psychodynamics, which may or may not have been associated with Leonardo, is very interesting.

So we consider the following possibility. Say Freud was working with a patient whose mental condition was, at least, similar to what Freud claimed to find in Leonardo. Say Freud was interested in indicating these psychodynamics but was greatly concerned that he not reveal the identity of his patient. Given the enrichment of his own understanding from dealing with the patient, Freud proceeded to write an account of Leonardo allowing himself a certain deliberate looseness. The end result was that Freud succeeded in communicating something that might be of great value in enhancing our understanding of people in general, possibly of value in enhancing our understanding of Leonardo—which is not so important—and succeeded in protecting the identity of his patient, the living "Leonardo."

Let me take from this. Suppose I am working with a patient. Suppose that my patient somehow makes me think of Marilyn Monroe, and with every clinical hour with her, my sense of the Marilyn Monroe narrative with which I am somewhat acquainted, but only from movies and reading, seems to fill out and become enriched. And maybe I can know Marilyn Monroe better than anyone might have known her even as I learn from my "Marilyn Monroe."

License me, as a professional psychologist, to write about Marilyn Monroe and tell her story as I understand it. I will not take the trouble to try to distinguish what my "Marilyn Monroe" has contributed to it. Nor will I claim anything more than that I came to understand Marilyn Monroe by an informed apperceptive mass that may, in point of fact, be largely out of my imagination rather than my apprehension. Indeed I will mention absolutely nothing explicitly about my "Marilyn Monroe." I will maintain that confidence meticulously.

But it is because of my work with "Marilyn Monroe" that I can say some things about Marilyn Monroe—and perhaps contribute more generally to psychology in this way.

So finally, let me say something about truth. We all feel obligated to tell the truth. And indeed, in scientific writing, deliberately telling untruths is totally unacceptable. But perhaps we need to make a distinction between *literal* truth and *real* truth. There is an old tradition, going back at least to Plato, that there can be a truth in madness, dreaming, poetry, or prophecy, which is higher than literal truth. A metaphor or a fiction might open a door that cannot be opened by approaches that are too weighed down by duty to literal truth.

References

Freud, S. (1961). Leonardo da Vinci and a memory of his childhood. In J. Strachey (Ed. and Trans.), *The standard edition of the complete psychological works of*

Sigmund Freud (Vol. II, pp. 59-137). London: Hogarth. (Original work published in 1910)

James, W. (1985). *The varieties of religious experience: A study in human nature.* Cambridge, MA: Harvard University Press. (Original work published in 1902)

❦ 2 ❦

Ethical Issues in Biographical Interviews and Analysis

Dan Bar-On

*I*nterviewing is a form of qualitative research through which we legitimately gather information that we further may analyze and publish (Rosenthal, 1987). The interviewer is supposed to be emotionally distant and close enough to be both empathic and critical toward the interviewees and their narration. In that sense, it is different from quantitative methods in which the interviewer has a much smaller active role and in which hypothesis and analysis are set in advance (Schon, 1983). It is also different from therapeutic interventions in which the clinician and patient function under a set of rules securing the role of the former and the privacy of the latter. When we take a closer look at interviewing as a method to gather qualitative information, however, especially within biographical research, it seems less like a formal research set of a priori rules and more like an intervention without the clear boundaries or a contract that a clinical intervention contains as a given (Bar-On, 1995).

When I call a new interviewee to set the first interview, there is (or at least should be) a moment where I stop and ask myself these questions: "Do you really feel like interfering in his or her life? Will you be able to live with the consequences of this encounter and intervention? Is it justified also from the interviewee's own perspective?" I can go on dialing when I believe that I will be able to follow through some unexpected consequences of the interview and when I assume that there is some value in the interviewing process also for the interviewee. Are these suppositions illusionary or self-serving biases? Do I talk myself into them only for the purpose of going along with my plan and research? I view it as a dilemma for which I have no clear-cut answer. I would like now to elaborate on this dilemma and bring a few examples from my study in Germany, interviewing children of Nazi perpetrators.[1]

The problem actually started with the idea to conduct such a study in the first place: It was clear from the outset that I am anything but an "honest broker"—an emotionally distant observer for my potential interviewees. I came from the side of the victims of the Nazis, and this would mean a deep emotional involvement in many of their potential responses. Before I started, I could imagine many of them avoiding me just for what I stand for. In relation to events like the Holocaust, however, an emotionally distant observer may have been and still is part of the problem itself. How could it have happened and what can we understand about its ongoing consequences (Laqueur, 1982)? On the other hand, no German social scientist had conducted such a systematic study: Why? Had I found such a report, I doubt if I would have proceeded with mine. I had first to clarify to myself that I was really interested in how the children live with their parents' atrocious deeds during the Holocaust. I remember training myself before going to Germany for the first time: What if someone would express an opinion or feeling that I would be very much hurt by (e.g., that the Holocaust was justified or had never happened)? How will I be able to go on conducting the interview? Or, alternatively, what if my questions will cause my interview partner to break down emotionally? Will I be able to take care of her or him? I had some clinical training and experience, but I also had to think through such possibilities and look for a local therapist to whom I could refer people if such an extreme outcome materialized.

I actually put off the idea of such a study for a long time ("neither a Jew or Israeli should conduct it"). As I had never been in Germany before, I was afraid that I might be completely unable to carry it out properly. At the outset, I even was not sure about my German—would it enable me to listen carefully to my interviewees, to understand what they were saying? I had spoken German only with my grandparents, who died many years ago. I set some limits, what I would not be able to cope with. For example, after interviewing "Ernst" (Bar-On, 1989b), I decided not to interview anymore perpetrators, even if they would be willing to talk with me. I was afraid of my own anger or despair, which I would not be able to handle. I felt differently about their children: They had not themselves done anything to my people. When I found out that I could feel empathy for their pain and anguish, I decided to go on and conduct more such interviews. These things I could not have predicted ahead of time: I had to deal with them only as they unfolded during the study itself.

There were several questions concerning the process of interviewing that became even more important in retrospect. For example, what to tell my interview partners about my research. I decided after some time to call it "family memories from the Third Reich." This had enough truth in it, as I was keenly interested in their very first memories from home, but it also covered up my other interests well enough: How do children of perpetrators cope with their parents' atrocious deeds? If I would have given them this name, I would have taken away the possibility that they did not define themselves as such or did not know about their parents' role in the extermination process. I remember a few cases (such as "Gerda" in the book)[1] in which I knew all along which atrocities her father had committed but I did not reveal it in the interview before she started discussing it herself.

I always declared who I was. It was important for me not to try to hide my real identity. Interestingly enough, however, it became a special problem for me when I called up a Jewish rabbi in Jerusalem ("Menachem" in the book), who was a son of a Nazi who had converted to Judaism. I did not know if people in his surroundings knew about that part of his biography (which came out to be a false suspicion) and was afraid if I said who I am and what I was after, he would just put me off. As it turned out, he was open with his people about his father's background, and the religious orthodox establishment showed an unusual openness in accepting him as a rabbi even with this background, perhaps owing to his own sincerity and openness.

I asked permission of all my interviewees to be taped and told all of them that in case I would publish anything, I would use pseudonyms and transform the identifying details. Only 9 people of 63 whom I called did not agree to be interviewed, and 2 more persons did not agree to be tape-recorded. During all these years, I had to withstand a lot of pressure from journalists to reveal my interviewees' identities, especially the prominent ones among them. I did that only after gaining their consent and after testing the hidden intentions of the journalists myself. Still, I did not use standard informed consent forms to be signed in the initial contact because I had a feeling that this formal procedure would introduce suspicion in a setting in which too many reasons for complexity were already there. This was the reason that I avoided any psychological tools as well. During my first trip, I still traveled around with a thematic apperception test (TAT) in my suitcase, which I have never used: As a matter of fact, what people narrated was so interesting that any such artificial tool was redundant and would have introduced unnecessary noise into a delicate situation.

People here in my home setting asked me how I could trust that my partners were telling me the truth. I was somewhat puzzled by their question because it said something about my friends' a priori stereotypes. For me, there was no one truth on their behalf. I could believe what people told me both if they tried to find out about what their fathers had done during the war and if they tried to avoid it. Interestingly, there was one case in which I became suspicious concerning what the interviewee was telling me. He was the only child of a perpetrator ("Dieter," in the book) who could report that his father told him in detail what he had "accomplished" as an Einsatzgruppen commander. My doubt stemmed from the fact that he was the only one who could report such details. When I tried to identify the unit the father was part of (by name and birth date—these details could be validated easily in Germany), there was no such unit stationed in that area. My fantasy was that the father was lying to his son, trying to be a big shot, though he may have been only a cook or a driver. The son, though being a historian and having his own doubts about his father's credibility, preferred a perpetrating father (but a "real" one) rather than a nonperpetrating unimportant cheater: an anomaly, specific to the outcomes of this era?

With time, I felt a lot of empathy and responsibility toward some of my interviewees' stories and their fate. Sometimes I even had to remind myself who were the real victims of this era. This is how I found myself one evening all alone in some friends' apartment in Munich, watching a 6-hour video about the Mydaneck trial. I also needed endless phone conversations with my wife, colleagues, and friends to "ventilate" the stories I had heard that day. Each time, I had to go home after 3 weeks because I could not take any more of these stories. I would use these pauses to have my tapes transcribed and translated into English, take a deep breath, and prepare myself for the next round. When I reached the sixth round, I just could not take in any more of these interviews (though by now I had many more on my list). Though these are more of my own psychological limitations than ethical issues concerning the interviews, I feel that they converge: Had I not considered my own needs, I am not sure I would have been able to listen to those of my interviewees.

At some point after about 3 years of conducting interviews, I felt a tremendous urge to publish something. That happened especially after Sichrovsky's (1988) book appeared, and I felt he took away the "primacy effect" of my study. I had to work through that feeling and accept the pace of my work: I could not yet come to conclusions because I was deep in my own interviewing phase, feeling totally committed to my interviewees, their own solitude, and the "conspiracy of silence" around them. I invited them to attend a conference at the University of Wuppertal, promising that there would be no name tags and they could maintain their anonymity. This shows again that I learned to see my interviews as an intervention that needed additional steps beyond just information gathering, from their own perspective and needs. It may also, however, have been my need to free myself from the commitment of the interviewer and be able to move to the next phases of analysis and publication.

Twelve of 92 decided to come to the conference at Wuppertal. There, they met each other for the first time. They also heard of the Dutch experience, of a self-help group of children of collaborators with the Nazis, which was functioning in Holland since 1981. My interviewees decided to form their own group. Because I would not be able to come to those meetings, I suggested a colleague from Berlin to facilitate this group. They felt that they had to go their own way, however, and after a couple of meetings with my colleague, they went on by themselves. This was actually the only group of children of perpetrators in Germany meeting for that purpose in a country where there must be hundreds of thousands of persons with similar biographies! I followed those meetings closely from Israel, and in 1992 while on sabbatical in Boston, I asked them if they would be interested in meeting with a group of children of survivors. The first such encounter took place in June 1992 (Bar-On, 1995), followed by three additional meetings.

Although the group was an unexpected offshoot from my interviews, I felt that it did help me move into my next roles, the analyst and the writer. I knew that they were being taken care of, at least those who felt they needed it. This was clearly the therapist in me who felt that I had become engaged in an intervention that I did not foresee and that did not have a clear a priori contract. I myself became more involved in the interviewee's perspective the further our contacts developed. This brought me to conduct follow-up interviews after 7 years, testing the long-term effects of the interviews themselves (Bar-On, 1996).

The change of roles demands a tremendous effort: It demands from the interviewer a growing distancing, a change of discourse, moving back and forth between different levels of conceptualization and abstraction. At the first stage of the transition, I even found myself in the role of the quantitative researcher, trying to test all possible hypotheses about independent variables and outcomes: demographic and socioeconomic variables, family structural ones—you name a variable that I did not try to quantify. The results were poor, as one could expect from such a small and varied sample. The only relevant outcome was that fewer children of perpetrators were married and more were childless than their control group (children of war in Germany) (Bar-On, 1990). Only after I became convinced that I had used this phase to distance myself from the interviewees and their stories did I get back to them and start my content analysis phase, followed finally by the phase in which I wrote my book presenting whole interviews with very little analysis on my part: Let them speak for themselves without my interpretations. I came to this conclusion convinced that they were so powerful in their own discourse that my analysis could only minimize and distort that effect.

At a later stage, a German colleague and I decided to test a hypothesis: Would my interviewees tell a different story to a German interviewer? My colleague approached one of my interviewees in an independent way, interviewing her under a different title ("life stories of the Hitler youth generation"). Our common analysis (Rosenthal & Bar-On, 1992) suggests that only minor details differed when comparing our separate interviews. Although this is only a very partial answer to our question, it went along with a previous feeling that once being able to talk about themselves (having someone listening to them carefully), the variations would not be interviewer dependent, if any were found at all.

In most cases, the interviews gave my interviewees a chance to free themselves of a burden: Just the opportunity to talk to a Jew and an Israeli about this complicated subject had a healing effect for them, as some of them mentioned manifestly, especially those who had never had an earlier possibility to discuss this aspect of their biography. But I also can see that in some cases, I may unwittingly have caused damage. At least in the case of "Hilda" (Bar-On, 1989b) it came out during the publication in English that she felt hurt and had avoided me ever since our single interview. This could suggest that one should never try to publish an interview if one cannot follow it up and observe its lasting effects on the interviewee.

The Phase of Analysis: Decontextualizing the Interviewee's Discourse?

Langer (1991) criticizes the literature describing the psychological aftereffects of the Holocaust on the survivors and their families. He starts with the interviewers, who did not listen carefully to what the survivors tried to tell them (especially their "unheroic" experiences, which the interviewers could not stand listening to). He follows with the concepts the researchers provided: He suggests that in some cases, rather than helping us get closer to and make sense of the experience of the survivors, the concepts helped the researchers defend themselves from the meaning and consequences of these experiences. In addition, it seems that many of these reports were loaded with psychoanalytic conceptualizations that were developed within the clinical setting (assuming personal abnormalcy under normal life circumstances). This in turn decontextualized the experiences of survivors, which may have been normal reactions to a rather abnormal situation in the first place (Bar-On, 1995).

From this perspective, it is extremely important which discourse analysts develop in analyzing their interviewees' narrations. I do not suggest that there is an a priori solution to this dilemma. Rather, it is an ongoing struggle in which the analysts try to describe their own understandings of the texts, to prove something, while also trying to remain faithful to the experiences of the interviewees and the way they themselves have formulated them. When one deals with such virgin material, such as my study with children of Nazi perpetrators, it was my personal initial decision that no a priori concepts should be consciously "proven" before the text was carefully read and reread. As I had never been in their role and had never encountered them before, I felt that previous concepts should be tested before being imposed in this specific context. There were two dangerous paths I tried to avoid in my analysis: (a) the overloaded meaning of psychoanalytic concepts and (b) striving for historical truisms that might lie behind every line of the interviewees' passages. The first would create a false analysis, in the sense that I "found what I was looking for all along." The second would cause one to disregard the variability of subjective meanings of a single historical truth or to undermine similar reactions that appeared under a variety of different historical truths. I will illustrate with a few examples.

When Professor Charny and I (1992) wanted to content analyze the interviews according to the moral argumentations of the interviewees, we had an a priori assumption that the interviewees would try to develop such arguments to defend themselves from the immoral deeds of their parents. We could even envision such arguments, based on previous knowledge: For instance, "the Jews did it to themselves" (and therefore it is not for me to carry the burden of my father's deeds). Or "the Holocaust has never happened or was justified" (and therefore this is not a moral dilemma for me). Still, we could not know ahead of time all the possible forms of such arguments. Neither could we predict whether the whole interview would develop around a central argument, an explicit or an implicit one. These were issues we could test only a posteriori. In addition, the arguments could appear verbally as we envisioned them or would have to be extracted from the text (in which were the hidden meanings of the explicit argument). This is a very complicated technique, which may invite charlatans— that is, finding the arguments that you assumed should be there and disregarding those that were unexpected or less interesting from the researchers' perspective. Our way to overcome these difficulties was by interjudge reliability, discussing and reanalyzing the discrepancies found between our interpretations. This is a cumbersome and time-consuming procedure, but I am afraid there are no short cuts in such a study.

One of the arguments we found a posteriori was the argument we called, "We suffered too." It was initially not seen as a moral argumentation because it was based on narrating real events that the interviewees had suffered from during the war and after it was over. When the interview would end without mentioning anything else, however, we thought that it became a kind of moral argumentation: Their own suffering helped our interviewees ignore the victims of the Nazi era and their suffering. We then developed a more detailed hypothesis: The capacity to relate to both one's own suffering and that of the victims of Nazism would be associated with working through the past. This hypothesis was further tested by a content analysis of each sentence of 31 interviews (Bar-On & Gaon, 1991).

Although I did use the psychological concept of *working through,* I felt it had to be redefined in relation to the children of the perpetrators: What did it actually mean to work through one's own father's atrocities? This became again a posteriori analysis, in which I defined five stages of that process, which only a very few of my interviewees have gone all the way through spontaneously (Bar-On, 1990). Also, the image of the *double wall* between perpetrators and their children and the *paradoxical morality* of the perpetrators were a posteriori conceptualizations that were developed after the interviewing phase while reading the interviews over and over (Bar-On, 1989a).

Today, I believe I would conduct this study differently. After learning the biographical analysis method from Professor Gabriele

Rosenthal (1987, 1989), I guess I would have preferred to conduct the interviews along those principles and do the analysis using her method because it maintains the discourse of the interviewee in its focus all along the analysis. This is what we did later when we interviewed families of Holocaust survivors, three generations in the family (Bar-On, 1995).

The Publication Phase: Starting All Over Again

As long as an analysis or a transcription of an interview lies in our drawers, the major ethical dilemmas between us and our interviewees have not yet begun. The issues become problematic once we have decided to publish the interviews (transcripts) or their analysis: Should we show these drafts to our interviewees before publication? Can they make sense of them? Can they veto a publication if they have changed their minds between the interview and the publication? These are difficult dilemmas, which have no clear-cut rule to follow.

In writing my book, I chose 13 interviews that I found most interesting, representing the variety of issues I had encountered during my study.[2] The interview with Peter Thomas Heydrich was definitely one of those, but it lost most of its meaning in not mentioning the name "Heydrich," especially because the interviewee himself spoke so much of the meaning of this name for him. I had promised pseudonyms, however, to all my interviewees. I called him up and asked his permission to use his explicit name. He gave it and sent me his written consent. Later, the publisher asked for the written consent of all the interviewees. I explained that I could not expose to them the real names of my interviewees. We finally agreed that I would receive written consents from my interviewees and mail them to the publisher without the names. After all this, when my book came out, "Hilda" wrote me an angry letter, saying that she did not expect her full account to appear in the book. My arguments about its importance did not convince her, and I had to promise her that I would not publish her chapter when the book would appear in German.

I sent each of my interviewees a copy once the book was published. I got five letters in which some of them felt misunderstood or tried to add details that now seemed important to them. In each case, I tried to follow through the arguments. In most of these cases, however, it became clear that these were additions in which the interviewee wanted now to adjust things he or she had said in a different way in the original text. In a couple of cases, the problem was not a careful enough translation of the transcript, in which some of the original meaning had been distorted or lost. In these cases, I tried to introduce these corrections in the following additions.

In my books (Bar-On, 1989b, 1995) I tell the stories of a friend and a client who I have cited in my text. When I showed them the citations before publication, they both responded using the same sentence: "Dan, it was not that way at all." Clearly, this could happen: In one case, I cited out of memory and in the other, out of my clinical reports (not from precise transcriptions). In both these cases, however, I am quite sure that this was not the issue. I could see their own agenda in not recalling the exact sequence of events. Because I had no transcribed texts, however, I could not clarify this question. I finally decided to publish my text, including their last commentary on it. But actually there is no way to make complete justice to your interviewees: Once the narrative has been analyzed, it is actually your text as well as theirs; the interviewees may be very happy or very unhappy with the way you have handled their texts, but it is still a point of view you wish to defend and clarify.

I believe that it is our responsibility to decide when to show what to whom. There are things we have to try and avoid altogether. For example, one of my German interviewees spoke about her father in a way that gave me the feeling that they had incestuous relations. She would not mention it openly, however, and even when I tried to suggest something to her indirectly, this did not yield a clear answer. Though I still feel so, in the analysis of her case I avoided writing about it because I knew she might read the text. Because I did not find a way to discuss it with her ahead of time, I had to skip its publication even though I feel that this case lacked some of its major features through the missing interpretation. I feel that finally, after all that we do, even when we think we are doing a lot of good to our interviewees, we have to take into account how they are thinking of themselves, how this is changing over time with or without any connection to our interventions, and what our published interpretations may cause them. I am afraid of my own urge to try and accomplish something, when I become impatient and want to see things formulated neatly: These are the issues around which I am making the worst ethical mistakes. In such cases, it is always helpful when there is someone around to make me alert, to rethink my moves, and to examine my ethical decisions. I have been lucky to have such good colleagues most of my professional way, but I am also aware of the few incidents in which I overlooked their advice and suffered from it later on. Although we are also only human, I feel we are responsible because in such a delicate kind of research, we hold the meaning of people's lives in our hands. Our successes will be gratifying, but our failures may become irreversible.

Notes

1. I interviewed 92 persons in Germany between 1985 and 1988 as part of my research concerning the aftereffects of the Nazi extermination process on the families of its perpetrators and bystanders (Bar-On, 1989a, 1990; Bar-On & Charny, 1992). My references to "the book" are to Legacy of Silence: Encounters With Children of the Third Reich (Bar-On, 1989b).

2. Whenever I was asked about the representativeness of my sample, I would answer, "Tell me the socioeconomic and demographic characteristic of the population of perpetrators in Nazi Germany and I will be able to assess the representativeness of my sample." Up to now, there is no such systematic information available in Germany.

References

Bar-On, D. (1989a). Holocaust perpetrators and their children: A paradoxical morality. *Journal of Humanistic Psychology, 29*(4), 424-443.

Bar-On, D. (1989b). *Legacy of silence.* Cambridge, MA: Harvard University Press.

Bar-On, D. (1990). Children of perpetrators of the Holocaust: Working through one's moral self. *Psychiatry, 53,* 229-245.

Bar-On, D. (1993). First encounter between children of survivors and children of perpetrators of the Holocaust. *Journal of Humanistic Psychology, 33*(4), 6-14.

Bar-On, D. (1995). *Fear and hope: Three generations of the Holocaust.* Cambridge, MA: Harvard University Press.

Bar-On, D. (1996). Descendants of Nazi perpetrators: Seven years after the first interviews. *Journal of Humanistic Psychology, 36*(1), 55-74.

Bar-On, D., & Charny, I. W. (1992). The logic of moral argumentation of children of the Nazi era. *International Journal of Group Tensions, 22*(1), 3-20.

Bar-On, D., & Gaon, A. (1991). We suffered too: Nazi children's inability to relate to the suffering of the victims of the Holocaust. *Journal of Humanistic Psychology, 31*(4), 77-95.

Langer, L. L. (1991). *Holocaust testimonies: The ruins of memory.* New Haven, CT: Yale University Press.

Laqueur, W. (1982). *The terrible secret.* New York: Penguin.

Rosenthal, G. (1987). *Wenn alles in Scherben fallt . . . Von Leben und Sinnwelt der Kriegsgeneration* [When everything fell into pieces . . . About life and meaning of the war generation]. Opladen, Germany: Leske & Budrich.

Rosenthal, G. (1989). Leben mit der NS-Vergangenheit heute: Zur Reparatur einer fragwurdigen Vergangenheit im bundersrepublikanischen Alltag [Living with the NS-past today: Repairing a questionable part of the German daily life]. *Vorgange: Zeitschrift für Burgerrechte und Gesellschaftspolitik, 3,* S. 87-101.

Rosenthal, G., & Bar-On, D. (1992). Biographical case study of a victimizer's daughter strategy: The pseudo-identification with the victims of the Holocaust. *Journal of Narrative and Life History, 2*(2), 105-127.

Schon, D. A. (1983). *The reflective practitioner.* New York: Basic Books.

Sichrovsky, P. (1988). *Born guilty.* New York: Basic Books.

❦ 3 ❦

Expert Witness

Who Controls the Psychologist's Narrative?

Terri Apter

*P*sychology is an intrusive and frequently cruel discipline. This cruelty is, I believe, generic to the discipline, not simply a by-product of some poor practices or crude studies. Criticisms of psychology and psychological practice are common enough. There is now a body of literature describing cruelty in mental hospitals, from their prisonlike status in previous times to their more modern enactment as centers of political or social control (Porter, 1987). Such suffering may be a result of ignorance, imperfect people, and depleted resources, and hence a product of the way psychology is practiced in our imperfect world, rather than a fault within the discipline itself. Certain outmoded treatments, too, such as lobotomy, may be unfortunate but incidental by-products of doctors' eagerness to calm their patients. Less drastic practices continue, however, such as the prescription of tranquilizers to tame rather than cure patients. In a study of Valium—a common tranquilizer—it was found that this drug was prescribed to help people tolerate roles "they found difficult or intolerable without the drug" (Cooperstock & Lennard, 1979, p. 336). A mother of four teenage children explained why she believed she needed the drug: "I take it to protect my family from my irritability." She described her children as normal and herself as yelling at them "because their normal activity is bothering me." In taking Valium, she could be "what my husband wants" (p. 136). The ways in which psychologists enforce prevailing norms meet with constant criticism. R. D. Laing was influential in reconceiving some mental illness as an understandable, reasonable, and indeed sane response to intolerable social and personal circumstances (e.g., Laing & Esterson, 1970). Family systems therapies now challenge the location of a problem within a single individual and, instead, work toward changing patterns of interactions among a network of individuals (e.g., Minuchin, 1984). These shifts away from seeing the problem as residing with the patient and toward seeing the context in which the person has to live as problematic have been pushed further by feminist critics of psychology. The prescriptions by Dr. S. Weir Mitchell, who believed that Dorothy Perkins Gilman's depression could be cured if she devoted herself to domestic work and child care, confined herself to a maximum of 2 hours' intellectual work a day, and "never touch[ed] pen, brush or pencil as long as [she] live[d]" (Gilman, 1935, p. 96), have been exposed as infantilizing and controlling. Gilman's longing for work and intellectual stimulation was declared to be dangerous and her frustration with the limitations of domestic and maternal roles was seen as something of which she must be cured. Sylvia Plath's electric shock treatment, which "took hold of [her] and shook [her] like the end of the world" and continued until she thought her "bones would break and the sap fly out of [her] like a split plant" (Plath, 1963, p. 151), has been revealed as a powerful device to persuade the fictional, but autobiographically grounded, Esther Greenwood that her resistance to feminine roles was wrong, that she had to learn how to "behave" herself so that the doctors and nurses who had tortured her would approve her "for the road" (p. 257).

In this article, however, I wish to put criticisms of specific treatments or therapies to one side. Instead I wish to focus on narrative issues in psychology. How do psychologists get the material they require for their narratives about their patients or their "subjects"? And once the information is available, who controls the narrative? In other words, who has the loudest voice, and how is the volume sustained?

Susanna Kaysen's (1993) novel, *Girl, Interrupted,* reveals a link between cruel therapies and the narrative presumption I wish to question. Kaysen's novel describes her 2-year confinement in a mental hospital. Her descriptions of these experiences are interspersed with the actual records made by the professionals who confined her. The diagnoses are sketchy and awkward yet carried the expert's credibility. A copy of the admission report reads, " 'Needed McLean [mental hospital] for 3 yrs. Profoundly depressed—suicidal, increasing patternless of life, promiscuous, might kill, sell or get pregnant' " (p. 10). The weight of this virtually illiterate diagnosis points to my terror of psychology: Knowledge is presumed, rather than proved or proposed.

The cruelty generic to psychology stems from three interconnected aspects of the study. First, there is the inevitable curiosity about that delicate instrument, the human mind; for psychology is more than a wish to observe the mind at its own work. Psychologists pose specific questions about the mind's working and its development. Strategies are then devised for getting the mind to reveal what the psychologist wants to know. These strategies, called studies, are often ruthless. Some blindness seems to strike psychologists as they position themselves as experts, explorers, or detectives. The minds investigated too often become the territory that is brutally charted or they are presumed to have criminal intent and need to be lured and tricked into self display.

Second, the cruelty inherent in psychology arises from a presumption of who has the knowledge about the person or people studied. In its belief in its expert status, psychology often silences the very voice that it purports to hear. Freud's (1953a) treatment of Dora is a widely recognized prototype of this presumption. Dora became distressed when, at 14 years old, a family friend aggressively sought a sexual relationship with her. Dora's life was further confounded by her father's infidelity and the mixed motives that led him to refer her to Freud. The psychoanalyst determined that her response to the older man's advances involved repression of sexual desire, and it was from this repression that her symptoms arose. Freud tried to inflict his interpretation on her. He heard her own story as a lie, a subterfuge. Yet he was the deceiver, purporting to elicit information from her in order to help her with the puzzle of her own responses, but in truth, he was waiting for sufficient information to prove his own theories. When she fled analysis to preserve something of her own, still confused story, Freud saw her as resisting the truth. The expert refuses to budge his narrative and sees others as stubborn or unenlightened or repressed.

Third, in its wish to become a body of knowledge, psychology engages in gross generalizations. This urge to construct general knowledge that can reveal facts about people not yet known reinforces the silencing of individual voices. When patients or subjects of a study give the psychologist information about themselves, many details of this information are cast aside so that it may be drawn and quartered into a favored theory rather than constructed into a personal narrative.

Not all generalizations distort and silence the wide variety of human experience, although psychological generalities tend to. "All happy families are alike, and all unhappy families are different in their unhappiness," Tolstoy posed as the opening sentence of *Anna Karenina*, and many readers think, "Yes, how true." The happy family runs with apparent simplicity along the line of mutual empathy and affection. You barely see what is going on because it all goes along so easily. Unhappy families glitch at different points. For some, irritation mounts to rage. For others, connection distorts to jealousy. The novelist's generality is not a universal statement but a lens through which one is able to see many similar patterns. When Nabokov, in *Ada*, counters Tolstoy's opening sentence by saying that in fact it is all unhappy, not happy, families that are alike, the reader can assent to that, too, because Nabokov's dissent highlights different aspects of similarity and difference. "Yes," one might agree, "in unhappy families there is that distinctive atmosphere of irritation and dread, a deep resentment and devastating disrespect. Yes, I see what Nabokov means," one can say, using this different highlighter. In short, the novelist's generality does not bully the reader. The reader has a certain freedom to identify—or not—with descriptions, to pick and choose, to use them where they apply and set them aside when they do not. Contrast the novelist's approach to generalization about the human condition with that of Sigmund Freud. Take, for example, *The Interpretation of Dreams* (Freud, 1953b). How can any dreamer escape the basic theory about the dream's aim and purpose? What freedom does the dreamer have to shift the context of the dream? Any which way the dreamer turns, any hoop the dreamer jumps through, lands him or her firmly in Freudian territory. Specific interpretations, of course, are highly negotiable—at least in theory. With a sensitive psychoanalyst, even the meaning of the image of tree might be negotiable. After all, a crucial part of psychoanalytic theory is that an interpretation of a patient's mental state is true only if the patient accepts it as true. But this theory may fall by the wayside. The agreement of the patient is often in practice the assent of someone who believes that the source of knowledge resides outside his or her own mind. Symptomatic of this imbalance is Freud's use of his daughter Anna as a subject of psychoanalysis. Where, in such a case, is the potentially dissenting voice? How likely is it to be heard?

I shall offer only a brief register of the psychological studies that I find particularly disturbing. This list is not complete but goes some way toward revealing the ruthless urge of some psychologists as they try to wrest the mind's secrets from itself. In the 1930s, Dr. Wayne Dennis (1948), at the University of Virginia in Charlottesville, wanted to discover how much of an infant's development was innate and how much was learned by watching adult behavior. To explore this question, he fostered twin babies from age 2 months to 14 months. During this time, he and his wife took sole charge of the babies and were careful not to respond in any way to the infants, to reward or punish them or instruct them—although, as quoted in Tucker (1994), he was curious to observe " 'the first reaction of the subjects to scolding and to a light slap on the thigh' " (p. 18). He refused to play with them or speak to them and heroically withstood responding when the babies "gazed into our faces and smiled" (p. 18). So convinced was he that maturation rather than actual experience was the crux of development that he attributed one baby's severe lag in motor development to "a partial hemiplegia which had not been noticed at an earlier period" (p. 20). In 1944, B. F. Skinner (1978) devised a thermostatically controlled box, which he called an "air-crib," in which an infant could be free to move about but would be removed from human sound and touch. So ignorant was he of his own cruelty that he subjected his own daughter to it—something Wayne Dennis was careful not to do, although his own baby daughter grew in tandem with the twins with whom he experimented and showed distress at the infants' cries she heard from behind the wall. J. B. Watson, in 1924, wanted to discover whether jealousy could occur early in a child's development. To work on this question, he pretended to abuse his wife in front of his 3-year-old son who " 'cried, kicked and tugged at his father's leg and struck with his hand' " (as quoted in Tucker, 1994, p. 18).

Curiosity about the mind seems to create moral blind spots. This is evident in a more recent study whose aim was to determine the moral strength or weakness of others. Stanley Milgram (1974) instructed his subjects to administer electric shocks to other people. Initially the subjects were instructed to administer shocks they knew to be harmless. Then they were instructed to increase the current beyond the danger point. Milgram was interested in discovering how obedient people were when given instructions that involved (apparent) infliction of injury to others. He wanted to measure the rate of compliance and resistance. Would people take a stand against authority and assume individual responsibility for what they were doing? Or were people more likely to obey instructions regardless of what damage they thought they were doing?

Does a psychologist have a right to put someone through this in order to observe what happens? Milgram (1963) admitted that some would exhibit stress. He thought at one point that he might "even start to wonder whether or not to abandon the study," but concluded that "momentary excitement is not the same as harm" (p. 377). Yet Milgram also noted this:

> I observed a mature and initially poised businessman enter the laboratory smiling and confident. Within 20 minutes he was reduced to a twitching, stuttering wreck, who was rapidly approaching a point of nervous collapse. He constantly pulled on his earlobe, and twisted his hands, at one point he pushed his fist into his forehead and muttered: "Oh, God, let's stop it." (p. 377)

The overlay of perception and blindness is characteristic of the cruel intrusion I wish to bring into focus. Milgram notes, logically enough, that momentary excitement is not the same as harm. With the sleight of hand characteristic of an expert who does not question himself closely enough, the logically correct remark is taken to mean that this momentary excitement does the person no harm. How does Stanley Milgram know that? How can this counterintuitive presumption rest easy beside the clear perception of the man's responses? Herein lie the astounding contradictions of psychological insight and psychological hubris. Just as Freud portrays Dora's struggle to preserve the integrity of her narrative while simultaneously describing his attempt to bring her in line with his interpretation, just as Wayne Dennis vividly describes the infants' needs for human comfort while simultaneously ignoring their significance, so too does Milgram portray the pain his participants suffer while denying it. This contradiction is the crux of the psychologist's cruelty—presumption and sympathy, blindness and perception.

Many years ago as a sophomore in college, I worked as an assistant on a study of children's motivation. My job consisted of greeting the first child and parent as they arrived at the research unit, handing the parent a permission and information form to fill in, and seating them in the room in which the study was to take place. After two more parent-child couples went through the same process, I brought out a large box filled with wooden blocks of different colors, sizes, and shapes and explained to the children, who ranged from 2 to 5 years of age, that they were to build the best tower they could build with these blocks and that someone would judge which child's tower was really the best. The parents were then led from the room. I told the children when to begin and when to stop, and gave a signal for the "judge"—a PhD student—to enter. He studied the towers closely, nodded from time to time, muttered to himself, and took notes. He then declared one or the other to be the best or the winning tower. This process was repeated three or four times before the session was declared to be at an end.

This procedure in fact had nothing whatsoever to do with assessing children's skills in building towers. The declaration that a tower "won" was random. The aim of the study was to observe children's responses to success or failure. Their responses were filmed and then analyzed by the researchers in charge. I never saw the films, but these scenes have never ceased their reruns inside my mind.

When I began this job, I knew nothing about and had no feeling for how children liked to be treated, for what adult behavior might be convincing or threatening or disturbing, or for how children might be responding to the world around them. That the public relations part I played so falsely was judged adequate by my employers may have indicated something about the quality of their intuitive judgment. In any case, my unsuitability for my role rapidly emerged for other reasons. I "disturbed" the study by comforting the losing child. I was insufficiently neutral as I described the process of the game; I sent messages to the children, even before they began, that the game should not be taken seriously.

It was not the youngest children who roused my runaway empathy. The 2- and 3-year-olds were in some ways hard work because they often had their own ideas about what they wanted to do with the blocks or whether they wanted to play with them at all, but on the whole, their winning or losing was of little import. Most of these very young children seemed to note their success or failure dispassionately. "Oh," they might say with a shudder of surprise, to either winning or losing; and whether they won or lost, they took great pleasure in demolishing the structure with one swipe. Some who won expressed surprise and looked at their tower with new respect. A few did, even at age 3, seem disappointed or angry. But the crestfallen face or the stamp of rage was transient. Within minutes, they were back into the game. Disappointment simply did not stick to them.

It was the slightly older children whose behavior turned my routine into torture. When these children "lost," a cloud seemed to settle over them and inside it they would contract. One girl sat with her eyes fixed on her tower and touched it gently with the tip of her forefinger, up and down, as though to protect it. When I spoke to her, she seemed too embarrassed to face me. A boy who had constructed his tower with the utmost concentration, knelt beside his "losing" structure and gazed at it from beneath, humming to himself as he dismantled it, slowly, brick by brick. He then stirred the wooden blocks into a pile as though to remove any sign of his former efforts. After two or three such failures to win, the children's diminished moods hung on. They became sullen and withdrawn and discouraged. They did not want to try to build another tower and expressed irritation with my attempts to encourage them to try again.

The oldest children in the study—the 5-year-olds—were enormously pleased when they won, but they also showed increasing despair at losing. After being told that his tower won, a child raised his eyes from his own work and looked triumphantly at the loser. His body stretched, his hands were thrown high, his pride became the central point of his experience. The losing child, on the other hand, hunched over. His body seemed to shrink. He crouched down, rocked on his feet, and then rested his chin on his knees, filling his gaze with his losing tower. His whole psychological field seemed to narrow as he studied that rejected product of his effort. Another child tried to cover his mood with an embarrassed smile. His mouth drew into a static grin and his eyes filled with tears. Some children were better at controlling their feelings, but the pain was still evident. One child looked at the winner with a forced smile but crouched low and hugged her ankles. Another's attempt at a smile was foiled by the twitching of her mouth and the quick pulling in of her lower lip. When I coaxed her into reluctant speech, her voice was dull. Hearing her voice crack, she ceased speaking.[1]

I remain fascinated with children's responses to success and failure, but I doubt that I could participate in studies that willfully subject children to experiences of failure—needless experiences that they could make no sense of because the results were random, having no link whatsoever to either their effort or attainment. On grant applications, I have been asked to sign a declaration stating that my research does not harm or disturb people. I still make such declarations with a clear conscience, but I know I cannot be certain that what I declare is true. Could I, as a researcher, be purely an observer—not interfere, not bully, just watch and listen? No, this is not feasible. So I entered the fray—but from the side door as an interviewer and observer of ordinary lives, not as a manipulator and quantifier. I thought I was safe from the psychologist's intrusion and presumption.

Of course, I was not, and each discovery of the ways in which I, too, manipulate, presume knowledge of others, and generalize thrusts me up against the criticism I harbor toward other psychologists. Each time this happens, I am taken aback as though surprised that I was not able to avoid something I knew, really, was unavoidable. In response to me, an interviewer keen to read a narrative of their lives, my subjects key into their story in new ways, wondering how it will be read by me and by others once I, the alleged expert, relay it.

One thing I discovered fairly early on is that different material comes up at different interviews. It is often as though people brood over what they have said at one interview and then modify it at the next—however long the interval between. They often seem to be checking their actual lives against the description they heard themselves give. Second interviews rapidly return to information given in the first. Or, if persons feel they gave too much away at a previous session, they may be guarded at the next, and I may not find out for some time why they feel some caution. "I shouldn't tell anyone certain things about my husband," Kate reflected. "Not anyone. I really do hope that what I said last time just won't figure—not in anything you do." The first interview had made her feel disloyal. Even 4 months later, her words haunted her. After all, those words took on a special life, a public narrative, in my tapes and possibly in a book. The effect such words can then have may make them seem unbalanced, incomplete—even untrue. This was a startling effect on teenage girls when their fathers read about their daughters' responses to them in *Altered Loves* (Apter, 1990). One 15-year-old said that when she saw the effect of her words—as written by me—on her father, she "felt kind of dizzy" and no longer knew if she had spoken the truth (Apter, 1993). The accounts of the adolescent girls in my study had to be carefully balanced within the context they were given. In publication, the context changed. They were no longer "passing remarks, but carved into the world, and not the way they were meant to be" (Apter, 1993, p. 164). One 16-year-old felt that her words had been "stolen": "I see how you got what you said. I'm not saying it's wrong, but when you read about yourself . . . Well, it's me, but not me. It's really weird."[2]

Like other psychologists, I would defend my procedures on the grounds that good comes from them, too. The changes in perspective that may be forced on people who read about themselves in someone's rendition of their self narratives can be enlightening and validating.

As these girls read their mothers' voices in my text, they gained a new sympathy. "She seems so big at home. You know what I mean?" Casey inquired.[3]

> Like, when she talks I feel she thinks she knows it all. When I hear her in your book . . . well, I read her and I can hear it clear as day. But it's different because you see the chinks in her armor. She's trying real hard . . . you know? You can see that. When I read what she says about me, I can see that she's trying and caring. But when you just hear it—the actual situation—it's like she's just nagging and doesn't see beyond her own nose.

In real life, as it were, girls would mock their mothers' concern, sigh in despair at their mothers' overprotectiveness, balk at the sheer silliness of their mothers' anxiety. Reading their mothers' voices, however, they lost that insouciance. In the psychologist's narrative, the mother's voice could gain their sympathy. The narrative offered a slant onto a mother's subjectivity that day-to-day reality had blocked.

The reasons why people respond so strongly to others' narratives of them, of course, give rise to further psychological questions. I am currently engaged in a series of home and classroom studies of young children's development of self-concept. The amount of emotion children invest in what others say about them can be seen at a very early age. They are quick to tune into, and join, conversations about who and what they are. There are direct and simple exchanges, in which 2-year-olds eagerly engage:

> Who's a clever little boy?
>
> Me!

But they also fall silent, stop what they are doing, or try to elicit a smile when they hear other people discussing them. The mother of 2-year-old Charlotte was discussing the girl's behavior toward her little brother. "He plays with something she hasn't touched in over a year, and she suddenly says it's hers and grabs it from him." Charlotte dropped the rabbit she was setting onto a chair and came over to her mother and turned her head upward so that her mother, looking down toward the baby in the playpen on the floor, would have to see her, and offered her a deliberately charming smile.

Even very young children are driven to correct negative descriptions of them. A grandmother, mopping up spilt coffee, said to 2-year-old Rachel, "Naughty thing!" Rachel, hopeful to deflect this label, said, "Not naughty." The grandmother insists, "You're naughty to spill the coffee." Rachel tried again, "Teddy did it. Teddy's naughty." "No, you're a naughty girl. You spilled it." When this second attempt to deflect the label failed, Rachel tucked her legs underneath her, pressed her fist against her cheek, and did not interact with the grandmother until the grandmother herself initiated interaction by offering to read the child a story. Judy Dunn (1988) observed how quick children were to key into situations in which they might obtain a compliment. She records a 2½-year-old monitoring a remark his mother makes to his younger sister. The mother tells baby Susie that she is a determined little devil, and the child remarks, "*I'm* not a determined little devil" (p. 179). Susie's brother uses his mother's playful description of the baby to remind his mother of what a good boy he is and perhaps to persuade his mother to turn her attention toward him. Adults quickly discover how easy it is to tease children by describing them in inappropriate ways:

> "You're a monkey-faced rascal," the father of 7-year-old Derek declared.
>
> "I'm not. I'm not . . . not 'monkey-face'!" the boy insisted.
>
> "Fish face, then?" his father suggested.
>
> "No!"
>
> "Then kangaroo nose?"
>
> "What? No!"

Clearly, Derek knew this was a name-calling game, yet the names he was called roused enormous excitement. His face color heightened and he jumped up and down, squealing his resistance, until the names were withdrawn. Other children are well aware of the pain they can inflict, and suffer, from name calling. "Sticks and stones may break my bones, but names will never hurt me," is uttered as a defensive hope, rather than a confirmed belief. From the age of 4, children become aware of themselves as specific persons who can be described both by themselves and by others. These descriptions are highly provisional. They can be modified, they can be changed, but children care deeply about them. These descriptions begin to structure a child's sense of who he or she is and they therefore are a source of fascination, pleasure, or terror.

When the psychologist's voice claims, or is presumed to have, an expert status, modification of the narrative is more difficult and the interpretation is more threatening. Even before it is voiced, many people who participate in a study—especially one involving interview sessions—guess the researcher's evaluation sheet. The context of the interview—expert assessor and naive informer—may give rise to defensiveness and irritation as the participants feel, already, that their stories will be taken from them. Each study raises different questions of influence. When I was led to ask teenagers and mature women about their feelings of envy, I often met with such irritation (Apter, 1995). Amy (aged 14) said that she believed that if she made an effort to get to know a girl and like her, then she could overcome her envy; but another girl (aged 15) said that she wanted to stay friends with Ruth "so that I can keep an eye on her." "What do you need to watch out for?" I asked. "I want to know how worried I should be, like whether she's racing ahead of me." "What do you do if she is?" I asked. "I feel awful," she replied, "but at least I *know*."

"What do you envy about her? I mean—why her?" I wanted to know, and she shrugged:

> She's so pretty, and smart. Like she's always smart. When she walks into the school, everyone feels different. She's really there. Well, if I say these things—they sort of fall apart. They sound silly but they're not! You know, clothes look different on her. White tennis socks, that red sweater she wears, with its wide ribbing set against her skirt, and her hair's always so—neat. She'll probably go to Stanford. She's all set up inside. I don't like talking about this. It isn't just

one thing, it's everything; but sometimes when I match up to her, like I get a higher grade or something, or when she messes up, I feel relieved. Okay? It just makes me feel better, because I'll know I don't have to envy her today.

Her relief at one small break from her envy registered its pain. But however familiar she was with it and however articulate she was about the range and details that aroused her envy, she could not locate its cause. This clearly bothered her. "OK?" she repeated. I had talked enough. I had made her feel stupid. I had made her reveal too much. I was stupid not to understand. Why should anyone know this about her. Such knowledge could be dangerous:

> When I talk to you sometimes I feel nothing I say is true. Like, I say something, and then when I explain it—'cause you ask—you know—"why so-and-so?"—it sometimes sounds bigger than it is. Like I'm not this green monster running around. But, sure, I envy some girls. Everyone does. But, like, what's this going to sound like? And where's my say? (Apter, 1995, pp. 222-223)

This is the great concern of people interviewed: that the psychologist will use their words, and take away their "say." Amy knows that what she says can be accurately reproduced, and yet she will feel silenced if the proportion and the context are in some way betrayed.

Roberta, 30 years older than Amy but struggling like a 14-year-old girl with her idealization of others, said,

> Something about another woman will just spark it off, and I'm burning with fury, asking "Why *her* and not *me*?" These feelings leave scars, and you never know when they'll open up again. I get so angry, and think and say such awful things. But it makes me ache, just feeling what it's like . . . for a minute you think what being her is like. And getting older— facing fifty!—well that's me locked out, isn't it? I feel trapped in my own life. I just don't see a way out. My friends will ring up and tell me their good news—phew—it's like being battered, one slap after another, and they just

keep on. Especially this one woman . . . she's been doing this
and that on the *Tribune,* and suddenly she's become real big,
travelling all over the place and covering everything. On and
on she goes about what new thing she's going to do. It's a
nightmare—she just won't stop, and I want to say, "Give me
a break; can't you just give me a break from all your fucking
triumphs." (Apter, 1995, p. 231)

Yet I observed Roberta in conversation with her friends, and she
prodded them into revelations about their triumphs. She would ask
how they were and what was happening at work and whether there
was any good news about this or that. I put this to her and she said,
"Yeah, that way I can brace myself for it; it won't jump out at me
unawares" (Apter, 1995, p. 231).

Like young Amy defeated by her adoration of another girl, Roberta
needs to know about their triumphs, to decide how much envy to
expend in a single day. Like Amy, too, the sound of what she had said
had unwholesome reverberations:

Why do I talk about these things? Why do you want to
know these things? It's going to make me look so bad. I
mean, sometimes we're talking and it's all right. There's a
string pulling in out, and it is fine. But sometimes I think
about what's unraveled, and I wonder whether it's right at
all. That's not me—not really me.

The words she had spoken so passionately, which had opened a
window onto the distorted suffering of envy, were now in a room she
wanted closed—not opened onto the world. But then it was too late.
The proofs were set. The deed was done. "But no one would recognize
you," I assured her. "No one would identify it as you." She nodded
and tried to focus on her concern:

No. I know. And I'm not worried about that. Not that. It's
just the image of me. Sitting there, filled with such awful feelings. They come, and I hate them. But then they go. Now
there's something about them that won't go. And when they
come, they're real, now, in a different way.

There were times during interviews with a group of midlife women when I knew the interviews were fashioning their thoughts. Some women sought approval or assent, which I tried to indicate was irrelevant. Sometimes I had to argue this and then saw that their need to argue with me was itself a process of thought and development. If psychology is a narrative, then psychology that makes use of narrative changes both the narrative and the psychology on which it is based.

The following quotes from a recently completed study (Apter, 1995, pp. 140-143) reminded me how common it is for people to do battle to take possession of their own psychological narrative. When I first contacted Beth Geist, she had recently become a vice president of a pharmaceutical company. She asked to be interviewed in her office. She allowed me the exact time we had agreed to before the interview. She was thoughtful, composed, and, I felt, fully in control of what she revealed and what she reserved. Her job was to explain her rapid success and the trick of being the first woman vice president in this firm. She was 45 years old.

The next interview, 3 months later, was canceled. She was too busy to keep the prearranged appointment and would be travelling soon after. Six months after the initial interview, she suggested that she drop out of the study. Things were changing too rapidly, she explained, for her to be able to talk coherently about herself and her work. She did not think what she had to say now should go "on record." I tried to persuade her that "off-the-record" stories had to be told. If they were hidden, then other women would think their off-the-record lives were freakish. The experience of this new generation of midlife women should be shared:

"That's not what I want to hear," she laughed.

"Why?" I asked.

"I guess you'd better come, so I can explain."

This time, too, she sat behind her desk, facing me. But instead of resting her folded hands on its top, she fidgeted with papers, paper clips, and pens and wheeled herself constantly first closer then further away:

"I don't think I have anything more for you," she began.

"But you do. I know you do. Why do you think you don't?"

"Because . . . " and she sighed at my slow uptake, "I'm going to be resigning. So," she continued impatiently, "I'm not exactly your model career woman."

"*My* model . . . ?"

"Well that's why you're here—isn't it? To find out how women become successful?"

"No. It's to find out about women."

   She held my gaze for a moment and then laughed. "All right. Here it is."

Beth had fought long and hard within the company, particularly on the issue of hiring and promoting women:

> After a series of interviews, we sit down to decide who will get the job. Now I'm not working with a bunch of archaically minded men. They know it's important to admit women into the firm. They know it's importance for fairness, and for their image. But when they sit down to decide any individual case, they go haywire when discussing a woman. Their criteria keeps changing, and they don't even see what they're doing. We need a woman in to manage one of our regional branches. We all agreed beforehand that we wanted a woman, because in that particular branch there are so many women employees, and there have been a series of complaints and problems, linked either to the fact there is a male manager or no woman there to oversee the problems. But of course we can't advertise the job like that. We have to advertise it straight, so we have lots of men applying too. The procedure's got to be fair—oh, they're very careful about fairness when it comes to making sure they're not discriminating against men! They start picking each female candidate apart. She's very good, but she also has a family, so that means she probably won't be able to spend informal overtime, which every firm needs to take for granted. If she

isn't married then she is either considered too young or not the sympathetic sort. When I try to point out what they are doing, I'm told that I'm veering toward reverse discrimination. I'm labelled a feminist, so everything I say in appointment discussions is undermined by that. I have this unwarranted identity thrust on me, and it means that whatever I say is counterproductive. Everything I say is heard with that assumption—that I'm going to be rooting for a woman just because she's a woman, so anything I say in defense of a woman is just brushed aside. I'm not really talking any more, just mouthing words. The feeling this gives me . . . It's not a feeling I want to live with. After the last batch of appointments, I decided to distance myself from it all, and I've realized that means I'll have to leave the firm. If I'm going to stay sane, if I'm going to wake up each morning without chips sloughing off my shoulders, then I'll have to find something else to do.

She wheeled her chair forward and launched into what sounded like a defense against an imagined accusation:

You have no idea how hard it will be to give up this job. Okay, I'll find something else. I'm not giving up work. But to walk out . . . when I think how much it's meant to me. But you can only say "Things will get better" for so long. And once you see they're not, you keep seeing them, and asking yourself . . . It's a headache, let me tell you.

Initially, Beth was so deeply committed to a standard of a successful careerist that she could not imagine that someone would want to see the person who might be at odds with that persona. The sets of feelings and experiences and needs that were at odds with her corporate life were assumed to be of no interest, not to be spoken of. She was receptive to my argument that women's disappointments or rough edges or off-the-record stories should be heard because she was already distressed about her collusion in sustaining unequal structures. Her argument to me ("You have no idea how hard it will be") is typical of an early midlife crisis phase in which others' judgments are still internalized and must be argued against. Like the adolescent girl who, in her mind's ear, hears her mother's remarks before they are spoken and fights her mother on these imagined grounds (see Apter, 1990), Beth imagined in me the objections she was beginning to overrule. The expectation of my judgment influenced her own narrative. It came out, as I have transcribed it, well argued—perhaps even rehearsed. The concern that I would not listen to her, in the sense that I would judge her by my own standards of what a model working woman was, made her prepare her own story. Even then, she was unsure of her control over the narrative: I had to assure her that I would listen to it before she told it to me.

The 80 midlife women in my study worked to establish their own narratives against the tide of other narratives of women and midlife women. Not all of these narratives were from psychologists. Not all of the narratives they battled against were accurately constructed. But each woman felt the burden of many so-called expert interpretations of her feelings and needs. Lottie, a midlife female character in Sue Miller's (1993) *For Love,* reflects that the generation coming of age in the 1960s were the first real post-Freudians:

> It was impossible to take yourself seriously. Every single thing was a dynamic. We knew everything was neurosis. And love in particular was made suspect forever, don't you think? Trivialized . . . See, in the nineteenth century, people could *feel* their emotions without second-guessing themselves all the time. They didn't have to realize that there was something ridiculously predictable and culture-bound—mundane— about even the most grand of them. (p. 130)

But Lottie's concern is less with psychoanalytic theories than with the stories other people tell of their lives, of the way we become minor characters in others' stories, and how the stories people tell about themselves become points of attraction in a game played in which people make themselves lovable. We are all possessive of the stories we tell about our lives—what we have suffered, what we desire, what we aim for, who we are. And other people tell different stories. But who owns the knowledge, who has power to tell the real story?

For women, midlife poses special challenges to a self narrative, as they catch glimpses of themselves as a type of woman they may once have marginalized and to whose marginalization by others they are highly sensitive. The women I interviewed for this project were also aware of themselves as having to change narratives throughout their lives. "I started out so sure of what I wanted, and I was so sure I could get it. That determination—" Patricia Galen laughed as it loomed up before her:

> And it isn't that now I see I was wrong or too idealistic—it's not that. No, I wasn't wrong, and I'm very pleased about what I've achieved, and how all that I've done will help me to do more. But as you get older—but it's more than getting older, isn't it? Yes, and it's certainly not getting old. No—there's a process—isn't there?—that you don't want just to call "maturity." It's as though the whole texture of your life changes, and you get better at touching it. (Apter, 1995, p. 319)

As Patricia and I shared enjoyment in her investigative description, I thought about the aptness of her terms, which blended problems in her work as a sculptor with life issues; but I also heard her utter what so many other women felt: that they wanted a hearing and wanted a structure for their changing narratives.

Psychology is one version of the power of the narrative. As with any power, it can be misused to wield power rather than to empower others. Yet such narratives are inescapable. We are all psychologists. People use psychology to make sense of their world—and sometimes to manipulate it or control it. Much of our behavior is influenced by psychological theories. We learn to monitor our own behavior and that of others. Being nice to someone, comforting someone, reassuring someone—all these behaviors are based on presumptions of what someone is feeling—and how someone will respond to what we say. We humans construct ourselves with stories about the meaning of what we do and what we have done. Our sense of character rests on presumptions about how we would behave in many hypothetical situations. The stories others tell about us affect us deeply. We feel outraged by unfair gossip, which we may hear in mangled form, and whose "behind one's back" discourse takes away our power to challenge or correct it. In the same way, we may feel devastated by a psychologist's manipulation of our story.

I continue to interfere in the narratives of the people I interview. What do I offer them that I can subject them to such risks? What protection can I give them? How do I minimize the risks? For I know all too well that narratives are not simple, that narratives change things, that the psychologist's narrative has a kind of privilege—often undeserved, but lack of desert does not reduce its power. Sometimes I worry about this and sometimes I don't. Many of my subjects, by whom I hope I really do mean participants and collaborators, get upset in the course of the interviews. Momentary excitement or harm? Perhaps they are letting it all hang out, and it is all to the good? I cannot answer; only they can answer. Therefore, I can conduct no experiments, no obfuscation, no withholding of information, no deceit. But I am the one who selects their quotes. I tease out revelations. I put together things that were not given to me already packaged. In some people's eyes, I am one of the so-called experts and therefore among the psychologists.

Yet psychology remains irresistible. Its very defects lure me on; they stimulate further questions. What is left out of current studies? What questions have not been asked or have been misconstrued? What theories silence us, and how can they be countered? In short, much of the impetus to do psychology comes from frustration with the narratives of other psychological experts. For there is exhilaration that psychology offers in overcoming its own limitations. It is a challenge that involves shifting away from fixed theories and keeping the information flowing and the perspective flexible. The crucial antidote to psychology's cruelty is a researcher's awareness of the undue power of a so-called expert narrative and of its undue claim to be a master narrative. People may construct their narratives in contradistinction to the ones they perceive us to represent. Their narratives, however, may be silenced or confused by those of a psychologist. Can researchers and therapists take on board the necessarily shifting ground of psychological narrative? Because this is the ethical mandate: to use whatever expertise we have to gauge the possible effect of our work on those we study and to be constantly on the lookout for effects that, in our blinkered hunt, we may have missed. Can we observe ourselves at work and the effects of our work? Can we describe the workings of mind while we let those minds get on with their own work? If not, can we disclose our political agenda and open it to debate? Only if we are able to do this will we mitigate the cruelty and intrusiveness of psychology.

Notes

1. I am not sure whether these particular studies were ever written up. I have come across similar studies, which I did not participate in, such as Heckhausen, H. (1982). Development of achievement motivation. In Willard Hartup (Ed.), *Review of Child Development Research* (Vol. 6, pp. 600-668). Chicago: University of Chicago Press.

2. This quote is from an unpublished transcript from the same 1992 study.

3. These quotes are from interviews taped in 1994.

References

Apter, T. (1990). *Altered loves: Mothers and daughters during adolescence.* New York: St. Martin's.

Apter, T. (1993). Altered Views: Fathers' closeness to teenage daughters. In R. Josselson & A. Lieblich (Eds.), *The narrative study of lives* (Vol. 1, pp. 163-190). Newbury Park, CA: Sage.

Apter, T. (1995). *Secret paths: Women in the new midlife.* New York: Norton.

Cooperstock, R., & Lennard, H. L. (1979). Some social meanings of tranquilizer use. *Sociology of Health and Illness, I*(3), 331-347.

Dennis, W. (Ed.). (1948). *Readings in the history of psychology.* New York: Appleton-Century-Crofts.

Dunn, J. (1988). *Beginnings of social understanding.* Oxford: Basil Blackwood.

Freud, S. (1953a). Fragment of an analysis of a case of hysteria. In J. Strachey (Trans. & Ed.), *The standard edition of the complete psychological works of Sigmund Freud* (Vol. 7). London: Hogarth.

Freud, S. (1953b). The interpretation of dreams (Vols. 1 & 2). In J. Strachey (Trans. & Ed.), *The standard edition of the complete psychological works of Sigmund Freud* (Vols. 4 & 5). London: Hogarth.

Gilman, C. P. (1935). *The living of Charlotte Perkins Gilman: An autobiography.* New York: Appleton-Century.

Kaysen, S. (1993). *Girl, interrupted.* New York: Turtle Bay.

Laing, R. D., & Esterson, A. (1970). *Sanity, madness and the family.* New York: Viking.

Milgram, S. (1963). Behavioral study of obedience. *Journal of Abnormal and Social Psychology, 67,* 371-378.

Milgram, S. (1974). *Obedience to authority.* New York: Harper and Row.

Miller, S. (1993). *For love.* New York: HarperCollins.

Minuchin, S. (1984). *Family kaleidoscope.* Cambridge, MA: Harvard University Press.

Plath, S. (1963). *The bell jar.* London: Faber.

Porter, R. (1987). *A social history of madness.* London: Weidenfeld & Nicolson.

Skinner, B. F. (1978). *Reflections on behaviorism and society.* Englewood Cliffs, NJ: Prentice Hall.

Tucker, N. (1994, November 18). Suffer little children. *London Times Higher Educational Supplement,* pp. 18, 20.

❧ 4 ❧

Personal Vulnerability
and Interpretive Authority
in Narrative Research

Susan E. Chase

*A*ll research based on in-depth interviews raises ethical and process issues, but narrative research demands that we pay special attention to participants' vulnerability and analysts' interpretive authority.

Sociologists who use methods of narrative analysis to interpret in-depth interviews focus on how individuals' stories embody general cultural processes or phenomena. We often select a small group of stories from a larger collection to serve as examples of the processes we want to study, and in our writing, we present those examples fully to demonstrate the relationship between specific stories and the cultural context. Thus research participants easily recognize themselves in our texts and readers who know them may recognize them, too, even when pseudonyms and other forms of disguise are used.

By contrast, readers of texts based on conventional methods of qualitative analysis are unlikely to be able to identify research participants—indeed, participants may not even recognize themselves (Rubin, 1976, p. 214). This happens because sociologists usually dissect individual interviews into pieces, looking for patterns across the entire set (Weiss, 1994), and they write about general themes that they demonstrate through a series of brief interview excerpts.

The extensive use of individuals' stories in narrative research clearly renders participants more vulnerable to exposure than conventional qualitative studies do. In turn, this greater vulnerability makes more acute the question of who should control the interpretive process. In this chapter, I discuss how I dealt with participants' vulnerability and how I claimed my interpretive authority in a study of the work narratives of women school superintendents (Chase, 1995). I also explore what good comes from or what purpose is served by narrative analysts' asserting such authority.

Attending to Narrators' Vulnerability

Between 1986 and 1989, my coresearcher Colleen Bell and I conducted intensive interviews with 27 women who led the nation's public schools in rural, suburban, and urban districts across the United States. We were interested in their work experiences in this overwhelmingly male- and white-dominated profession—95% of school superintendents are male and 96% are white. At the time of the interviews, we explained that we intended to publish work on the basis of the interviews, but we did not know specifically what kind of writing we would do or what our interpretations or analyses would be. As highly educated professionals, the women we interviewed were no strangers to research; two thirds hold doctorates and so have conducted research of their own at some point in their lives. We spoke in general terms about how publication of their stories would be helpful to other women. In retrospect, it is interesting that we did not say that our analyses would be helpful to them personally. Indeed, both we and they took for granted that our research would be especially useful to women at earlier stages in their careers who aspire to positions these educational leaders already held. They seemed to experience their participation in our study as a pleasurable part of their professional responsibility to younger women.

After Colleen and I finished interviewing, we wrote several coauthored papers and also decided that each of us needed to produce some singly authored texts because coauthored work is less valued in the professional world of academe. I had developed an interest in treating the interviews as narratives and began to work on narrative analyses of specific interviews.

Because women superintendents are public figures in their communities, and in some cases have national reputations in educational circles, I felt a special responsibility to make sure that I disguised their identities well and that I did not publish material that made them feel too vulnerable. I sent copies of the transcripts to those women whose interviews I wanted to use extensively and asked for permission to use certain sections that I marked on the transcripts. I also informed them of ways I planned to conceal their identities and reminded them of the possibility that some readers might recognize them despite my attempts at disguise.

All of the women I contacted granted me permission to use their stories. At the same time, some pointed out details that they wanted me to either exclude or handle carefully. In one case, we discussed at length the ways I would change the details of a story to ensure that her identity was protected. In general, I found that they felt most vulnerable about statements they had made about colleagues or persons in their communities or about political controversies in which they were embroiled. I sensed that they felt such statements might anger their colleagues or constituents (if my attempts at disguise were unsuccessful) and thus damage their professional relationships or local reputations. In other words, they were most concerned about possible negative effects on their jobs or work situations. By contrast, none expressed concern about publication of passages in which they described painful emotions generated by problems encountered at work—such as discrimination—or in which they recounted non-work-related difficulties.

In each case, I honored their requests to conceal or exclude specific details and hoped that this would eliminate any potentially negative effects of publication of their stories. In addition, the long germination of researching, writing, and publishing a book mitigates vulnerability; the interviews took place between 1986 and 1989, and the book, *Ambiguous Empowerment: The Work Narratives of Women School Superintendents,* was published in 1995. Moreover, three of the four women whose narratives I eventually chose to analyze in depth have moved from the jobs they held at the time of the interviews.

Claiming My Authority as Narrative Analyst

Sending transcripts and asking for permission to use specific passages gives a certain amount of control to participants and reduces the vulnerability they might feel from exposure of their stories. I did not, however, share my work in progress—my interpretations—with the women whose narratives I had analyzed extensively. At the time of the interviews, or later in granting me permission to use specific parts of the transcripts, several women expressed interest in "the final product," but none asked to read work in advance of publication. Nonetheless, by not asking them to read my interpretations, I made a methodological decision that has consequences for the research relationship. As I sat down to write about this decision, I realized how much I had struggled with it. Professional pressures, feminist issues, and my intellectual commitment to narrative analysis became distinct but entangled influences in this decision.

Professional Pressures

In writing *Ambiguous Empowerment,* I was racing against the tenure clock, and I had good reason to believe that my achievement of tenure was contingent on finishing the manuscript and securing a contract for publication. The writing process would have slowed considerably had I sought to negotiate interpretations with research participants. More seriously, if, for some reason I had not anticipated, any of the four women whose narratives I had devoted an entire chapter to decided that she wanted her narrative excluded from the book, completing it would have been delayed.

In addition, I knew that failing to finish the manuscript because of interviewees' responses to my interpretations would not be looked on favorably by many of the people evaluating my record. Although some feminist researchers attend to participants' responses to their interpretations, conventional social science is indifferent to if not dismissive of such a practice (Cancian, 1992). If I lost an entire chapter at the request of an interviewee, those evaluating me would treat that as a sign of failure rather than a serious methodological commitment on my part.

On the one hand, then, I did not want to jeopardize my career. I felt I had adequately fulfilled my ethical responsibility to participants by sending them their interview transcripts and asking for permission to use specific passages. I had already done more than most social scientists who usually stop at obtaining signatures on informed consent forms. On the other hand, I felt tugged by my feminist commitments.

Feminist Issues

I conceive of my work as feminist—by which I mean, in part, that it is guided by my desire to contribute to our understanding of how women make sense of their lives in an inequitable social world and of how social change becomes possible. In this sense, my work is for women rather than for those who have the power to control women's lives (Chase, 1989; Harding, 1987; Westkott, 1979). A growing literature argues, however, that feminist commitments should inform research methods as well as substance. Feminist methodologists challenge the conventional hierarchy of researcher and researched and resist the potentially exploitive aspects of the research relationship by raising questions about authorship and ownership: Who should control the interpretive process and who should benefit from publication of results (Cancian, 1992; Harding, 1987; Lugones & Spelman, 1993; Mbilinyi, 1989; Reinharz, 1992; Shostak, 1989; Stacey, 1988; Wolf, 1992; Zavella, 1993)?

In terms of conducting the interviews, my coresearcher and I worked at making the context comfortable and collaborative—we aimed to produce interactive conditions that would encourage participants to tell their stories fully. Nonetheless, as we wrote our coauthored papers (Bell & Chase, 1995; Bell & Chase, in press; Chase & Bell, 1990; Chase & Bell, 1994), we chose to exercise control over the interpretive process rather than share that control with participants. Later, when I began to analyze individual narratives, my feminist commitments surfaced and nudged me to share my work in progress with those individuals. I was (and still am) attracted to this idea because it breaks down the barrier between researcher and researched. It acknowledges that my research depends on your story and that you have good reason to be particularly interested in what I have to say about your story. If my narrative were the subject of someone else's book, I would certainly be curious about how my words were interpreted. Does the researcher portray me sympathetically? What can I learn about myself from the analysis? Of what is my story treated as an example? How might my feedback make the analysis stronger?

Interestingly, when I searched the literature for examples of feminist research in which the researcher had shared her work in progress with those she studied, I discovered that such collaborative attempts often resulted in less than sanguine reactions from participants. Margaret Andersen (1987, p. 187) found that her sociological characterizations angered the corporate wives she had interviewed, and Arlene Kaplan Daniels (1983, pp. 205-206; 1988, pp. xiv-xv) had a similar experience with upper-class women volunteers. Both Andersen and Daniels state that, with the help of participants, they revised and strengthened their interpretations. In her study of a working-class women's union drive at Duke Medical Center, Karen Sacks (1988, pp. viii-ix) reported that she, too, encountered criticism from participants that she used to improve her analyses. In addition, one woman requested that her story be deleted from the final manuscript, a request Sacks honored. Judith Stacey (1990, pp. 272-278) gave the last word to the two women who dominate her ethnography of family life by publishing in an epilogue the women's reactions to her book. Whereas one woman declined to say much, the other spoke passionately about how Stacey's presentation of her story failed to capture fully who she was.

These "tales of the field" (Van Maanen, 1988) gave me pause. On the one hand, some participants' displeasure seemed to arise from researchers' initial, unfair characterizations. On the other hand, some of it seemed related to the interpretive process of transforming particular stories into examples of larger social phenomena. If a participant expects that the researcher will capture fully who she is, then it must be disconcerting to have her story analyzed for the social processes it reveals rather than preserved in its uniqueness.

I began to feel that there may be no easy solution to the question of how to integrate feminist commitments into one's research methods. Sharing work in progress with participants does not necessarily lead to agreement on how interpretations should be made, what is sociologically significant, and what should be published. The researcher must decide how to respond to, negotiate, or present disagreement, and in so doing, she continues to exercise control over the research process (Mishler, 1986, pp. 126-127).

Susan Krieger's (1991) discussion of this feminist dilemma helped me to resolve it for myself, at least with respect to my narrative analysis of women superintendents' stories. She suggests that the researcher's analysis, no matter how oriented to participants' points of view, reflects more than anything the researcher's interests, choices, and concerns. She writes,

> I saw repeatedly that my work looked like itself more than like anything else. It had themes whose source was not in the external world so much as in my consciousness of it. In addition, I found that the people described in my studies usually preferred to have the studies seen as mine and not theirs. . . . There was more to their stance, I thought, than a desire to deny unwanted truths. There was a basic recognition that a study, or story, was the work of its author: it might include aspects of the lives of other people, but the person most responsible for putting those aspects together would be held accountable for the work in the end. (p. 53)

Rather than suggesting that researchers attempt (futilely) to subordinate their interests to those of participants, Krieger argues that researchers should acknowledge their interests and how they may differ from participants' interests. This encouraged me to take responsibility for my desire to author certain kinds of interpretations of women superintendents' narratives, interpretations grounded in the growing field of narrative analysis. I concluded that although feminist commitments require that we address questions of authorship and authority, no specific rules can be outlined for answering them. Who should control the interpretive process in any particular case depends in large part on the aim or purpose of the research and thus what kind of material needs to be collected and what kind of interpretation best suits that material. Moreover, as long as decisions about these questions are made by the researcher (for example, the researcher may decide to invite certain kinds of collaboration), the researcher continues to exercise authority not shared with participants. Fully collaborative ventures, in which the distinction between researchers and participants evaporates and all share equally in authorship and the benefits of publication, may suit particular kinds of studies. But I contend that projects in which the researcher controls the interpretive process are not necessarily less feminist. In the latter case, however, I believe that claiming and acknowledging one's interpretive authority is imperative.

Narrative Analysis as a Theoretical Commitment

In my view, a simple distinction between narrators as storytellers and narrative analysts as interpreters is misleading. Storytellers do more than chronicle events; they also evaluate how and why events occur, determine their meaning, and interpret characters' actions and motives (Labov, 1972; Polanyi, 1985). In addition, the in-depth interview context, at least as my coresearcher and I organized it, allows for more than a rigid exchange of questions and answers. It becomes an interactive process of telling, listening, clarifying, and understanding (Chase & Bell, 1994). During the interviews, our shared goal as narrator and listeners was to hear and understand the narrator's story in full detail.

As I began to analyze women superintendents' narratives, however, I felt a disjunction growing between my interest and their interest in their stories—a disjunction between my interest in how culture shapes narrative processes and their interest in articulating and explaining their experiences. As a sociologist, I was already familiar with the general content of their experiences because they had been recorded by innumerable studies, not necessarily of women superintendents but of women in other white- and male-dominated professions (Edson, 1988; Epstein, 1983; Kanter, 1977; Lorber, 1984; Shakeshaft, 1987). Indeed, professional women's stories of achievement and discrimination had become common fare in the popular media. Instead of presenting yet another version of the familiar, I wanted to analyze the cultural processes that are taken for granted in such stories. In articulating my interest, I do not mean to denigrate the content of women's stories; a focus on content is inherent in all storytelling and listening. Like our interviewees, we, too, concentrated on content during interviews, on understanding the specific events, actions, characters, and feelings they described.

Nonetheless, in my view, narrative analysis consists of a different form of interpretation from that which occurs during engaged story-telling and listening. I was interested in how women superintendents' narratives embodied general cultural phenomena. As I analyzed the narratives, I focused on a set of language processes that are taken for granted in everyday speech: the use of cultural discourses for making sense of individual experience; the development of narrative strategies in relation to conflicting cultural discourses; and the communication of meaning through linguistic features of talk (such as pace and intonation as well as words) (Bruner, 1987; Heilbrun, 1989; Mishler, 1986; Personal Narratives Group, 1989; Polanyi, 1985; Riessman, 1990; Rosenwald & Ochberg, 1992; Stromberg, 1993). In the course of our everyday lives—including interviews—intelligible and effective communication requires that we simultaneously depend on and ignore these language processes. They become visible or audible only through a reflective, retrospective standpoint.

Thus, in my analytic work, I focused on how women superintendents narrated their experiences of achievement and discrimination within the context of an overwhelmingly white- and male-dominated profession. Through this analytic focus on narrative processes, I hoped to show how successful professional women inevitably encounter and must find some way to respond to a significant disjunction in U.S. culture: the disjunction between taken-for-granted, individualistic, gender- and race-neutral discourse about professional work and con-tentious, gendered and racialized discourse about inequality. More generally, I aimed to show that language constraints (such as that dis-cursive disjunction) are much more taken for granted and invisible than even the structural constraints shaping women's professional lives.

Given this analytic focus, I decided that it was not necessary to send participants drafts of my analyses and to ask for their feedback. When researchers share their work in progress, they are often attempt-ing to answer certain questions: Have I gotten it right? Do I under-stand what you mean? (Reinharz, 1992, p. 21). But I did not need to ask for this kind of clarification and validation because my primary aim was not to analyze what participants intended to say. Rather, I aimed to interpret the meanings expressed implicitly in their use of cultural discourses, their narrative strategies, and their linguistic practices. This was not a case, then, where the narrator's agreement with my interpretation would have validated it in any special sense. In terms of evaluating my interpretations of the discursive, narrative, and linguistic processes embedded in their stories, they would have been in a position similar to that of any other reader. Thus I chose colleagues familiar with methods of narrative analysis as readers of my work in progress.

In sum, I claimed my authority as narrative analyst by articulating a distinction between what I wanted to communicate through my interpretations and what women superintendents wanted to communicate by narrating their experiences. Although initially in conflict, my feminist and intellectual commitments grounded this exercise of authorship. My intellectual interest in cultural and language processes pushed me to develop my own story about women's narratives, whereas my feminist interest in nonexploitative research relationships pushed me to articulate the consequences of claiming authority in this way. The professional pressure of my impending tenure review lent urgency to the process of figuring out how to claim my interpretive authority while respecting women superintendents as research participants.

In articulating the difference between my work and participants' stories, I created a distance between myself as researcher and those whose narratives I studied, a distance that may seem typical of conventional social science that ignores the research relationship after tipping its hat to standard ethical issues. I contend, however, that acknowledging the difference between my and participants' interests makes room for rather than precludes conversation. The analytic story I tell invites readers—including the women whose narratives I have interpreted—to listen to professional women's stories in new ways. Furthermore, I suggest that listening in these new ways is pivotal to women's engagement in social change in their professional settings. Although I was not oriented to what these individual women may have wanted me to do with their stories, I hope my research serves their interests in a deeper sense by analyzing the cultural discourses that shape and constrain their understandings of their experiences of accomplishment and discrimination.

The Purpose or Good of Narrative Analysis

What, then, is the purpose of narrative analysis? What good is served when narrative analysts acknowledge the difference between their interests and those of participants and claim interpretive authority? The aim of narrative analysis is not to impose immutable or definitive interpretations on participants' stories or even to challenge the meanings participants attach to their stories. Rather, its goal is to turn our attention elsewhere, to taken-for-granted cultural processes embedded in the everyday practices of storytelling. With this shift of attention, questions of content become deeper and more complex. Understanding the meaning and significance of a story requires understanding how it is communicated within or against specific cultural discourses and through specific narrative strategies and linguistic practices.

More specifically, what good might come from my analyses of women superintendents' narratives? How are my analyses *for* women superintendents? How might a focus on the disjunction in contemporary U.S. culture between discourse about professional work and discourse about inequality, and an analysis of the narrative strategies women developed in relation to that disjunction, be useful to the women I wrote about? How might it be useful to women in other male- and white-dominated professions? What can a professional woman learn from such an analysis that would make a difference to her professional life?

Although it is difficult to answer such questions about one's own work, I venture the following. By shifting attention to the cultural processes embedded in women superintendents' narratives, my analysis invites readers who are themselves professional women to listen for the discursive disjunction that constrains their stories about achievement and discrimination and thus constrains their understandings of their experiences. As I suggest in the conclusion of *Ambiguous*

Empowerment (Chase, 1995), this reflection will lead professional women to ask themselves new questions:

> In what contexts do I speak more and less freely about my competence and accomplishments? Are these the same contexts in which I speak more and less freely about my experiences of sex or race discrimination? What narrative strategies do I use to tell my stories? Do I exclude my subjection when I want to highlight my achievements or ambition . . . or do I integrate stories of success and subjection . . . ? When I recount experiences of discrimination, what vocabularies do I draw on to understand what happened, to come to terms with the pain of subjection, to decide what action I should take, and to negotiate my relationships with those who discriminated against me? (p. 215)

By reexamining their stories through such questions, professional women can begin to "identify how their stories preserve or unsettle the individualistic, gender- and race-neutral discursive realm of professional work" (Chase, 1995, p. 215). And in so doing, they can begin to imagine what they would need to cultivate alternative forms of discourse and action in their work contexts, especially discourse and action oriented to collective struggles for social change.

Concluding Thoughts

If we as narrative analysts ground our interpretive authority in the idea that we achieve these kinds of goals through our work, do we have a responsibility to tell participants that we are going to reframe their experiences through the methods of narrative analysis?[1] Should the informed consent form for narrative research be different from that for more conventional methods of qualitative research?

We could tell prospective participants that during the interviews we want to hear about their experiences fully and in detail but that our analyses will reframe their stories through connections to the broader cultural context. We could tell them that narrative analysis often requires extensive use of some and minimal use of other individuals' stories. We could promise to inform them if we choose their narratives for close analysis and assure them that we will honor their requests to change or exclude details to protect their identities. Finally, we could explain that, given the nature of narrative analysis—its dependence on and embeddedness in the stories they recount—we cannot tell them in advance which individuals' stories we will select for detailed analysis and which specific aspects of the broader cultural context will be significant to our analyses.

I find appealing the idea that informed consent should be tailored to the processes involved in narrative analysis and even to the processes of specific narrative projects. At the same time, however, I think we need to remind ourselves as well as prospective participants that narrative research is a contingent and unfolding process, the results of which we cannot anticipate or guarantee. An informed consent form cannot possibly capture the dynamic processes of interpretation and authorship. Even if—or perhaps especially if—narrative analysts offer participants some form of ongoing negotiation over the use of their stories, we should also acknowledge to them that, in the end, we claim authority over the interpretive process.

Note

1. Ruthellen Josselson raised this question in her initial response to this chapter.

References

Andersen, M. L. (1987). Corporate wives: Longing for liberation or satisfied with the status quo? In M. J. Deegan & M. Hill (Eds.), *Women and symbolic interaction* (pp. 179-190). Boston: Allen & Unwin.

Bell, C. S., & Chase, S. E. (1995). Gender in the theory and practice of educational leadership. *Journal for a Just and Caring Education, 1*(2), 200-222.

Bell, C. S., & Chase, S. E. (in press). The gendered character of women superintendents' professional relationships. In K. D. Arnold, K. D. Noble, & R. F. Subotnik (Eds.), *Remarkable women: Perspectives on female talent development*. Cresskill, NJ: Hampton.

Bruner, J. (1987). Life as narrative. *Social Research, 54*(1), 11-32.

Cancian, F. M. (1992). Feminist science: Methodologies that challenge inequality. *Gender & Society, 6*(4), 623-642.

Chase, S. E. (1989). Social science for women: A reading of studies of women's work. *Humanity and Society, 13*(3), 246-267.

Chase, S. E. (1995). *Ambiguous empowerment: The work narratives of women school superintendents.* Amherst: University of Massachusetts Press.

Chase, S. E., & Bell, C. S. (1990). Gender, ideology, and discourse: How gatekeepers talk about women school superintendents. *Social Problems, 37*(2), 163-177.

Chase, S. E., & Bell, C. S. (1994). Interpreting the complexity of women's subjectivity. In E. M. McMahan & K. L. Rogers (Eds.), *Interactive oral history interviewing* (pp. 63-81). Hillsdale, NJ: Lawrence Erlbaum.

Daniels, A. K. (1983). Self-deception and self-discovery in fieldwork. *Qualitative Sociology, 6*(3), 195-214.

Daniels, A. K. (1988). *Invisible careers: Women civic leaders from the volunteer world.* Chicago: University of Chicago Press.

Edson, S. K. (1988). *Pushing the limits: The female administrative aspirant.* Albany: State University of New York Press.

Epstein, C. F. (1983). *Women in law.* Garden City, NY: Anchor.

Harding, S. (1987). *Feminism and methodology.* Bloomington: Indiana University Press.

Heilbrun, C. (1989). *Writing a woman's life.* New York: Ballantine.

Kanter, R. M. (1977). *Men and women of the corporation.* New York: Basic Books.

Krieger, S. (1991). *Social science and the self.* New Brunswick, NJ: Rutgers University Press.

Labov, W. (1972). *Language in the inner city: Studies in the black English vernacular.* Philadelphia: University of Pennsylvania Press.

Lorber, J. (1984). *Women physicians: Careers, status, and power.* New York: Tavistock.

Lugones, M. C., & Spelman, E. V. (1993). Have we got a theory for you! Feminist theory, cultural imperialism and the demand for "the woman's voice." In M. Pearsall (Ed.), *Women and values: Readings in recent feminist philosophy* (2nd ed., pp. 18-29). Belmont, CA: Wadsworth.

Mbilinyi, M. (1989). "I'd have been a man": Politics and the labor process in producing personal narratives. In Personal Narratives Group (Ed.), *Interpreting women's lives: Feminist theory and personal narratives* (pp. 204-227). Bloomington: Indiana University Press.

Mishler, E. G. (1986). *Research interviewing: Context and narrative.* Cambridge, MA: Harvard University Press.

Personal Narratives Group. (Ed.). (1989). *Interpreting women's lives: Feminist theory and personal narratives.* Bloomington: Indiana University Press.

Polanyi, L. (1985). *Telling the American story: A structural and cultural analysis of conversational storytelling.* Norwood, NJ: Ablex.

Reinharz, S. (1992). *Feminist methods in social research.* New York: Oxford University Press.

Riessman, C. K. (1990). *Divorce talk: Women and men make sense of personal relationships.* New Brunswick, NJ: Rutgers University Press.

Rosenwald, G. C., & Ochberg, R. L. (Eds.). (1992). *Storied lives: The cultural politics of self-understanding.* New Haven, CT: Yale University Press.

Rubin, L. B. (1976). *Worlds of pain: Life in the working class family.* New York: Basic Books.

Sacks, K. B. (1988). *Caring by the hour: Women, work, and organizing at Duke Medical Center.* Urbana: University of Illinois Press.

Shakeshaft, C. (1987). *Women in educational administration.* Newbury Park, CA: Sage.

Shostak, M. (1989). "What the wind won't take away": The genesis of Nisa—The life and times of a !Kung woman. In Personal Narratives Group (Ed.), *Interpreting women's lives: Feminist theory and personal narratives* (pp. 228-240). Bloomington: Indiana University Press.

Stacey, J. (1988). Can there be a feminist ethnography? *Women's Studies International Forum, 11*(1), 21-27.

Stacey, J. (1990). *Brave new families: Stories of domestic upheaval in late twentieth century America.* New York: Basic Books.

Stromberg, P. G. (1993). *Language and self-transformation: A study of the Christian conversion narrative.* Cambridge, MA: Cambridge University Press.

Van Maanen, J. (1988). *Tales of the field: On writing ethnography.* Chicago: University of Chicago Press.

Weiss, R. S. (1994). *Learning from strangers: The art and method of qualitative interview studies.* New York: Free Press.

Westkott, M. (1979). Feminist criticism of the social sciences. *Harvard Educational Review, 49*(4), 422-430.

Wolf, M. (1992). *A thrice-told tale: Feminism, postmodernism, and ethnographic responsibility.* Stanford, CA: Stanford University Press.

Zavella, P. (1993). Feminist insider dilemmas: Constructing ethnic identity with "Chicana" informants. *Frontiers: A Journal of Women's Studies, 13*(3), 53-76.

❧ 5 ❧

On Writing Other People's Lives

Self-Analytic Reflections of a Narrative Researcher

Ruthellen Josselson

All action and all love are haunted by the expectation of an account which will transform them into their truth.

—Merleau-Ponty
(1964)

*I*n the fourth act of Shakespeare's *Much Ado About Nothing,* Dogberry, the illiterate constable, is insulted by one of Don John's men who tells him bluntly, "Away! You are an ass, you are an ass." In response, Dogberry declares plaintively and fervently, "Oh, that he [the scribe] were here to write me down an ass! . . . Oh, that I had been writ down an ass." With this longing, Act IV ends.

We might wonder why, if Dogberry has been so grievously insulted, he would wish the insult to be written down. Shakespeare, in this exchange, calls our attention to the power of the written word. What is written is real; what is written really happened. Only if it were "writ" could Dogberry show that he *had* been grievously insulted; the act would be recorded. Written events gain a substantiality above that carried by memory or speech.

Although narrative researchers have begun to explore the ways in which our exchange with participants in the interactional phase of our research may affect those who share their lives with us, we have paid less attention to how what we write down may affect those about whom we write. And although we recognize that our hypotheses and conclusions about people originate in our own complex conceptual processes, we often lose sight of the additional authority our words and ideas carry when transferred to the permanence of print.

Judith Stacey (1988), in a widely cited, influential paper, raised the question of whether it is possible to have a truly feminist ethnography, whether it is possible to have an approach to research that is authentic, reciprocal, and fully intersubjective: "I find myself wondering whether the appearance of greater respect for and equality with research subjects in the ethnographic approach masks a deeper, more dangerous form of exploitation?" (p. 22). Not only does the field worker risk engaging in complex relationships with those she or he is observing, relationships that might be betrayed by full reporting of the material they provide, but the ethnographer must acknowledge that

> the research product is ultimately that of the researcher. With very rare exceptions it is the researcher who narrates, who "authors" the ethnography . . . [which is] a written document structured primarily by a researcher's purposes, offering a researcher's interpretations, registered in a researcher's voice. (p. 23)

Stacey's concerns, experiences, and cautions echoed my own apprehension in regard to narrative psychology.

How Does It Feel to Be Written About?

In this chapter, I want both to report and to analyze my interactions with participants about our experiences with the "writing down" process.

Perhaps because of my training and long experience as a psychotherapist as well as a narrative researcher, I am rarely uncomfortable talking to people about their lives—even hearing intimate details or bearing painful emotions. I do not worry that the interview will be injurious. Usually, these talks are cathartic, and I trust that my ability to understand another person's experience is affirming to him or her. And I do not worry much about betraying "confidentiality." I disguise in such a way that I am certain that no one else could recognize the people about whom I write and I have never, never disclosed anything to anyone that could lead to such recognition. But I worry intensely about how people will feel about what I write about them. I worry about the intrusiveness of the experience of being "writ down," fixed in print, formulated, summed up, encapsulated in language, reduced in some way to what the words contain. Language can never contain a whole person, so every act of writing a person's life is inevitably a violation.

I was interested in learning about how what I have written down about people I have studied has affected them. I pursued two sources of information about this. The first came from spontaneous comments and letters from women I had interviewed when they were 21 years old and again when they were 32, women who I then wrote about in a book called *Finding Herself* (Josselson, 1987). Six years after the publication of the book, I contacted them to interview them yet again. Some had read the book; most had not. Although I had promised to do so, I had not sent each of them a copy of the book—in part, because I was too uncomfortable about how they might respond to what I had written. If they read it, it was because they searched it out or came across it. But those who had read it shared with me their reactions at the time of this later interview.

My second source of information was from people who I had interviewed about their history of relationships for a book called *The Space Between Us* (Josselson, 1992). Because this was not a hypothesis-testing study, several of the participants whose life patterns I reported in detail were people with whom I have ongoing relationships in other contexts and this, I had thought, made it likely that I could have open, honest conversation with them about how it felt to have been written about. (Most of these people had seen what I wrote before publication, but none had asked me to make any changes.)

Before considering what I learned from these follow-up interviews about people's reactions to being written about, I want to reflect on the process of asking my participants to tell me about their experience of being fixed in print. I was surprised to find that this was a much more anxiety-provoking and difficult topic to discuss than were the interviews that explored their life histories. Although I had talked easily with these people about the most private details of their lives, I felt intensely anxious and uncomfortable talking with them about how it was for them to find their lives in print—and in words that I had written. My impression was that they were also anxious and uncomfortable with this topic.

For many of them, the first line of defense was to assure me that it was "fine" and that they had no reaction whatever to being written about (by me). But I didn't allow myself to be put off by this polite reassurance. What did you do with the book? I asked those from *The Space Between Us,* because I had sent all of them copies. Said one,

> Well, I have it in my office, but [very apologetically] I haven't read it again—maybe I should have since I knew you wanted to talk about it today, but I didn't have time [he had read the manuscript version] and I had been meaning to take it home, maybe even to show it to my wife, but I didn't.

We both recognized that this observation pointed to some possible conflict about so much of his internal, intimate life appearing in print, and I found myself growing anxious at this point. But, although I tried several avenues, this participant either would not or could not explore the ambivalence that was so apparent. (He simply reverted to asking if I wanted him to reread the book so that he could have a reaction. I didn't.) Here I learned from what could not be said—there is something discomfiting here but no matter, the book can be buried among the hundreds on the shelf and, I felt, we would tacitly agree not to speak about his being in the book, much as people may dissociate from an old love affair in the interests of working together—just pretend it never really happened. But I was left with the distress of not being able to name and understand my own discomfort, which felt like some mixture of shame, guilt, and dread.

In fact, I felt the same feelings in each of the other interviews that I initiated with the participants in *The Space Between Us.* Even when

I interviewed two of the participants with whom I did not have an ongoing connection, I felt the same. And I was aware of the same unpleasant feelings when, with those *Finding Herself* (Josselson, 1987) participants who had read the book, the conversation turned to their response to having read it. I will return to these concerns later. At this point, I wish only to stress that talking to people about how being written about has affected them was not an easy matter.

What My Participants Said

One participant (and now I don't even want to identify them by their original code names)—but let me call her Janice here—said that she had showed "her" section of *The Space Between Us* to her children in hopes that they could now better understand her. They had known about the trauma of her early life, but she hoped they could more fully appreciate how it affected her by seeing it in print. (Here, Shakespeare's "Oh, that I had been writ down" is relevant.) Despite the disguise of the material, she felt I had captured something essential about her, but she seemed ashamed to be using the book in this way. She was embarrassed that it had become important to her—and so was I. She countered this by then mentioning one passage where she felt I had got her wrong, where it didn't "feel" like her. Somehow, this was easier for both of us to discuss.

Participating in this process of sharing one's life to be written about by someone else stirs up a welter of narcissistic tensions in both the participant and the researcher. Inevitably, what we take into our possession as we collect people's life stories is people's narcissistic experience of themselves. Unwittingly, we may provoke what Kohut (1971) has termed a *mirror transference* in which our participants may regard us as carriers of core aspects of themselves (i.e., *selfobjects,* to use Kohut's phrase). Our writings then become for them highly concrete selfobjects and evoke the vicissitudes of powerful selfobject transferences. Serving, even temporarily during the interview, as validating, affirming selfobjects for our participants, we risk evoking the dynamics that emanate from the unconscious grandiose self (Kohut, 1971).

In fact, we *have* aggrandized our participants—we regarded them as important enough to write about. But the experience of the grandiose self is always accompanied by shame and by an unconscious conviction of being in complete control of the Other, and this, I think, complicates people's experience of being written about. In my interaction with Janice, it was my discomfort in bearing her shame about her excited feeling of aggrandizement that made me anxiously take refuge in my own narcissistic injury (my not having done a good enough job).

Similarly, failure to report in the written presentation something of great importance to the participant can be narcissistically wounding. Kohut (1971) commented on how trivial to the analyst may seem something "the patient, after so much time, labor, and intense inner resistance, has ultimately brought into the light of day" (p. 148). The revelation, Kohut goes on, may not have a strong emotional effect on the analyst. Analogously, what the narrative researcher is paying attention to may differ from those confessions that are central to the participant, but this becomes apparent only after the report is published. Very likely, some of my participants may have had an experience of my leaving out something that felt central to them, but they would certainly have felt too ashamed to tell me.

In reading what we have written, our participants are left to deal alone with our inevitable failure as selfobjects, with their injured or overstimulated grandiosity and with their recognition that they were not in control of us. And, being so close to the narcissistic core of personality organization, none of this can be easily discussed.

I think that the difficulties in managing the overstimulating aspects of the experience of grandiosity may also underlie some of the embarrassment of my *Finding Herself* participants who I asked how it felt to be written about. These are women who I have been following for 20 years who have, on occasion, expressed surprise that I would go to so much trouble to keep tracking their lives. Many who had read the book refused to discuss their reactions beyond "It was fine," and I suspect that shame-filled grandiosity in part shaped their reluctance to engage more fully with the question of what it has meant to them. One participant was, however, able to say simply, "I'm glad you thought my life was interesting enough to write about."

Integrating Interpretations

Besides the problem of maintaining narcissistic balance in the wake of the experience of being written about are the issues of managing the intrusiveness of the researcher's meaning-making efforts.

From Lydia, a participant from the *Finding Herself* study, I received a letter after I sent her a copy of the book, just after our third interview when she was 43 years old. After reading it, she wrote,

> Let me begin by telling you how much I enjoyed our interview session last month. What a luxury to talk about myself to an interested listener for three hours! As I later told my family and friends, it was a very therapeutic experience for me in that it allowed me the opportunity to make connections with my past. I appreciate having had that chance and sincerely hope that we can do it again in another ten years.
>
> As for the book, to me it is no less than a cherished gift. Of course it does wonderful things for my ego to read about myself as "Lydia." You were certainly right: I easily recognized myself and cannot help but feel flattered with much of the description. Except for a few exceptions (the geography, some of the timing and the dream), it was all quite accurate. To say that I was "pleased" is an understatement. But more importantly, your explanation of why I made the choice I made was a welcome enlightenment for me. . . . You have put together some pieces for me that hadn't quite fit before, and for that I shall always be grateful.

She goes on to discuss in detail how my explanation of why she had chosen the men she chose at various points in her life made great sense to her, more sense than the understanding she had been living with.

One would think that this letter, full of admiration and gratitude, would have made me feel elated, appreciated, and valuable. Instead, what I felt was dread and guilt. I felt that even though Lydia found my comments useful to her, I had intruded on her and on her life in a powerful way. Whatever sense she was making of her life was, after all, her sense. What right had I to impose my meaning making on her?

This is, after all, different from psychotherapy, in which someone invites, even pays for, my interpretations. And therapeutic interpretations are co-constructed in a very precise interpersonal context. Lydia merely agreed to talk to me. She never agreed to subject herself to my interpretations of her life.

But is this any different than if Lydia would have read a self-help book? I ask myself. After all, my ultimate hope is that others will learn from Lydia's life, as I have portrayed it, something that might be useful in their own. But someone other than Lydia gaining insight from Lydia's life is different from Lydia reading my interpretation of what she lived. Lydia is not reading about women in general or about some other woman in whose life she finds echoes of her own. What she reads is about her, about my summation and analysis of material she offered me. Perhaps I ought to be able to say, "How nice that I have however inadvertently been helpful to Lydia" and leave it at that. But I think that to do so is a way of blinding myself to the intrusiveness of this work—intrusiveness that is perhaps only harder to recognize when it seems to be valued by the one who is intruded on.

There are those who have contended that psychotherapy, in its essence, is just a way of renarrating someone's life (Schafer, 1992; Spence, 1982). If this is so, then the renarrating we do when we write about someone is a form of psychotherapy, cloaked not in the authority of the therapist-patient relationship but in the authority of the written word. To renarrate a life unasked, therefore, robs the Other of a piece of his or her freedom no matter how exhilarating an experience it may be.

Lydia's response also makes me wonder about "oracle" fantasies that our writings may induce in our participants. Especially to those who credit psychologists with knowing more than we do, we must, in our pronouncements, seem rather like oracles or like the angels who might appear at the end of life to tell a person what it all meant. I don't think we can underestimate the projected, imagined powers our apparent authority, which rests on our access to print, invokes.

Unlike Lydia, Jim is a participant in one of my studies who is himself a psychologist and a psychoanalyst, who has undergone a lengthy and thorough psychoanalysis, and is no stranger to commentary on his life. In one of my papers, I presented his life as an example of a way of

growing through the use of idealizable selfobjects—idealizing others
and then internalizing or trying to internalize what he perceived as
exemplary in them. In this follow-up interview, he spoke to me about
feeling "haunted" by what I wrote about him:

> It's as though your categorization of me is something I al-
> ways have to react to, something I have to support or dis-
> prove. How you categorized me is something I can't ignore.
> Sometimes I hear myself talking to people about someone
> new who I met or someone I heard lecture and then I find
> myself asking myself—so, does this reflect my tendency to
> idealize? I feel it's something I am trying to correct. So I find
> myself using your categorization to reflect on my relation-
> ships and approach to people. I say, "This is what Ruthellen
> wrote about me." In some ways, it has been an insight, but I
> feel it there as your perception and I use it to see how I'm
> really doing it and sometimes I think, "see, she was right."

What Jim was telling me about was his feeling that I had invaded
him—and in a way that he had not felt about his analysis. I had
"captured" him in a category that he could either explore or escape
from, but it was a cell that bounded how he could think about himself.
Of all the other terms through which he could process his experience,
somehow the one that I had written about seemed more powerful. I
had "writ him down an idealizer."

I think that what is important here is that Jim did not feel criticized
by my portrait of him. Indeed, I had presented him as admirable. I
hadn't suggested that there was anything unhealthy or undesirable
about his functioning. Rather, with the power of words, I had named
him and this naming came to feel like something he always had to
wrestle with.

My reinterview with Abby was, perhaps, the most surprising,
upsetting, and instructive. I had presented Abby, in *The Space Between
Us,* in a most appealing light. Hers was a story of growth and
enlightenment, but I sensed, in this reinterview, her profound discomfort with her role in my book. "Look," she finally brought herself to
say, "there was a lot I didn't tell you." From there, she began to unfold
a story of an aspect of her life of which she was deeply ashamed,

something horrifying, something, in all truth, I preferred not to know. For Abby, her discomfort with what I wrote down was that it was not the whole truth about her. She felt she had lied, had cheated me. In meeting the written text, she had a sense of, "Oh my God, I did not tell all the truth." What she found in my report was what she felt was a dishonest version of herself, and this only increased her shame about the part of herself she regards as a black spot on her soul. My written account reminded her of the ways in which she hides from the world. Her stifled narcissistic rage at having participated in my study was about seeing in the textual mirror the "false self" she presents to the world.

Have I harmed any of these people? I don't really think so. And I may have contributed to their growth. With time, Janice will undoubtedly integrate and modulate her high hopes for what being written about might create in her life, Lydia will go on to other kinds of meaning making, and my categorization of Jim will fade for him. Abby will continue to live with what she has to live with. Their tenure as characters in my books will become just one more of the many life experiences in which a person learns about himself or herself. In the end, I am not that powerful. But these issues for narrative research persist.

Saying What Is Hard to Say

My analysis here suggests that the discomfort that attended these interviews about effects derives from stirring up dormant narcissistic tensions. It was not an easy matter for me and my participants to acknowledge to each other the importance of what we did together. And it was perhaps hard (and courageous) for them to acknowledge the effect it had on them. Perhaps one can comfortably participate in such a study only by keeping its implications at a safe narcissistic distance.

But that leaves me still to understand my own discomfort—the dread, guilt, and shame that go with writing about others. These interviews helped me to some insight here. The dread is easiest to trace. There is always the dread that I will have harmed someone, that I will be confronted with, "How could you say that about me?"

The guilt is more complicated. My guilt, I think, comes from my knowing that I have taken myself out of relationship with my participants (with whom, during the interview, I was in intimate relationship) to be in relationship with my readers. I have, in a sense, been talking about them behind their backs and doing so publicly. Where in the interview I had been responsive to them, now I am using their lives in the service of something else, for my own purposes, to show something to others. I am guilty about being an intruder and then, to some extent, a betrayer.

And my shame is the hardest to analyze and the most painful of my responses. I suspect this shame is about my exhibitionism, shame that I am using these people's lives to exhibit myself, my analytical prowess, my cleverness. I am using them as extensions of my own narcissism and fear being caught, seen in this process.

Proceeding Nonetheless

Doing narrative research is an ethically complex undertaking, but I do not advocate that we stop doing it. Rather, I am suggesting here that although this is important work, it is work we must do in anguish. That we explore people's lives to make them into an example of some principle or concept or to support or refute a theory will always be intrusive and narcissistically unsettling for the person who contributes his or her life story to this enterprise. I don't think that there is any measure one can take to prevent this (beyond the usual safeguards, of course). No matter how gentle and sensitive our touch, we still entangle ourselves in others' intricately woven narcissistic tapestries. When we write about others, they feel it in some way. Yet I would worry most if I ever stopped worrying, stopped suffering for the disjunction that occurs when we try to tell an Other's story. To be uncomfortable with this work, I think, protects us from going too far. It is with our anxiety, dread, guilt, and shame that we honor our participants. To do this work, we must contain these feelings rather than deny, suppress, or rationalize them. We must at least try to be fully aware of what we are doing.

I arrive then, at a place similar to where Janet Malcolm (1990) ended in her reflections on the ethics of journalism:

> The wisest know that the best they can do . . . is not good enough. The not so wise, in their accustomed manner, choose to believe there is no problem and that they have solved it. (p. 162)

References

Josselson, R. (1987). *Finding herself: Pathways to identity development in women*. San Francisco: Jossey-Bass.

Josselson, R. (1992). *The space between us: Exploring the dimensions of human relationships*. San Francisco: Jossey-Bass.

Kohut, H. (1971). *The analysis of the self*. New York: International Universities Press.

Malcolm, J. (1990). *The journalist and the murderer*. New York: Knopf.

Merleau-Ponty, M. (1964). *Signs*. Evanston, IL: Northwestern University Press.

Schafer, R. (1992). *Retelling a life: Narration and dialogue in psychoanalysis*. New York: Basic Books.

Spence, D. (1982). *Narrative truth and historical truth*. New York: Norton.

Stacey, J. (1988). Can there be a feminist ethnography? *Women's Studies International Forum, 11*(1), 21-27.

❧ 6 ❧

Narrating a Psychoanalytic Case Study

Pirkko Lauslahti Graves

*T*he psychoanalytic case study is a special form of narrating lives. It is a narrative of a dialogue in which one person, the analysand, tells his or her life story, which is elaborated by the listener, the analyst, "along psychoanalytic lines" (Schafer, 1983, p. 219). This narrative, the case study, is the most compelling means of documenting clinical findings, which form the prime ground to develop and document psychoanalytic concepts and theory. But as numerous analysts have indicated, writing a case study exposes the writer—the analyst—to several conflicting forces. Foremost is the conflict between the recognition that detailed clinical material is essential for the furthering of clinical knowledge and the recognition that publishing the material contradicts the patient's rights for confidentiality and privacy. Freud (1905/1957), it is known, struggled with the conflict from early on. On the one hand, he stressed one's duty to publish clinical case material to further scientific and clinical understanding; not to do so was "a disgraceful piece of cowardness" (p. 8). On the other hand, he stressed the obligation toward the patient and advised publishing "as long as he [analyst] can avoid causing direct personal injury to the single patient concerned" (p. 8).

In my experience in writing, psychoanalytic case studies are among the most taxing and demanding. They force me to wrestle with a number of problems that I do not encounter when writing other kinds of reports. I shall reflect on some of the problems as I have experienced them. It is possible that they are idiosyncratic and need not represent a common fate in writing of case studies. I tend to believe, however, that at least some of the issues resonate as familiar concerns among many colleagues. And although I shall focus on a psychoanalytic case study, similar concerns emerge in all case studies that are grounded on long-term intensive treatment.

I shall first address some of the issues that relate to me as a reporter of my work. Motivations to write case studies can vary greatly. On occasion, it is to fulfill a requirement: As part of psychoanalytic training, one is expected to prepare annual reports; when the analysis is completed, another report is in order. Several additional reports need to be prepared for graduation from one's training institute, for certification by the umbrella organization, the American Psychoanalytic Association, and for other steps requested for promotion in the psychoanalytic hierarchy. These case studies, however, are not typical case studies because they aim to illustrate the writer's technical knowledge and understanding of the clinical process.

A different category of motivation is involved when I "volunteer" to write a case study. Intriguing theoretical or technical aspects may have emerged as the patient's narrative of his or her life has unfolded in treatment. These aspects may convince me of the importance to inform others or to initiate a dialogue with colleagues. Or I find myself challenged in my work by responses on my part, puzzling at first because they scarcely represent my typical modus operandi. Close scrutiny, more often than not, will lead to a novel understanding of the patient and of myself. And although such experiences may not be directly applicable to others' experiences, some commonality can be recognized so that my observations become worthwhile to describe and report.

Other motivations can be unearthed as well, such as a wish to impress others, pridefully to show my talents, or a desire to leave my mark in psychoanalytic writings. These are important motives because they help me to sustain the task of writing and to carry me over the main hurdle that invariably appears and with which I wrestle through most of the writing. The hurdle is the intensely self-revelatory nature involved in my writing about my work as analyst. This writing exposes, more than I like, my mistakes, blind spots, and other limitations, not only my strengths and capabilities. It happens because my understanding of a case study is inherently a study of the analytic dialogue. This dialogue is a continuous, widening, and deepening exchange, both verbal and nonverbal, between analyst and analysand. Far from being a Delphic oracle, I bring into my work my personality, life experience, my identity as analyst. I endeavor to use these highly personal qualities, filtered through training, work experience, self-knowledge, and discipline, to assist my aim in analysis: to help the other person, the analysand, understand his or her past and present life more fully and so improve his or her capacity to make choices.

It is perhaps this highly subjective nature of the analytic work that led Freud to challenge himself—and others—to have the courage to write. This very subjectivity of analysis also makes it closer to an artistic creation, less "science" with its expectations of measurable, quantifiable, and reproducible characteristics.

This view of analysis carries as its consequence certain responsibilities toward the analysand. Because the analysand is an active collaborator in the analytic process, I cannot claim sole ownership of the clinical material. It follows that the analysand's permission is essential before I can use the material for a publishable case study.

This view, this necessity to obtain a permission, raises a multitude of problems and complicates the writing of a case study. Foremost is the question, How will the project to write influence the analytic work? If I request a permission during an ongoing analysis, how does the patient's knowledge that my interest contains motives other than wanting to help affect his involvement in analysis? Perhaps an initial reaction of benevolent agreement, which may prompt the granting of a permission, is but a prelude to a host of other kinds of reactions, such as elatedness and specialness but also a sense of being misused, manipulated, or betrayed. And although the various emotional reactions have a personal significance to the patient and, therefore, would be likely to emerge in the course of the analysis, it is possible that my request, as an arbitrarily introduced influence, grossly interferes with the exploration of the meanings of these reactions because it has broken the natural unfolding of these feelings in transference.

"Informed consent" is perhaps the most widely considered form through which patients would authorize the use of clinical material for purposes such as teaching, research, and publication. Some clinics and institutes routinely introduce an informed consent form to persons applying for treatment. To my knowledge, very few analysts working in a private capacity follow that procedure. Of the many concerns that surround the use of informed consent, two are particularly troublesome. Patients, frequently having only a vague notion of the nature of the treatment process, may initially agree to sign the consent form without fully grasping its implications. Only much later, when the treatment has gained more personal meaning to them, will they be able to evaluate the significance of the agreement. It would seem reasonable that therapists should pay attention to the changing meanings that informed consent may hold for patients and evaluate its use accordingly. Another often-voiced concern and criticism is that such a consent would seriously interfere with the development of trust and a sense of safety, essential in psychoanalytic treatment. Because these concerns are important, they should prompt systematic studies that would help remove the concerns from the realm of speculation to factually supported considerations.

Some information is available about analysts' experiences in publishing case studies: how they solved the problem of informed consent and what effect publishing clinical material had on their patients (Lipton, 1991; Stein, 1988a, 1988b; Stoller, 1988). It becomes apparent that no single response characterizes patients' reactions but that the reactions vary greatly in accordance with the patient's pathology (Lipton, 1991). These writers' valuable contributions need supplementation by others so that a bank of information can become available for general consideration.

Most writers, following Freud's example, postpone publication until the treatment is terminated. As is known, Freud waited 4 years after ending his contacts with Dora before he published his case study. In my published works, I have followed this guideline, although the time span in some instances has been considerably longer (Graves, 1984, 1991, 1994). Two cases stand out representing opposite reactions to my request to use their clinical material for publication. Both had terminated their treatment with me 2 to 4 years previously. The first, a young woman, had continued sending me notes on major holidays about events in her life. When I requested her permission, explaining my project to her by phone, she gave it to me without hesitation, and her feedback to my written report, which I subsequently sent to her, was thoughtful and helpful. But her feedback was the last message I obtained from her; her customary notes no longer appeared in my mail, and subsequently, I learned she had resumed treatment with another therapist. I was left with the unpleasant consideration that my report played a major role in her stopping her contacts with me. In retrospect, I became convinced that I should have discussed her personal reactions to the report with her. I had not paid enough attention to the fact that the report, reminding her of aspects of our work, which had already become re-repressed, could be quite disturbing and cause undue anxiety and pain.

In the analytic process, inaccessible unconscious conflicts are brought into more meaningful relationship in the conscious mental life (Abend, 1990). Wishes, impulses, memories, fantasies, and the defensive operations of the ego and superego are woven into increasingly specific transference patterns, which allow for their recognition, experience, and interpretation. In the subsequent working through, important reorganization takes place and brings relief from anxiety and intrapsychic conflict. At the same time, the no longer "useful" transference elements are re-repressed but—as analytic follow-up studies demonstrate (Hartlaub, Martin, & Rhine, 1986; Pfeffer, 1963)—can be resurrected under special circumstances. Work on my patient's strong self-sacrificing and masochistically submissive tendencies when faced with demands and hardships of life led to significant changes in her sense of her own value and her assertiveness. My write-up, I suspect, was a painful reminder of aspects of her that were no longer in accordance with her present sense of self. It is possible that her ready collaboration with my project represented a resurrection of her overly submissive, self-sacrificing attitudes in transference. In addition, the effect of the written word should not be minimized. No matter how tactfully and respectfully one describes the clinical material, the written word has a unique power that is different from spoken statements.

The importance of discussing patients' personal reactions to written reports about them, akin to brief psychotherapy, became clear with another person. With him, I used my previous learning and offered a series of meetings to discuss his reactions to my report. Many important and useful aspects came forth. Most significant, perhaps, was the opportunity for him to work through, once more, aspects of himself that the report made him recall. He was able to use the experience further to integrate the "old" and "buried" aspects of himself with his current sense of self. He was explicit about the pain he felt when being reminded of the, by now, forgotten material. But he was also able to realize that this forgetting repeated his old major defensive strategy: to isolate, repress, or otherwise block painful experiences from awareness. For him, this brief encounter with his "earlier self" made him more whole and, therefore, stronger.

Although I consider the analysand's permission and subsequent approval (or nonapproval) of my written report as central, they represent but one step in the process of writing a case study. Inherent in the request to publish are the multiple concerns regarding confidentiality. Confidentiality, I think, addresses two separate aspects: (a) a need to protect the person's individuality from recognition by others and (b) a need to protect the unique and private information that treatment invariably produces. The first aspect, protection against recognition, has received the most attention and is, perhaps, the least complicated to achieve. Name, age, education, occupation, and other information that identifies the person in others' eyes can be deleted or replaced by a broad, approximating description. Some writers have reversed the sex of the person as the surest means to safeguard against recognition. This procedure, however, has the danger that important information becomes misleading and misrepresented—after all, many observations and their validity are highly gender specific.

Protecting the unique and private information poses a more complex problem, both conceptually and pragmatically. As the analysis progresses, thoughts, feeling experiences, and fantasies emerge that may have never been expressed before or may condense past and current experiences to unique, highly personal forms. Their emergence is largely dependent on the sense of safety in the analyst-analysand relationship fostering security and trust. And whereas the very uniqueness of these expressions may often be the main reason why I want to write about them, the writing may form a breach of the very essence that guarantees the progress of the analytic work. It may be argued that this very personal nature of the clinical material is, in and of itself, a protection against recognition by others: The feelings and fantasies are the result of the unique interplay between the analyst and the analysand and rarely find direct expression in the analysand's everyday life. Yet the very uniqueness of the material requires special consideration. This requirement, to me, is the source of the greatest difficulty in preparing a case study, one that challenges my professional and ethical integrity the most. My solution has been to write thoughtfully, keeping the patient as my audience, so that my description of his contribution is colored by the same regard of his personality that I want to show in my treatment contacts. The very private nature of the material is, in my opinion, the most compelling reason to seek the patient's permission. And, as I have learned and described, it is essential to offer the patient the possibility to discuss his reactions to my written report.

Last, there are the issues of selectivity, simplification, and compression that require consideration in the narration of a case study. The accumulated material about a case is extensive and complex in nature: No case study can include all of it. Selectivity is necessary both in the light of the enormous amount of information that analysis provides and in the light of the need for clarity in communication. It is primarily guided by the purpose for which I want to write the case study, be it for technical considerations, for elucidating the clinical process, or for exploring a clinical concept or diagnostic entity, to name a few. This purpose dictates what is included but also highlights the vast amounts of information that cannot be used in a particular case study. In addition, other factors play a role in selectivity. For example, when I write a case study, I want it to be a story: a vivid narration of the particular nature of exchange between me and a particular person. This may lead to my selecting more dramatic samples of exchange or samples that best condense the features that I wish to illustrate. Again, many other, perhaps equally telling exchanges cannot be included.

Thus the narrative of a case study does not replicate the treatment narrative as it has unfolded in the course of analysis. This latter narrative, as I define it, is a product of interaction between analyst and patient and is scarcely more than an approximation of the patient's actual past experiences as they originally occurred. For many, this is a bitter acknowledgment: that neither clinical treatment narrative nor clinical case study can satisfy the criteria of objectivity, reproducibility, or reliability, which are the hallmarks of "true science." Yet intuitively graspable, although beyond scientific verification, is the notion that these narratives may well capture the essence of human experience, its ambiguity and subtlety, with more accuracy and reliability than does "historic truth," consisting of objective historic and discrete inner events.

References

Abend, S. M. (1990). The psychoanalytic process: Motives and obstacles in the search for clarification. *Psychoanalytic Quarterly, 59*, 532-549.

Freud, S. (1957). Fragment of an analysis of a case of hysteria. In J. Strachey (Ed. and Trans.), *The standard edition of the complete psychological works of Sigmund Freud* (Vol. 7). London: Hogarth. (Original work published in 1905)

Graves, P. L. (1984). Life event and art. *The International Review of Pycho-Analysis, 11*, 355-365.

Graves, P. L. (1991). The little riddle-maker: A case presentation. *Psychoanalytic Study of the Child, 46*, 255-275.

Graves, P. L. (1994). *The unraveling of a severe obsessive-compulsive neurosis.* (Manuscript in preparation).

Hartlaub, G. H., Martin, G. C., & Rhine, M. W. (1986). Recontact with the analyst following termination: A survey of seventy-one cases. *Journal of the American Psychoanalytic Association, 34*, 895-910.

Lipton, E. L. (1991). The analyst's use of clinical data, and other issues of confidentiality. *Journal of the American Psychoanalytic Association, 39*, 967-986.

Pfeffer, A. (1963). The meaning of the analyst after analysis. *Journal of the American Psychoanalytic Association, 11*, 229-244.

Schafer, R. (1983). *The analytic attitude.* New York: Basic Books.

Stein, M. H. (1988a). Writing about psychoanalysis: I. Analysts who write and those who do not. *Journal of the American Psychoanalytic Association, 36*, 105-124.

Stein, M. H. (1988b). Writing about psychoanalysis: II. Analysts who write, patients who read. *Journal of the American Psychoanalytic Association, 36*, 393-408.

Stoller, R. J. (1988). Patients' responses to their own case reports. *Journal of the American Psychoanalytic Association, 36*, 371-392.

❦ 7 ❦

Who Benefits From
an Examined Life?

Correlates of Influence Attributed to
Participation in a Longitudinal Study

Gail Agronick
Ravenna Helson

*T*hose of us who study lives are aware that we influence the lives that we examine—perhaps very little, perhaps a great deal. Typically, we interview, observe, or have other interactions with selected individuals, sometimes making contact with family members and acquaintances as well. Our interests structure their recollections and may form new patterns of association. We may make interpretations of their lives that we share with them while preserving their anonymity, or in the case of prominent figures, we may even change the way they are perceived by the general public.

Although it is important for us to be concerned with our ethical responsibilities for these people, it has become widely recognized that respect for participants in a psychological study includes recognition of their own powers of evaluation and self-determination (e.g., Harre & Secord, 1972; Rogers, 1951). The degree to which a person is influenced by being studied depends a great deal on her or him. In this chapter, we explore the characteristics of women who felt they had been influenced most and least in the Mills Longitudinal Study.

The study began in 1957 as an investigation of creativity, leadership, and plans for the future in modern women. Initially tested as graduating seniors of the classes of 1958 or 1960 at Mills College (a private women's college in Oakland, California), members of the study participated a second time at about age 27 in 1963 or 1964, again at an average age of 43 in 1981, and most recently, at an average age of 52 in 1989. Approximately 100 women provided inventory and questionnaire data at each follow-up, with larger numbers contributing demographic information. (Articles providing considerable detail about the study include Helson, 1993; Helson & Moane, 1987; and Helson & Wink, 1992.)

Let us briefly describe the nature of our contacts with these women. As seniors, two thirds of the participants filled out inventories and questionnaires administered in a large lecture room. The other third attended these sessions and also came in groups of 10 to be assessed at what is now the Institute of Personality and Social Research at the University of California, Berkeley. The procedures included interviews, tests of cognitive styles, projective tests, and group interactions of various kinds. Some of the assessed women wondered whether they had been selected for their talent or promise, and, indeed, the sample consisted of seniors who had been nominated by the faculty for their creative potential and a comparison group matched with the creative nominees on verbal aptitude and college major.

For all of the participants, whether assessed or not, the urgencies of life must have diluted the influence of the study over the next three decades: There were gaps of many years between the appearances of our inventories and questionnaires, which were delivered by mail in bulky brown packages. Nevertheless, the study was not entirely distant and impersonal. We (the second author with the help of others) interviewed a sample of women at each follow-up. We gave talks or held group sessions at several alumnae reunions. We corresponded with participants in the course of inviting their continued involvement in the study, sending feedback, or requesting permission to use their personal material in articles we wrote. Most important, perhaps, was the fact that our questionnaires were quite extensive, covering many areas of life with both ratings and open-ended questions. The material that the women supplied is copious and often quite personal or painful. "You know more about me than anyone on earth," commented one of the women.

During the three decades from 1958 or 1960 to 1989, the sample developed from late adolescence to mature middle-age in a society undergoing dramatic social change. Lives of three fourths of the women turned out differently from their college-age expectations (Helson, 1993). Letters and notes that we received from time to time suggested that at least some of the women were using the study to adjust to new conditions of life. In 1990, when we sent out a report about the preliminary findings of the follow-up at age 52, we decided to ask all of the women about their experience of the influence of the study. On a sheet that inquired about additional feedback they would like, we squeezed in a few questions that had been overlooked when we first sent out the materials. Among these was the following: "Having participated in the Mills Study has affected me ___ quite a bit, ___ some, ___ not very much." Then there was a small space in which to "elaborate if you are so inclined."

This was not a context conducive to careful consideration of the topic. Single-item questions are generally distrusted, and there is certainly no assurance that replies would have been similar if the question had been asked in earlier stages of the study. Nevertheless, 72 women responded, of whom 22 checked "quite a bit," 34 checked "some," 14 checked "not very much," and 2 commented on the nature of the influence without making a rating. We will first analyze the elaborative remarks that were made, then correlate personality and life data with the ratings to fill out a portrait of who it was that felt most and least influenced by the study. We will describe the women at ages 43 and 52.

Themes of Comments on the Influence of Participating in the Mills Study

Of the 72 women who responded to the question about the influence of the Mills Study, 38 made elaborative comments. Remarks came from almost three fourths of those who rated the influence *strong,* from about two thirds of those who rated it *moderate,* and from less than one fourth of those who rated it as *slight.* Influence attributed to the study was not significantly associated with whether the woman had been included in the assessment sample.

Most of the comments contained one or more of four themes: 22 women said that participating in the Mills Study had brought them psychological perspective or insight, 14 said it had provided support or validation, 7 mentioned that it had increased their awareness of social change or of their place in social history, and 4 said it had given them a chance to contribute to a worthy research undertaking. These themes show no clear relation to the ratings of strength of influence, perhaps because so few women who assigned little influence to the study wrote comments. Women who assigned lower ratings were more likely to say that what they learned about themselves through the study had not changed their basic personality or that emotional involvement was largely confined to the period of filling out the questionnaires.

Psychological Perspective or Insight

Most of the comments in this large category are concerned with intellectual understanding, though some refer to affects:

> The Mills Study has given me the opportunity to periodically step back and look objectively at my lifestyle, relationships, priorities, etc. Consequently, I have made conscious changes in some areas (i.e., in friendships, after the 1981 study).

> It was quite valuable to pause during several points of my life to take a longer view of directions. This process gave a perspective to my progress and regresses I would not normally have had.

> Often when I cannot answer a question in a way that is "computer friendly," this is the very question that occupies my thoughts and opens new perceptions.

> [The] study has required me to crystallize concepts and perspectives that might have remained elusive, as well as

[provided] reports that give me an awareness where others are, and what they have experienced.

[The study] has always generated feelings as I have reviewed where I've been and where I am going—precipitated some grieving.

I am naturally inclined to introspection. However, participation in the study forced me to write down and therefore clarify my thoughts, especially during a period of major upheaval and change.

Support or Validation

Several women said that the study had been a source of support during difficult times, or that they appreciated the interest taken in them:

I feel, in a way, you have "talked me through" some difficult times.

Freelance writing is lonely. It's wonderful knowing that a small group of professionals, somewhere in California, care (professionally and to some extent personally). Sort of like finding out at age 26, 43, and 52 that there really is a Santa Claus.

Some women felt validated by Mills research studies. A woman who had been included in an article on the lives of women who scored high on Loevinger's measure of ego development (Helson, Mitchell, & Hart, 1985) wrote this:

Since my life and pursuits are somewhat unorthodox, it felt pleasurably validating to be considered so successful by a university-based study.

Other women felt supported or validated for different reasons:

Learning about the group has made me realize my life is on course.

> I am glad to know [from the reports] I'm quite normal and much happier than many of my classmates.

Awareness of Social Change

Several women mentioned a connection between their participation in the Mills Study and awareness of their place in social history or of women's changing social roles:

> It has helped me to keep up with (stay aware of) the evolution of my personality and the relationship of that evolution to social changes.

> I think about women and changes evolving for us as a group more often than I would have if not involved.

> Similar to workers in the Hawthorne experiment—I feel part of a special study—and part of a special period in history.

Opportunity to Make a Contribution to an Important Research Program

Several women said they were glad to be socially useful through their participation in the study:

> I can see the study as being helpful in future research and education. I enjoy the concept of being a part of this.

Summary

The women described their experiences of participating in the Mills Study in very different ways. The most common theme was that the study had given them an expansion or clarity of perspective (psychological or social) or stimulated an intensification of reflection. The next most frequent theme was that participants appreciated what they felt was our encouraging interest in them as individuals and our encouraging support for the legitimacy or continued viability of their lifestyle through uncertain times.

We proceed now to an examination of personality and lifestyle characteristics associated with the women's ratings of the importance of the influence of the study. The number of cases contributing to our analyses fall between 65 and 70, except where specifically mentioned, and all findings are significant at or beyond the .05 level.

Personality and Life Characteristics at Age 43

Descriptions of the Women by File Raters. At age 43, the women filled out extensive questionnaires, including many open-ended questions about their work, couple relationships, children, parents, health, and experiences since graduation from college. Graduate students in personality and clinical psychology read this material and rated each woman on the 100 items of the California Q Sort (Block, 1978), using the customary 9-point scale and the assigned normal distribution for this procedure. Reliability was satisfactory (for details, see Wink, 1991). Table 7.1 shows items that were correlated with the participants' ratings of the influence of the Mills Study on their lives at age 52.

The items in Table 1 describe the women who would later attribute "quite a bit" of influence to the Mills Study in terms such as *expressive* (facially, gesturally, or verbally, with expression of hostility specifically mentioned), *valuing independence, assertive,* and *intellectual,* as compared with those who would attribute least influence to the Mills Study, who were described in terms such as *having flattened affect, conservative,* and *not inclined to express themselves verbally.*

The items of the Q set can be sorted by expert judges to describe exemplars of various constructs. These prototypical descriptions can then be correlated with each individual's Q-sort description. The correlations are used as individual difference measures of the construct under study. If the correlation is high, the individual is assumed to have the characteristics associated with the construct. In the Mills Study, we used prototypes developed by Mallory (1989) to measure achieved, moratorium, foreclosed, and diffuse ego identity statuses as conceptualized by Marcia (1966; Marcia, Waterman, Matteson,

TABLE 7.1 Personality Characteristics (Age 43) Correlated with Influence Attributed to the Mills Study (Age 52)

Facially or gesturally expressive	.44
Verbally fluent	.38
Values independence	.38
Expresses hostility directly	.38
Assertive	.36
Talkative	.35
Values intellectual matters	.33
Interesting person	.33
Stretches limits	.32
Judges conventionally	−.32
Submissive	−.32
Moralistic	−.33
Overcontrolled	−.33
Uncomfortable with uncertainty	−.33
Communicates through behavior	−.36
Favors conservative values	−.40
Is emotionally bland	−.44

NOTE: Items are abbreviated phrases from the California Q Set. All correlations are significant at the .01 level; $N = 68$.

Archer, & Orlofsky, 1993). Influence of participating in the Mills Study was not significantly correlated with either achieved or diffuse identity but it was correlated positively with scores on moratorium identity status ($r = .43$, $p < .001$) and negatively with scores on foreclosed identity status ($r = -.36$, $p < .01$). According to Marcia and other contributors to the literature on ego identity, individuals in moratorium identity status value independence; are introspective, intellectual, nonconforming, and anxious; and have a history of exploration of options with difficulties making and sustaining commitments. Those with foreclosed status have emotional control and follow socially approved paths.

Ego Development. Loevinger's Sentence Completion Test (Loevinger & Wessler, 1970) for the assessment of ego development was among the instruments included in the follow-up at age 43. Individuals high in ego level are described as not necessarily well adjusted but as having complexity of outlook, long-range goals, tolerance, and a sense of autonomy combined with respect for the autonomy of others. They

also value relationships. Those average in ego level tend to be confor-
mists and to think in terms of social roles; however, they have some
awareness that they themselves do not conform in all ways and that
the particulars of a case need to be considered (Loevinger, 1976).
Characteristics of those who score very low (below the conformist
level) in ego development are not described because there were only
three such individuals in our sample of college-educated adult women.
Influence attributed to the Mills Study showed a correlation of .34,
$p < .01, N = 57$, with ego level.

Social Awareness. One page of questions that the women filled out
concerned how much they had been affected by their particular cohort
membership and place in social history. Influence attributed to the
Mills Study at age 52 was substantially correlated ($r = .41, p < .01$)
with influence accorded to one's place in social history at age 43.

Lifestyles. The lifestyles of the women were also associated with the
influence to the Mills Study at age 52. Women who were most
influenced had careers rated higher on the Mills Status Level Scale
(Helson, Elliott, & Leigh, 1989) and were more likely to be divorced
mothers; those who were least influenced received lower ratings on
work status and were more often in intact marriages with children.
All correlations were significant but modest (between .25 and .30),
due in part to restriction in range of the life path variables.

Summary. These findings show a consistent picture. The women who
attributed "quite a bit" of influence to the Mills Study were described
by raters at age 43 as open, complex, independent, and assertive. They
scored high on ego level, indicating complexity and moral seriousness.
They had many features of moratorium identity status, suggesting that
they liked to explore options. Indeed, they were forging new, less
conventional life paths and, as one might expect, showed an awareness
of their place in social history. In contrast, women who attributed
little influence to their participation in the Mills Study were described
as emotionally bland, conservative, overcontrolled, submissive, and
cautious. They scored relatively low on ego level. Their characteristics

fit the foreclosed pattern of identity, and, indeed, these women followed life paths that were conventional for middle-class women.

Personality and Life Data at Age 52

Personality. Q-sort descriptions of the women by file raters are not available at age 52, but the California Psychological Inventory (CPI; Gough, 1987) shows correlations with influence of the Mills Study significant at both age 43 and age 52 on scales for Dominance, Self-Acceptance, and Independence. These results support the portrait of the women who reported more influence as consistently assertive, self-confident, and independent in comparison with the women who reported less influence. Regression analysis of change between ages 43 and 52 on CPI scales showed a significant negative correlation on the Self-Control scale: Women who felt quite a bit of influence from the Mills Study had not increased in regulation of anger and impulse as had women who reported little influence.

At ages 43 and 52, the women rated a set of "feelings about life" on a 3-point scale. Here we will be concerned with 31 items that were the same at the two times of testing. At age 52, influence of the Mills Study was positively correlated with *feeling very much alone* and negatively correlated with *a new level of intimacy* and *worry about the children*. Regression analysis of change in ratings of these items showed that women who reported much influence from the Mills Study described themselves as enjoying less intimacy at age 52 than at age 43 but also as worrying less about their children. Women who attributed little influence to the Mills Study tended to experience more intimacy at age 52 than at age 43 but worried more about their children.

Lifestyle. This pattern of findings is related to lifestyle differences among the women. As at age 43, influence of the Mills Study was correlated positively with status level in work and negatively with living with a partner. But conditions of life had changed. At age 43, most women in this group who were without partners had children, but by age 52, the children had left home. More than half of the 22 women who reported most influence were living with neither partner nor children. So they were "very much alone." Some of these women expressed the desire for a partner but said that they did not know men who would provide the egalitarian companionship they wanted. Though many of the "most influenced" women had difficulties in satisfying their need for intimacy, their independence and investment in work may have aided them in letting their children become adults because these women did not worry about their children at age 52. On the other hand, some did feel strain from the amount of effort their careers demanded. Others felt discouragement from lack of room at the top or limitations due to physical aging—a dancer said, "I just can't jump as high."

Among the 14 women who attributed least influence to the Mills Study, only 1 was living alone at age 52. By this time, several women with difficult, demanding husbands had divorced, and all except one had remarried. An alcoholic husband was in recovery. Thus there did seem to be a new level of intimacy. On the other hand, several women had children still at home, either because they were young or because they had some problem (e.g., drugs) that made it more difficult for them to leave. Some children who left home, such as daughters who were felt to have married unsuitable partners, were also the source of worry.

Adjustment and Life Satisfaction. There were no significant correlations between influence of the Mills Study and overall ratings of life satisfaction, health, marital satisfaction (for those in couple relationships), or enjoyment of work, which were generally quite high at age 52. The women who reported most influence relative to those who reported least influence, however, described themselves as feeling less healthy than they remembered themselves to be at age 43, more set in personality, more afraid of competition with other women, more angry at men and masculinity, and less optimistic. Though these correlates may be due in part to the greater willingness of the women who attributed much influence to the Mills Study to entertain and admit negative emotions, they probably also attest to the relational deficits and work strains experienced by many of these women.

Closing Thoughts

At the launching of each follow-up, we proposed to the women in the Mills sample that they would personally benefit from continued participation in the study and at the same time make an important contribution to longitudinal research on women's lives. We believe that this statement is generally true. Through the preparation of this chapter, however, we have sharpened our impression that the members of the study have benefited from it in quite different ways and that participation has been more important to some than to others.

Being influenced by the study was associated with the cognitive characteristics of being intellectual and open to new ideas; the affective characteristic of expressiveness, especially the expression of negative emotions; and the traits of independence, assertiveness, and self-confidence. We have seen that these characteristics fit fairly well the pattern of identity in moratorium. Individuals searching for an identity would be expected to be receptive to the opportunity to explore themselves and to be interested in the feedback the study provided. Being influenced by the study was also associated with ego development, and certainly one would expect that women with cognitive openness and moral seriousness would be interested in examining their lives. In this sample, characteristics such as independence, openness, and assertiveness led the women to new life situations— being a careerist, getting divorced, beginning a lesbian relationship. Such risks in lifestyles must surely have increased the woman's interest in herself and her place in social history.

The women who said they had been least influenced by the study may be understood in terms of their risk avoidance, manifested in their emotional control, their guarded or sparse responses, lesser assertiveness and independence, and attraction to a traditional marriage. Some lived conventional lives with a "secret" such as an alcoholic husband or with commitments such as caring for a handicapped child that absorbed all their energies. Some were private persons who guided their conduct by religious principles that discouraged the expression of negative feelings or criticism of family members. An artist who finally agreed to be interviewed was neither conventional nor religious but extremely evasive and disinclined to connect different parts of her life experience. What these women had in common was either a desire not to reveal themselves or, being preoccupied with others, a lack of strong interest in examining their own lives. So of course it seems reasonable that the study would have relatively little to offer them and understandable that a number of them have needed special coaxing to participate. Having laid out their characteristics, we feel even more grateful for whatever combination of altruism, loyalty to alma mater, courtesy, need to be included, and moderate interest has led to their continuation in the study.

If ratings of the influence of the study had been obtained at the follow-up at age 43, we believe that they would have been similar to those obtained at age 52. It may be important, however, that the women who attributed strong influence to the study described themselves as lonely, less healthy, and somewhat pessimistic at age 52, a time when life satisfaction in the sample as a whole was most significantly related to health and to being in a couple relationship (Mitchell & Helson, 1990). Therapists tell us that loneliness and frustration in achieving our goals, rather than success, lead to the development of inner life. Participation in the Mills Study gave the opportunity for self-reflection, which was most valuable to women who had both the need to examine their lives and the interest and resources to use the study for this purpose.

References

Block, J. (1978). *The Q-sort method in personality assessment and psychiatric research.* Palo Alto, CA: Consulting Psychologists Press.

Gough, H. G. (1987). *CPI: California Psychological Inventory administrators guide.* Palo Alto, CA: Consulting Psychologists Press.

Harre, R., & Secord, P. (1972). *The explanation of social behavior.* Oxford, UK: Blackwell.

Helson, R. (1993). The Mills classes of 1958 and 1960: College in the 50s; young adulthood in the 60s. In K. D. Hulbert & D. T. Schuster (Eds.), *Women's lives through time* (pp. 190-210). San Francisco: Jossey-Bass.

Helson, R., Elliott, T., & Leigh, J. (1989). Adolescent personality and women's work patterns. In D. Stern & D. Eichorn (Eds.), *Adolescence and work: Influences of social structure, labor markets, and culture* (pp. 259-289). Hillsdale, NJ: Lawrence Erlbaum.

Helson, R., Mitchell, V., & Hart, B. (1985). Lives of women who became autonomous. *Journal of Personality, 53,* 257-258.

Helson, R., & Moane, G. (1987). Personality change in women from college to midlife. *Journal of Personality and Social Psychology, 53,* 176-186.

Helson, R., & Wink, P. (1992). Personality change in women from the early 40s to early 50s. *Psychology and Aging, 7,* 46-55.

Loevinger, J. (1976). *Ego development: Conceptions and theories.* San Francisco: Jossey-Bass.

Loevinger, J., & Wessler, R. (1970). *Measuring ego development* (Vol. 1). San Francisco: Jossey-Bass.

Mallory, M. E. (1989). Q-sort definition of ego identity status. *Journal of Youth and Adolescence, 18,* 399-412.

Marcia, J. E. (1966). Development and validation of ego-identity status. *Journal of Personality and Social Psychology, 3,* 551-558.

Marcia, J. E., Waterman, A. S., Matteson, D. R., Archer, S. L., & Orlofsky, J. L. (1993). *Ego identity: A handbook for psychological research.* New York: Springer-Verlag.

Mitchell, V., & Helson, R. (1990). Women's prime of life: Is it in the 50s? *Psychology of Women Quarterly, 14,* 451-470.

Rogers, C. R. (1951). *Client-centered therapy: Its current practice, implications, and theory.* Boston: Houghton Mifflin.

Wink, P. (1991). Self- and object-directedness in adult women. *Journal of Personality, 59,* 769-791.

PART II

❦ 8 ❦

Interpreting Life Stories

Richard L. Ochberg

I think that many of us were first drawn to interviewing because it promised to bring us closer to the experience of the people we study. More traditional styles of research can be alienating; questionnaires, for example, limit our informants to narrow menus of preselected questions and answers. In contrast, interviews let informants choose the events that matter to them and put their own construction on them. I share this preference for conversation; therefore, it may come as some surprise that in what follows, I advocate a way of listening to the stories people tell that systematically refuses to take them at their own word. In the past few years, any number of writers have pointed out that the stories people tell about themselves are not merely descriptions but efforts at persuasion. Narrators try to convince others, and themselves, to take a particular view of their lives: to see them as coherent, dedicated, triumphant—or perhaps as unfairly constrained. Often, these efforts at narrative persuasion matter because of the contrast they draw between a preferred account and a less palatable alternative: a latent subtext, which is never described explicitly but which is always threatening to emerge.

The problem, of course, is that this interpretive attitude is not at all what our informants expect. If I say to you, speaking of the wedding I attended last week, "And then there was the most amazing coincidence!" I expect you to reply, "Really? What happened?" I will be surprised and not especially pleased if instead you say, "Isn't it interesting how you make ordinary events so dramatic?" To pay attention to speakers' rhetoric seems to rob them of authority: It suggests that narrators do not know what they mean to say or cannot find the way to say it and that someone else—the interpreter—can do a better job. Interpretation does not have to be insulting, however. First of all, the stories that people tell are one way of reclaiming some measure of agency. No matter how buffeted one has been by events, at least one can take charge of how the story is told and, in this way, rescue oneself from passivity. To tell a story allows one to make something of experience and, thereby, of oneself. In turn, for an interpreter to show the rhetoric at work in a narrative is not to demean the narrator but to appreciate this act of self-construction. Yet to see this, we must listen to the account not as it was intended—as a literal description—but as an effort at persuasion.

The idea that a life story conceals a negative subtext (as well as partly alluding to it) strikes many investigators as more troubling. It suggests that speakers are unable to tell some portion of their story. This seems especially demeaning when our informants have been oppressed; here, listening to an account on any terms but those on which it is offered seems an act of further disenfranchisement. Yet it is no insult to point out how our informants' abilities to tell their stories have been stunted by coercion. For example, Gilligan (1990) shows how girls become less sure of their own experience as they enter adolescence; this is an indictment of our culture—not an insult to women. Liberation depends on recognizing how social codes have entered into partnership with self-censorship. Interpretation reveals what one might say if only one could speak freely, but we can see this only if we are willing to look beyond what our informants tell us in so many words.

In this article, I explore what this interpretive approach implies for a writer speaking to a reader. When I interpret a life story, I try to show what an informant accomplishes by recounting his or her history in a particular fashion. To succeed, I must undermine the usual assumption: that people say what they mean and mean only what they say. I lead a reader through the account showing how everything that has been said has other meanings, ulterior purposes.

The case that I will describe is drawn from an interview study of middle-aged businessmen. I focused on the distinct way each man described the trajectory of his career: One drifted with events, another took dramatic and risky chances, still another—the subject of this essay—trampled his opposition underfoot. I came to believe that this style of telling a story—we might call it "the manner of the plot"—was a symbolic bridge between what men said aloud about their careers and what they did *not* say about their relationship with their fathers. The men themselves were quite aware of their own styles of climbing the ladders of careers; they did not see that this style might refer to anything else. In what follows, I describe how one might go about taking them at something more than their word.

Creating a Focal Puzzle

"Interpretation," Taylor (1987) says, "is an attempt to make clear . . . a text, or a text analogue, which in some way is confused, incomplete, cloudy, seemingly contradictory—in one way or another unclear" (p. 33). It is a reasonable way to approach the accounts people give of their lives except for the fact that these accounts are not often, or at least not obviously, problematic. In practice, listening to people talk about their lives is rarely like stumbling across cuneiform in the supermarket. People talk—not quite in the words we might have chosen—about the things they have done—again, not quite what we might have done in their place. Yet, for the most part, neither their actions nor their talk is extravagant. By and large, there are no obvious puzzles to be deciphered. Because no interpretation is likely to win us over unless we believe that there is some puzzle worth understanding, the interpreter must persuade us that something does not make sense on its own terms.

Consider, for example, Geertz's (1987) famous account of the Balinese cockfight. Cockfighting, after all, is a peculiar focus for an anthropologist. It has no obvious connection to kinship or social class, economics, or worldviews, though in the course of his exegesis, Geertz eventually implicates all of these. He starts, however, by persuading us that Balinese cockfighting is worth our attention. It is a national obsession. Furthermore, it is immoderate behavior: The Balinese typically gamble for far higher stakes than they seem able to afford.

Finally, it is anomalous behavior: Although men become obsessed with caring for their birds, Balinese are usually averse to everything animal-istic. By the time Geertz has finished his opening remarks, we are ready to believe that the cockfight holds a significant and peculiar place in Balinese culture. Something worth understanding is happening here.

In much the same spirit, I find it useful to organize a case history around some focal incident. I try to find something that my informant has done or said that I can make puzzling enough to hold my readers' attention. What kind of incident do I want? Something serious enough to matter to the protagonist. (One way to put this is that, were the informant to appear as a client in therapy, the focal incident might be his or her answer to the question, "Why are you here?") At the same time, just as the presenting problem in therapy is only a point of departure, so the focal incident is only a hook on which to hang a larger interpretation. Geertz (1987), after all, points out that cock-fighting is no more the master key to Balinese culture than baseball is to ours. Like the dead body in a mystery, it announces a puzzle. Here is an example.

In October, Mike Doyle, the owner of Green's Furniture Store, launched what he called a *Dutch auction*. Each day for a week, he reduced prices by 10%. The sale proved an enormous hit: The store was filled with customers who bought every stick of furniture. Mike claimed that the sale was a triumph of advertising, but publicity came at an exorbitant price. By Wednesday, he was selling goods for less than cost; by the end of the week, he had lost $50,000; by March, he was bankrupt.

"Did you ever consider calling the sale off, say, in the middle of the week?" I asked him. "I wouldn't even think of halting it, not in my wildest imagination," he replied. "My concern was that we might have a mob." Later, he suggested that the customers were "panic buying," and that the sale had acquired "an evil connotation" in people's minds: They thought he was going out of business. It was partly to combat this evil rumor that Mike felt obliged to pursue the sale to its fatal conclusion, although one might have thought that a merchant who hoped to remain open would set aside some stock for the weeks to come.

The Dutch auction was not Mike's first adventure in salesmanship. Six months earlier he had held what he called his First Annual Horse's

Ass Sale. A large newspaper ad proclaimed, "Tired of feeling like . . . ? [Here appeared a picture of a horse's backside.] Well, we are." Mike explained to me,

> That ad said three things. One, that we are a little bit angry; second, that we are going to semi-insult you if we have to; and we are just going to have a hell of a lot of fun. We are going to gently but directly hit them in the teeth, and kind of defy them to come down to see us. We'll see if we can't elicit more of a response from people. We'll get them, erode away; eventually we will crack that facade that you have and get right down into your hot little buttons; make you recognize what it is that we are.

Mike's language suggests that he felt not only disappointed in Green's financial prospects but personally affronted. Why should this be? Before buying Green's, Mike spent 15 years in corporate sales; Green's—a venerable old store in a small midwestern town—was to have been his retirement from the fast lane. His office displayed photographs of the store from the 1920s, he described his staff as being like a family, and he suggested that people should be willing to pay Green's higher prices (the malls at the edge of town were cheaper) because they were all part of an extended community. In this context, the personal note in Mike's frustration made more sense. Mike had worn his heart on his sleeve and been rejected.

Now what kind of story is this? I do not mean Mike's account; I mean my own. Ostensibly, I have simply reported what Mike told me. Yet my retelling makes this narrative more puzzling to a reader than it was to Mike himself.

Mike drove himself into bankruptcy. He sees this as a financial miscalculation, not as a puzzle requiring life-historical interpretation. I, however, have called attention to certain ways that his experience seems peculiar. Mike claimed that the sale was a great success although it ruined him. Was the sale successful in terms of some other interest? Mike worried about implausible dangers: that his customers would panic and turn into a mob. He felt insulted when sales were low: This seems to be taking things too personally.

In pointing to these peculiarities, I am looking ahead to the kind of explanation I mean to provide. I want to explain Mike, but I also want to use him to illustrate a larger point: that the plot of a life story can operate as a symbol. In anticipation of this argument, I call attention to the way events in Mike's life seem to be *unstoppable*—he could not call off the sale—and I emphasize the implausibleness of his reason. I might have asked, "Why is Mike so aggressive?" or "Why does he feel so personally rejected?" Instead I ask, "Why didn't he call off the sale?" The question is reasonable—it is consistent with the events—but it is certainly not the only one I could have asked. I construct the puzzle with an eye not only to understanding Mike but to showing how he illustrates a larger idea. (In the same way, Geertz—I assume—is especially fascinated not by cockfighting but in the possibility that we can read culture semiotically.) We choose our focal puzzles not simply because they epitomize the character of a particular informant or culture but because they let us demonstrate the power of an interpretive strategy that matters to us for some larger reason.

Discovering the Rules for Making Sense

An interpretation shows us that a narrator is not simply describing events but construing them. Sense is made, not passively recorded. To see this, we must recognize the rules that a narrator is following to construct a story. Furthermore, if we are to learn anything new from a case study, an interpretation must show something that we did not already know about how stories may be constructed. The point of interpretation is not to understand a single individual but to enlarge our conception of how sense might be made—or deformed.

Here I hope to show that the focal puzzle in this account—Mike's fatal sale—can be understood as a coded reference to his childhood. The larger point is that we can interpret the formal structure of a plot. By *plot* I mean, roughly, the style in which one event leads to another: how the story builds to a climax. I will try to show that the stories Mike tells about many different episodes in his life have strikingly similar plots. Usually, Mike starts out as a provocateur. He irritates people, arouses them, stirs things up. Once events are in motion, the scene seems to gather unstoppable momentum and culminates in a destructive crash. (Carrying the sale to its bitter end is one example.) By telling his stories in this fashion, Mike makes a larger claim about himself: that throughout his life he has never backed away from a fight.

The interpretation offered here invites a reader to discern meaning in an aspect of narration that we do not ordinarily consider. By way of analogy, an art historian might interpret a medieval altarpiece by explaining how the figures it depicts refer to biblical themes. No one would suggest, however, that the artist alluded to these themes through his choice of paint or the type of wood used for the frame. In the same way, many interpreters assume that the thoughts and feelings expressed by characters in one episode may allude to other scenes, but we do not ordinarily suppose that the tempo of the plot is allusive in the same fashion. This proposed extension of how we might interpret is what makes Mike's case interesting.

Mike pictures himself as a provocateur. Here, for example, he describes his local organization of merchants who were losing business to the malls on the edge of town:

> If I were involved in that group, I would want to get right in under their goddamn skin and make them bloody mad, realizing what is happening, and that there are things we as a merchants group can do about it.

This description should sound familiar: Speaking of his Horse's Ass Sale, he said, "We will crack your facade and get right down into your hot little buttons."

Sometimes Mike suggests that other people try to provoke him but that he is too mature to be easily roused. Early in his career, Mike said, a supervisor became intimidated by Mike's high score on a test of management:

> He tried to make my position demeaning; I would not let him get a rise out of me. He would try to embarrass me in front of clients. . . . Had I considered him more of a threat, I would have gotten angry.

Yet Mike is hardly immune to provocation. Here he describes eating lunch with an old business partner, who said, "I have always enjoyed humiliating you." Words led to blows; soon the two men were wrestling in the alley behind the restaurant:

> He wouldn't quit. I stopped in the middle. We were both in suits, and I am cut to shreds in the glass, and I started laughing at the ridiculousness of two businessmen fighting. I started to walk away. He grabbed me, said he was going to kill me. That was when I got mad. Up until then I was not mad. Right then and there I really beat the shit out of him.

This episode captures something that we have heard before. Once the action starts—whether Mike or someone else is the instigator—Mike finds it difficult to walk away. In fact, the signature of his stories is their unstoppable momentum.

Mike started college with the intention of finishing a 4-year program in 3 years; when he fell short, he quit. His account, however, suggests that he was too fast:

> I'd be too far ahead, waiting for the rest of the class to catch up. I always went in with a full head of steam, like a bullet fired into the air. It takes off like a banshee but eventually it reaches its apogee and that's it. It runs out of steam and just falls down.

After college, Mike became a sales representative for Pratt-Whitney. He rose rapidly through the ranks—to the consternation, he suggests, of those above him: "The managers over me felt fairly threatened. I recognized that and enjoyed it, relished it." Eventually the company offered him the manager's position in a new division; Mike, however, turned it down, feeling that the company had lost its aggressive edge. "They had turned Milquetoasty. They were slowly but surely turning away from being an established world leader."

Several jobs later, Mike started his own company selling industrial pipe systems, then merged his outfit with a larger organization. Once again, he emphasizes his unstoppable velocity:

> My achievements have not been easy victories. For most people, it would have been enough to just build a successful company. To others, enough to merge it with a larger organization. Or another step further, to be given responsibility for a whole corporation. That wasn't enough for me. I had to have the whole everything, and let everyone else sit back and clip their coupons.

Mike suggests that his rapid ascent made others fearful—just as it did at Pratt-Whitney. Speaking of his fellow stockholders in the piping company, he said, "The bastards were not going to let me own any more stock; they were scared to death of me." Finally, this story—like his history at Pratt-Whitney—ends when the craven old men above him backed away from a fight. The board of directors refused to support him in a contest with a union, and Mike quit the company.

I am suggesting that these vignettes are similar in terms of both their subject matter and their formal structure. Each story draws a contrast between Mike—a young conquistador—and the timid (usually older) men who stand in his way. More formally, the plot of each story has a quality of relentless momentum. Mike will not be held back—and if he is, he loses interest and quits. Here is one more example. When Mike was a child, he led a small gang in a running war with the police:

> They were building a new police building. They were all on the first floor; we got up on the third floor, and lo and behold, what is up there but a great big double-doored safe? I said, "Come on, let's get this thing moving." We pushed it right through a fucking wall. It was too big to go through the window. That sucker went right through a brick wall, down three flights, through the frickin' sidewalk. The cops came roaring out the front door; we went out the back.

Does this episode have anything in common with Mike's various jobs? Mike has been telling us about the unstoppable momentum of his career; is it stretching the metaphor too far to include the unstoppable momentum of the safe? Perhaps—but we might notice that once again, Mike starts the action, and once started, the action is unstoppable. We might also notice that once again, he is the young rebel, striking terror into the older authorities beneath him.

History and Subtext

If Mike's way of describing his life is symbolic, what is the referent to which this symbolic talk alludes? The simplest answer might be that accounts of adult life allude to the formative experiences of childhood. Among other things, this answer may be a welcome respite from the ambiguities of interpretation. Unfortunately, it is too simple.

In the archaeological metaphor of interpretation, by the time we have worked our way down to childhood, we feel that we have "gotten to the bottom of things." Descriptions of childhood do not appear to refer to anything else; they seem to be the literal rendition of what is represented symbolically everywhere else.

There can be some relief in this idea. Interpretation, after all, leads us into a land where nothing is taken at face value. We may put up with this ambiguity if it promises to pay off: Maybe we will learn why Mike drove himself into bankruptcy. Yet we fervently hope that when we arrive at the childhood events to which this sale refers, we will be in possession of facts whose meaning is unambiguous. We hope, in short, to escape from the territory of interpretation into that of literal fact.

There is another reason that we may be tempted to abandon interpretation when we listen to accounts of childhood. These descriptions are often poignant: The early chapters of even average lives often feature parents who were inattentive, unaffectionate, or abusive, or who were lost to death or divorce. These events may be so compelling that it seems indecent to focus on the narrator's rhetorical technique. Rather than paying attention to how the story is told, we are tempted to focus on the events themselves.

There is good reason, however, not to abandon interpretation too quickly. Accounts of childhood are no less rhetorical than any other part of a life story. Narrators choose what events to tell us and what construction to put on them to preserve their idealized histories. If we ignore this, we lose the opportunity to see what the account is trying to accomplish.

If a focal event does not refer symbolically to what happened in childhood, however, to what then does it refer? The alternative, I suggest, is that it alludes to a subtext. Here again, Geertz's (1987) discussion of the cockfight is helpful. If we agree that cockfighting is symbolic, we may be tempted to imagine that it represents some other aspect of public life. Yet this is not exactly Geertz's conclusion. He says,

> Balinese go to cockfights to find out what a man, usually composed, aloof, almost obsessively self-absorbed . . . feels like when, attacked, tormented, challenged, insulted, and driven in result to the extremes of fury, he has totally triumphed or been brought totally low. (p. 236)

Yet if we ask, "Where is it that Balinese men are really insulted, infuriated, and brought low?" we find that there is no literal answer. The cockfight does not refer to some other event; instead, it represents a kind of potential experience, something that never actually happens but that is always a latent, if disavowed, possibility.

In the same way, an interpretation does not explain a puzzling focal event by showing how it refers to other events. Instead an interpretation shows how one story—told about the focal puzzle—refers to another story: one that is not told aloud but that is nevertheless latent. It is as if the narrator were saying, "Someone else might describe my life in a different fashion, one that I would find unappealing. But he or she would be wrong—as my account demonstrates."

To take this point of view, however, is to return to the central theme of this discussion. The task of the interpreter is to show that an account is a construction and not merely a report. This is as true of childhood as everything else. With this, we can return to Mike:

> My father was an absolute tyrant, and I would never knuckle under. The combination was nitro and glycerin. Until I was 8 or 9 [years old], he would get me up in the middle of the night and beat the living shit out of me; kick me out of bed

and make me sleep on straw. He would tell me if I was going to conduct myself like an animal, I would sleep like an animal. He would wake me up, find that the bed was wet, beat the living crap out of me, and make me sleep on straw. Defiance, whatever his philosophy was, whatever reason I was wetting the bed, he felt that was an instance that I was not trainable. And his capacity to understand, be compassionate, whatever is necessary, was not there.

What are we to make of this description? Do we need to "make anything" of it at all? Our first reaction is likely to be one of relief; finally, we have escaped the murk of interpretation. Who could doubt that these beatings left their mark on Mike's character? If we were imperfectly persuaded that his sale was puzzling or that the unstoppable momentum of his stories is metaphoric, here at last we seem to have emerged into the sunlight of an unambiguous event. Or have we?

How did Mike feel about being beaten? We might guess that he was frightened and humiliated—but this is not at all Mike's construction. He says, "I would never knuckle under," and in that defiant line we hear an echo, projected back into the past, of the man he now claims to be. This account of childhood, in short, is not simply a description in the literal sense; it is an attempt to persuade us about who he is and has always been. Yet to see this clearly, we must notice what else he is not saying.

Mike's description of his childhood is a curious mixture of bitterness and bravado. Though he is blunt about his father's mistreatment, he denies that his father ever succeeded in frightening him. For example, he said, "His approach was just shattering, not so much to me but to my mother." Should we believe that his mother was more shattered than Mike himself? (We might remember that he described his customers as panicked, though it seems more likely that he was the fearful one.)

Mike continued, "Ninety-nine percent of the beatings I deserved; I covered a lot of territory when I was kid." This last line alludes to his adventures as a petty delinquent. After regaling me with a string of these escapades, Mike concluded,

Surprisingly, I was one of the smaller boys in school. I had
altar boy looks: platinum blond hair and blue eyes, and
maybe I looked like a pushover type. The undercurrent was
[here he started laughing] there wasn't any kid who covered
more ground than I.

So his provocative behavior—pushing a safe through the window of
a police station—stands counterpoised to the false impression that he
was a pushover.

In a different passage, he described his brother: "As a kid he was
a wimp; the sickliest kid you ever saw. I don't know how many times
I used to want to pound his daylights out." Why would Mike want to
beat up his sickly brother?

If we are willing to go beyond what Mike says explicitly, then the
following construction seems plausible. Mike may have been terrified
of his father but perhaps also ashamed, and he chose to cover up his
shame with a child's bravado. That would help make sense of his
insistence that his mother was more frightened than he and that he
brought those beatings on himself. Furthermore, we noticed that he
contrasted his juvenile adventures in crime with the false impression
that he was a pushover type—who sounds suspiciously like his detested,
sickly brother. Could he be telling us, without ever quite recognizing
what he is saying, "Sometimes when my father beat me I felt like a
weakling and a coward. I hated this image of myself (and the way my
brother reminded me of myself) and fought this image by deliberately
becoming a little hellion." If this makes sense, we can now understand
what provocation means to Mike. Better to provoke other people's
rage—and thereby preserve at least one's pride—than suffer passively
and be both beaten and humiliated.

There is another part of this story. Despite the beatings, Mike feels
considerable affection for his father, but his father seems never to have
acknowledged this:

He never really knew how to love. He doesn't have a friend
in the family, and he doesn't realize that I am the only friend
he has got. I really love my Dad, even though I consider him
a classic prick. I can tell him to his face that I love him, not

for what he has done but for what he is, my Dad, and I can't get that through his fucking head.

We have heard that Mike finds it unbearable when people do not recognize his overtures of affection. This was why he felt so personally insulted when his customers abandoned his "family" at Green's in favor of the malls. Faced with rejection, Mike tries to provoke an emotional reaction: "We will get down into your hot little buttons and make you recognize us for what we are." His problem is that the experience of trying to provoke affection lies so close to the provocation of rage. With this, we can return to his final, fatal sale.

He began his First Horse's Ass Sale in what he intended to be a playful, affectionate manner, "We are just going to have a whole lot of fun." But the provocativeness and the aggression were never far from the surface: He was going to "gently kick people in the teeth." By the time of the second sale, Mike was caught up in the more combative connotations of provocation, a struggle that he could not honorably quit.

The sale was never wholly about making money. It was yet another edition of the story Mike performs over and over in his life: one in which he provokes a struggle and defies everyone to the bitter end. The purpose of this idealized story is to contradict the less palatable alternative that Mike fears someone—including himself—might tell: that he was once afraid and ashamed. To see this, we must look beyond what he has told us, in so many words, about any chapter of his life.

Conclusion: Making Sense

When we interpret a life story, we do not simply report what our informant told us. Instead, our retelling changes the story in a much more fundamental way than the kind of light editing we take for granted. We do not simply tell a shorter story, one that distills the highlights from a long and repetitive transcript, nor do we simply organize events chronologically or group them into themes. Instead, we convert what we have been told from one kind of account into another.

We systematically call into question the ordinary assumption that our narrator is simply reporting what happened. We show that our narrator's account of some focal event is puzzling: in fact, we make the description of that event more puzzling to a reader than it was to the narrator. We show that the way the story is told is allusive; it tacitly refers to more than the narrator officially acknowledges. Even when we deal with the early, formative chapters of life history, we show that we have not reached "the bottom of things," but that there is still another, unspoken subtext. All of this converts the story from a description into an argument. More exactly, we show how it has been an argument all along—though not explicitly so.

Why do we do this? What justifies paying attention to an account in so radically different a fashion than our informants intend? Here we might consider the variety of interests that interpretation serves.

Sometimes we want to show how the kind of sense people are able to make of experience changes as they develop (Perry, 1968).

Sometimes we want to show what a narrator gains by making sense of experience in a particular way. Mike's story, for example, turns his passive experience of abuse into active provocation. Other rhetorical strategies can persuade us that a narrator's life has been coherent or moral (Mishler, 1992; Modell, 1992).

A story can connect a narrator to a particular community by telling the individual history within the imagery that that community favors. An account can also allude to the relationship between the narrator and the interviewer (or the jury of potential witnesses that this interviewer represents). In so doing, the story alters the identity of both the listener—one who will understand, forgive, or be converted—and the narrator—one who can be understood, forgiven, and so on (Harding, 1992).

Sometimes we want to show the connection between individual lives and social practices. Mike, for example, acts out his style of unstoppable movement within the cultural practice of careerism. This psychosocial perspective can show us both how identity depends on social recognition and how subjectivity can be stunted by the internalization of social coercion. We may, for example, want to show what a given way of speaking conceals—and at what cost (Rosenwald & Wiersma, 1983). This idea is central to the liberative interests of both psychodynamic and critical social theories (Geuss, 1981; Rosenwald & Ochberg, 1992). For example, men's preoccupation with career advancement may help them suppress their discomfort with the affiliative dilemmas of middle-class work (Ochberg, 1987).

Sometimes we want to show how groups of people differ in the sort of sense they deem sensible. A feminist reader, for example, might point out that plot may be a useful way of appreciating men's experience but not that of women; it emphasizes individualism at the expense of relatedness (Gergen, 1992). This would lead us to see plot not as a natural and inevitable dimension of stories—the way physicists regard mass or velocity—but as a particular narrative choice: one that carries with it certain questionable assumptions about how lives are lived and how identities are constructed.

No doubt there are still other theoretical agendas that interpretation may serve. What all of them share, however, is the idea that people do not simply register experience passively. Instead, sense is made. We are all more like painters than photographers (with all due apology to the constructivism of photography). Interpretation is interested in the possibilities and limits of this constructive activity, but to see this, we must first deconstruct the unreflective assumption that our narrators are simply describing what happened.

This is not the way our informants intend to be heard. Listening to them from an interpretive point of view, however, is not demeaning. It is, rather, the only way that we can notice both the power and the limits of our narrators' attempts to make something of their experience—and, thereby, themselves.

References

Geertz, C. (1987). Deep play: Notes on the Balinese cockfight. In P. Rabinow & W. Sullivan (Eds.), *Interpretive social science: A second look* (pp. 195-240). Berkeley: University of California Press.

Gergen, M. (1992). Life stories: Pieces of a dream. In G. Rosenwald & R. Ochberg (Eds.), *Storied lives: The cultural politics of self-understanding* (pp. 127-144). New Haven, CT: Yale University Press.

Geuss, R. (1981). *The idea of a critical theory: Habermas and the Frankfurt school.* Cambridge, UK: Cambridge University Press.

Gilligan, C. (1990). Teaching Shakespeare's sister: Notes from the underground of female adolescence. In C. Gilligan, N. Lyons, & T. Hanmer (Eds.), *Making connections: The relational worlds of adolescent girls at Emma Willard School* (pp. 6-29). Cambridge, MA: Harvard University Press.

Harding, S. (1992). The afterlife of stories: Genesis of a man of God. In G. Rosenwald & R. Ochberg (Eds.), *Storied lives: The cultural politics of self-understanding* (pp. 60-75). New Haven, CT: Yale University Press.

Mishler, E. (1992). Work, identity, and narrative: An artist-craftsman's story. In G. Rosenwald & R. Ochberg (Eds.), *Storied lives: The cultural politics of self-understanding* (pp. 21-40). New Haven, CT: Yale University Press.

Modell, J. (1992). "How do you introduce yourself as a childless mother?" In G. Rosenwald & R. Ochberg (Eds.), *Storied lives: The cultural politics of self-understanding* (pp. 76-94). New Haven, CT: Yale University Press.

Ochberg, R. (1987). *Middle-aged sons and the meaning of work.* Ann Arbor, MI: UMI Research Press.

Perry, W. (1968). *Forms of intellectual and ethical development in the college years.* Cambridge, MA: Harvard University Press.

Rosenwald, G., & Ochberg, R. (1992). Life stories, cultural politics, and self-understanding. In G. Rosenwald & R. Ochberg (Eds.), *Storied lives: The cultural politics of self-understanding* (pp. 1-18). New Haven, CT: Yale University Press.

Rosenwald, G., & Wiersma, J. (1983). Women, career changes, and the new self. *Psychiatry, 46,* 213-229.

Taylor, C. (1987). Interpretation and the sciences of man. In P. Rabinow & W. Sullivan (Eds.), *Interpretive social science: A second look* (pp. 33-81). Berkeley: University of California Press.

❧ 9 ❧

Telling From Behind Her Hand

African American Women and the Process of Documenting Concealed Lives

Gwendolyn Etter-Lewis

> *Breaking out of silence means more than being empowered to speak or to write, it also means controlling the form as well as the content of one's own communication, the power to develop and to share one's own unique voice.*
>
> Marsha Houston and Cheris Kramarae
> (1991, p. 389)

*E*xploration of the inner workings or process of interview-based research is at once intriguing and intimidating. For oral history narratives in particular, it is intriguing because we have the rare opportunity to examine the intricacies of collaboration as well as the quality of the final product.

On the other hand, it is intimidating because it means making public those miscalculations, unanswered or unasked questions, unexpected reactions, and other problems that researchers are trained to keep private. Thus, unveiling the actual process in broad applications, rather than the edited version of our findings, is equivalent to telling secrets or disclosing information that usually is left in our rough drafts, in our notes from pilot projects, and on the cutting-room floor, so to speak. In fact, this undertaking reminds me of watching my great-grandmother in church. Whenever she had a juicy bit of gossip to convey to another church lady, she would raise her right hand to her mouth (a protection against those who could read lips) and whisper forbidden information into the ear of an eager listener. It was a kind of ritual gesture that falsely implied that the act of concealing her mouth would keep the secret hidden. Thus, it is from behind this symbolic hand that I offer the following discussion.

Some Preliminary Considerations

That is why for a black woman to write about black women is at once a personal and an objective undertaking.
—Paula Giddings
(1984, p. 5)

In general, the experience of conducting interview-based research is a challenge on several levels. On a theoretical level, there is the continuously debated question of subjectivity and the accompanying issue of the interviewer's own personal bias. On a practical level, there is concern about the interviewee's personal bias as well as the accuracy of her or his memory. Regardless of whether or not these issues can be resolved appropriately,[1] it is also important to note that these same questions are more likely to be raised in the context research that focuses on so-called minority groups, such as people of color or women. There was no great outrage when Zora Neale Hurston's biographer, Robert Hemenway (1984), excused the great Ernest Hemingway for not telling the truth but, at the same time, condemned Hurston for doing the same thing:

> Autobiography is not history. The autobiographical act incorporates emotional truths that inevitably distort public events

and private experiences. No one expects Ernest Hemingway to tell the "truth" of the lost generation in *A Moveable Feast*. He recasts events as he remembers them from the advantage of age, reporting only the emotional reality of a man settling scores for posterity. "If the reader prefers," he warns, "this book may be regarded as fiction." Yet Hurston's ten-year memory lapse reveals something about her relationship with the *Dust Tracks* reader: she tests that reader's good faith, challenges credibility and asks for a considerable suspension of scrutiny. (pp. xii-xiii)

Although critics may argue that autobiography is different from interview-based research, the principle is the same—the elite and the privileged are exempt from moral codes-ethics of conduct as are those who study them and become gatekeepers of personal myths. Returning to the issue of oral narrative studies, again we find few expressions of concern when researchers take liberties in interpreting someone else's life: "Understandably, she was constructing a text by which she wished to be remembered—not necessarily reconstructing the actual record of her life" (Steward, 1989, p. xxiii). How does the researcher know this? Did she tell him so? Is he a contemporary who can verify the facts of the narrator's story?

This subtle implication of lying or distortion on the part of the narrator also reveals something about the interviewer—a bias on his part that slants or otherwise alters the final product. Although it is humanly impossible to conduct bias-free research, it is reasonable to expect that interview-based data be interpreted within the context of the narrator's world view rather than that of the interviewer-researcher's. If we continuously map our own perspectives onto those of the interviewee's, then we will learn nothing.

As an African American woman conducting research on other African American women, there is always the risk of being perceived as indulging in self-serving research that ultimately will be "ghettoized" because "African American women" are a group too specific and too disenfranchised to yield widely generalizable data.[2]

If there existed hundreds or thousands of studies of African American women in the majority of academic disciplines, I might be discouraged. This, however, is not the case. We are still struggling to uncover and disseminate information about African American women's lives, thoughts, inventions, discoveries, and other general successes. (We have already heard too much about our failures.) How many books and studies purport to be about women only to include white women, middle-class women, or both exclusively? When I pick up a title like *Women's Personal Stories,*[3] I expect to find or see some representation of myself and my experiences, but this usually does not happen because the term *women* is not extended to women of color. So out of necessity, I find my own research filling gaps as well as carving out new ground. So I must ask, who can better reconstruct the life story of an African American woman than another African American woman? Beyond purely academic and historical value, interviewing these women was for me an act of liberation as well as a labor of love.

Another issue that I have encountered in conducting interview-based research on older African American women is that of anonymity. The majority of the 88 women that I interviewed (see Etter-Lewis, 1993) agreed to participate in my study only if their names would not be made public.[4] At that point, I had to decide which was most important: naming names or recording-preserving these life stories.[5] I had to offer them safe conditions for telling their own lives. It was not easy for them to reveal their past to a stranger-researcher and in turn to an audience (reader-public) of nonkin "others."[6] African American women, a group historically exploited by researchers and do-gooders alike, have every right not to be forthcoming about the innermost details of their lives.

Many scholars have argued that anonymity (and sometimes pseudonymity) diminishes if not thoroughly destroys the credibility of interview data. Although I agree with this notion up to a certain point (see Jean Fagan Yellin's introduction in Harriet Jacobs's [1987] *Incidents in the Life of a Slave Girl*), I do not think that it holds true in all situations. Excluding writers such as Samuel Langhorne Clemens, Amatine Lucile Aurore Duping, Gloria Watkins, and others,[7] several major narrative studies (too numerous to name individually) have been conducted, published, and used without using narrators' real names (see issues of the *Oral History Review* between 1988 and 1995). Also, there is the "scientific" practice of blind and double-blind studies created to eliminate potential biases. This kind of anonymity is not only encouraged but required in some research designs. So lack of names or labels is not necessarily a negative trait or quality. Furthermore, even though naming names may appear to enhance a narrative's authenticity, there is no guarantee that this particular story or text is more truthful than one that does not include names.

Asking Difficult Questions

Mama, are you a virgin?
—April Sinclair
(1994, p. 3)

One of the most sensitive areas of my study of older African American women was that of their personal lives. The majority of women spoke candidly about their birth families, education, and career experiences but felt uncomfortable revealing details about their romantic relationships (regardless of whether or not marriage had been the ultimate outcome), family problems and dynamics, and personal attributes such as age. Once I discovered this tendency, I wanted to know, (a) Should I ask questions about a narrator's personal life if there is the possibility that she will resist or feel uncomfortable? (b) Is it more important to document African American women's achievements rather than their personal lives? (c) Should I ask for details about sex, childbirth, illness, and other private topics that usually are not discussed in public? These were complex questions that had no simple or easy answers.

A biologist and ex-college president, born in 1924, for example, spoke of her marriage and subsequent divorce as events that occur in life's unpredictable twists and turns. She did not express remorse but, rather, a wise acceptance of the situation. As a researcher and a woman, I wanted to know if the divorce had been caused by the fact that her former husband was not in the same field, so I asked,

Q: Uh, was it difficult to be married to a nonscientist?

A: Yes. No, it's not so much of the nonscientist, but it's the kind of person that you're married to. Whether they understand science, and it's much more complicated than that for reasons which I really don't need to put into public view. Um, some personality difficulties associated with his own, uh, situation with relation to his brother and his family. Uh, but we had, from a social point of view, we had lots of good things together, but my being a scientist was something that he really did not accept privately. He accepted it publicly, but privately uh, it was something that was not uh, necessarily pleasant. We never shared discussions about my lab. He never went to visit my laboratory. He never really wanted to acknowledge my, my involvement in research. It was as if my scientific research and writing was another man. It was kind of: "I'm not part of that world. I'm jealous of it. I don't want to hear about it" kind of concept [for him]. So it was a little difficult to say the least. (57:3, 1)[8]

The narrator's initial yes-no response appeared to be a spontaneous reaction to the question. That is, yes, it was difficult to be married to someone not in her field, but no, that was not the primary cause of marital difficulties. She points out the disparity in their public and private lives and implies that their personal intimate relationship was strained, "it was something that was not uh, necessarily pleasant." It is also interesting that she felt her husband regarded her work in the same way that he would have appraised an extramarital affair, "It was as if my scientific research and writing was another man." Without going into lengthy details, the narrator offers some insight but also protects the confidentiality of the particulars of her marriage: "And it's much more complicated than that for reasons which I really don't need to put into public view." I did not press for more details about her marriage and subsequent divorce because she volunteered more information as the interview continued, and I supported her desire not to reveal all of the details of her life. Unlike newspaper reporters who believe in the myth that they are entitled to any and all information about a person's life (especially those who are public figures), oral history researchers must keep the narrative process humane and preserve the personal dignity of narrators. Otherwise, we usurp the power of the interviewee's authority and what we have left is not collaboration but coercion.

My most difficult elicitation of a life history occurred in 1987 when I interviewed a retired school teacher who refused to give her age.[9] She welcomed me into her home warmly and without reservation. Yet as the interview proceeded, she became very anxious, impatient, and abrupt. After the interview, she resumed a hospitable attitude. I can only speculate that she was uncomfortable with the tape recorder (even though she was blind) or felt uneasy talking about her life, or, to put it plainly, maybe I got on her nerves. In any event, she did talk about her life at length. Again, I did not know age was a sensitive issue, so I asked that question not expecting the answer that I received.

Q: How old were you when you finished high school?

A: I don't tell my age to anybody!

Q: Alright uh, I'm simply asking that because a lot of the women that I've interviewed finished high school at 15.

A: Well, I don't know, I guess I finished high school before then. Um, about fourt . . . no, no, no, not high school. Um, let's see . . . finished around fourteen. (26:1, 2)

At this point, it was important for me to establish her early graduation from high school, so I pressed for an answer even though I risked the possibility that she would terminate the interview on the spot. Nonetheless, the narrator continued and had fascinating stories to tell, but she was always on guard about the issue of age. In turn, I proceeded to ask questions (sometimes disguised, embedded in other information, or otherwise indirect) throughout the interview that would require some indication of date or age. She never explicitly told her age, but I never gave up trying to find out (in a polite manner, of course).

By the time I interviewed the next narrator, in 1988, I was well versed in ways to get around particular problems. Yet nothing prepared me for this interaction. The interviewee was a retired university professor born in 1911. She told her story with pride and aggressiveness (she interrupted me more than any of the other interviewees, for example). When I asked her age, she did not flinch, but when I asked about her marital status, she adamantly refused to talk about it:

> Q: Now one thing you haven't talked about and I wanted to ask you about any, at any uh, point in time after high school or at any point was there a marriage and family for you?
>
> A: Well, I'm going to tell you that, that's uh, that's an aspect that does not require, nor does it need validation in this interview, because I would want to be very honest and frank with you and I don't want to call names because people . . .
>
> Q: (interrupts) You wouldn't have to call names.
>
> A: No, so I wouldn't, I, I won't go into that. I'll just simply say that there were two young men that . . . lived in my household since 1954. . . . I've never formally adopted them, but they are, I guess they are as near to me as children could be. . . . I wasn't proud that they left their wives, but for the last four and a half years, I was glad they were home. . . . So I'll have to drop that right here.
>
> Q: All right. I respect that.
>
> A: All right. (laughs) (30:1, 32-33)

As our exchange indicates, the narrator places the subject of marriage off limits. At first, she tries to evade the question by bringing up the question of confidentiality,"I don't want to call names because people . . ." When I agree with her, she simply refuses to go further, "I won't go into that." Instead, the narrator chooses to talk briefly about her role as surrogate mother without revealing many particulars. Even though I was extremely interested in women's opinions about married life versus single life, I conceded to her wishes. It was more important for me to allow narrators to control the interview (in order that their views prevail) than to continuously probe for intimate details that may or may not have considerable influence on the whole of their lives. Also, it was important not to alienate the narrators from the text or the interview process, for they are the authorities of their own life stories.

Differences Within

We were perceived as an elite family, since our parents were
college-educated and had important jobs. But honestly, money
was very tight.

—Sarah and A. Elizabeth Delany
(1993, p. 51)

Like telling personal secrets from behind a hand, controversies and
issues within the African American community are not easily made
public. Some narrators resist for fear of "airing dirty laundry," or
exposing information that should be kept within the confines of the
community. Others have been witnesses to or victims of exploitive
research that either misinterprets the African American community or
habitually dwells on negative aspects of individuals or the group.
Social class-status is one such issue that recurs in the life history
research that I have conducted over the past 10 years. Therefore,
situating African American women in the social hierarchy of their own
communities has not been a straightforward undertaking. A host of
variables, including geographical location, education, family background, and so on, must be a part of the equation. Independent of
formulaic determinations of social class, I also was interested in how
these educated women viewed themselves within the social boundaries
of their own communities: Did they see themselves separate and apart
from the whole? Did they view themselves as members of an elite
social class, an impoverished social class, or neither? Did they feel that
they had privileges that other African Americans did not? In an effort
to elicit answers to these questions, I asked each woman about social
and economic differences between people in their respective African
American communities. The retired school teacher previously mentioned (my most difficult interview) was neither forthcoming nor
helpful in her response to the question:

Q: What did black women do then when they were your contemporaries if they didn't get an education? What were the
things that they were to do with their lives?

A: They did domestic work, I think I read in a thesis from the University of Cincinnati. Mostly domestic work and, I think that's about all. What else is there to do, for people to do if they don't have an education?

Q: I mean especially your contemporaries.

A: Well, I think my contemporaries did what anybody would do. What anybody is doing now. . . . So um, I, I, can't think of what they might of been doin'. What could, what might they have been doing?

Q: I, I don't know. I was just asking. If you had made that observation that maybe . . .

A: (interrupts) Well, I don't know, and I can't think of it right off. I can't remember because, you see maybe I was associating mostly with people who were in the same category that I was. And I didn't observe too much of what others were doing. (26:1, 13)

The narrator's initial reply to my question was not helpful because the information came from someone else, "I think I read in a thesis . . ." The second time I try to ask the same question also is not successful. She seems completely at a loss for an answer and reacts by asking me the question, "What might they have been doing?" However, I thought her next response was very informative: "I was associating mostly with people who were in the same category that I was." "Category" hints at a social class division and places her in a group of people who were well educated and upwardly mobile. Later in the interview, she talks about friends who went on to college and assumed careers after graduation.

My second most difficult interview proved equally taxing. The university professor previously mentioned would not admit to social class divisions within her own community.

Q: Uh, was there a dichotomy, was there a tension in the community that you grew up in between the black people who could afford to go to private school and those who could not?

A: No, 'cause everybody could afford a dollar and a half a year. (laughs)

Q: But I mean . . .

A: (interrupts) Yeah, I don't, I don't know anything like that, never, I uh, I guess you're talking about a development of a kind of class consciousness . . .

Q: (interrupts) Yeah, yeah.

A: No, no. Uh, no, I, I, no I don't remember anything like that, because I uh, I'll let you know very quickly we were not the most well-off black family. We did all right, but I mean you, uh, we had, we had doctors there, black doctors. . . . I'm sure they made more, and uh, undertakers. So don't think it was just our little lonesome family over there. Yeah, so, but I don't know of any, any great uh, situations [extremely poor families]. (30:1, 19)

Although the narrator does acknowledge a hierarchy within the black community, "we were not the most well-off . . . ," she does not elaborate on this issue. It may be that the social class divisions that exist within the African American community generally are considered part of the dirty laundry that should not be made public. Insiders know, however, that there are not only different social classes but also distinctions based on skin color, hair texture, location of residence (urban vs. suburban, urban vs. rural), length of residence in a particular city or town (native born, lifetime vs. newly arrived), and so on. Even though most of these divisions exist in other communities, women in my study may have felt uncomfortable discussing this topic because the African American community, ravaged yesterday by slavery and today by racism, can ill afford such divisions if disunity is the result.

Alliances

Words create and maintain relationships of power as surely as do prisons and arms.

—Aldon Lynn Neilsen
(1988, p. 3)

The interview process often has been acted out as an elaborate configuration of stances between two people in an asymmetrical relationship: the researcher, who is always in control, and the interviewee— the knower, but the one who is controlled. This adversarial approach may work sometimes, but ultimately, it is unproductive. When researcher and narrator enter an interactive framework that automatically pits them against one another, then the resulting text cannot be a reflection of a joint effort but rather a final product forged into existence through opposition rather than cooperation and usually dominated by one person's (usually the researcher's) view. Thus I tried to avoid the traditional interview dichotomy by deferring to the narrator and offering an open-ended format. This does not mean that I had no say or input or that we talked about anything and everything in a structureless interaction, but my intention was to establish cooperation rather than dominance. Notwithstanding, if one view had to be primary, it should be that of the interviewee. Again, the retired school teacher did not hesitate to put me in my place:

> Q: You know one story that you, that you mentioned to me once, when I was here last time was, I think the black ministers asked the [female] school teachers to quit their jobs so men could have them. Do I have that story correct?
>
> A: What you sayin'? No, you don't have it right!
>
> Q: All right, would you tell me?
>
> A: See there were so many graduates every year. And the only thing they could do was teach. So consequently when black women got married, the black ministers here and some others went to the Board of Education . . . (26:2, 2)

She goes on to tell a story of how many African American women lost their teaching positions when they got married due to the influence of local ministers who lobbied for more jobs for African American males (that meant firing women and hiring men). Yet before she could recount this very interesting story, she expressed her irritation with me by shouting, "No, you don't have it right!" I admit that I was startled by her outburst, but eventually it worked in our favor because this time she told the story with more feeling and more details. She rightfully asserted her authority in the telling of her own life story.

The university professor also caught me off guard by her response to one of my questions. It made me wonder if she understood or accepted my motives and purpose as I had initially described them to her (i.e., to collect the life stories of older African American women):

Q: You were the first generation of your family to go to college?

A: Well, they called that school that they went to, but there was not a formal college. I can't say I was the first because you know these people I tell you about, first cousins to my father . . . one had gone to college to be a priest, and Aunt Mary was teaching school in Michigan, so there wasn't a situation like that, that I was the first. Nobody ever talked about stopping school. So I didn't have anything pushing me except the sense that I knew I was going on to whatever heights there were. . . . That was in me . . . so I can't say that anything was pushing me to go to college, that I was crying at night and wondering, and that kind of thing, whether I was going or not, no . . . I wish I could make that sadder. (laughs)

Q: No, I don't want a sad story, I want your story. (30:1, 23)

I really wanted to know if her parents had attended college (and I asked that question later), but I did not insist at this time.

It was her last statement that was disturbing: "I wish I could make that sadder." I silently wondered what I had done to give her the impression that I wanted a "sad" life story. On the other hand, it may have had nothing to do with me and everything to do with traditional and stereotypical images of African American women as victims—impoverished, long-suffering casualties of a merciless patriarchy. Needless to say, that was neither my intention nor my viewpoint. I do not know if she ever believed me.

In another instance during the interview, I asked this same narrator what I considered an innocent question. I wanted to know how she envisioned her life during her early years, before her extraordinary success both at home and abroad:

Q: Uh, did you . . . at what point in your life did you make all of these plans and goals, like . . .

A: (interrupts) Didn't make them. I keep telling you that. I never made them, except to go as far as I could go, yeah I never made any other plans. Much just happened. Just being in the right place at the right time. (30:1, 32)

Under different circumstances, I would have argued that the habit of being in the right place at the right time *is* a plan, but this was her story, not mine. In response to her charge, "I keep telling you that," obviously my impression of her life did not match her view of her own life or the words she used to describe that life. When she spoke of going back to school, for example, "Then in 1939 I decided to go back to school . . . and I went back. I completed the doctoral program in '44 or '46," I assumed some amount of planning and goal setting had to be involved, but she would always say, "I was just lucky."

The bottom line is that both the researcher and the interviewee are working toward the same goal. Methodology should be designed accordingly, and in the instance of life history interviews, the narrator's outlook must prevail. Researchers lose nothing in sharing the process (reaffirming the narrator's authority of self), which naturally is interactive and collaborative rather than autocratic. In other words, narrators must participate in this alliance with the power to know, correct, and teach, whereas the interviewer must be a willing learner whose external knowledge (i.e., information outside of the narrator's experience) guides (not dominates) the elicitation process.

Postscript

As I have said before, interviewing older African American women was a labor of love as well as an act of liberation. If their stories inform and redirect our lives, then my efforts have not been in vain. If what they have said frees us in some small way, then we have achieved much more than merely recording history. We have gained our selves.

Notes

1. See the discussion in Gwendolyn Etter-Lewis (1993), *My Soul Is My Own: Oral Narratives of African American Women in the Professions* (pp. 128-144).

2. The idea that African American women's life experiences yield inconsequential and insufficient information is valid only if we posit white middle-class American women's experiences as the norm.

3. Fictional, used as an example.

4. All interviewees gave their oral consent and most signed agreement forms.

5. I also considered this a multiphased project in which the first phase primarily was concerned with the process of "telling" under secure and nonthreatening conditions.

6. Since the publication of *My Soul Is My Own,* several of the women in my study called or wrote and said that they were ready to reveal their own names because, after all, it was *their* own story.

7. Mark Twain, George Sand, bell hooks.

8. 57 = transcript number, 3 = third side of the tape, 1 = page number (of the written transcript).

9. With the help of archival data, newspaper clippings, and information obtained from the narrator's close friends, I estimate her birth date to be approximately 1910, which means she was in her late 70s when I interviewed her.

References

Delany, S., & Delany, A. E. (1993). *Having our say: The Delany sisters' first 100 years.* New York: Kodansha.

Etter-Lewis, G. (1993). *My soul is my own: Oral narratives of African American women in the professions.* New York: Routledge.

Giddings, P. (1984). *When and where I enter: The impact of black women on race and sex in America.* New York: Bantam.

Hemenway, R. E. (1984). Introduction. In Z. N. Hurston, *Dust tracks on a road* (2nd ed., pp. xii-xiii). Urbana: University of Illinois Press.

Houston, M., & Kramarae, C. (1991). Speaking from silence: Methods of silencing and of resistance. *Discourse & Society, 2*(4), 425-437.

Jacobs, H. (1987). *Incidents in the life of a slave girl: Written by herself.* Cambridge, MA: Harvard University Press.

Neilsen, A. L. (1988). *Reading race: White American poets and racial discourse.* Athens: University of Georgia Press.

Sinclair, A. (1994). *Coffee will make you black.* New York: Avon.

Steward, J. (1989). Introduction. In B. Jones, *For the ancestors: Autobiographical memories* (p. xxiii). Athens: University of Georgia Press.

❧ 10 ❧

Ethics and Understanding Through Interrelationship

I and Thou in Dialogue

Melvin E. Miller

*S*o often, we who have dedicated ourselves to the study of lives over time engage in this endeavor alone. We fret away in isolation, full of doubts, questions, and uncertainties. Not only do we typically struggle with the vagaries and low points of this work alone, we usually experience any high points, triumphs, and joys alone as well. This volume offers a welcome relief. It affords fellow researchers an opportunity to share questions and insights with one another. It permits us the chance to interact and dialogue within a community.

AUTHOR'S NOTE: I would like to thank Susanne R. Cook-Greuter, Dina DuBois, John McKenna, Loren H. Miller, and Alan N. West for their helpful comments and suggestions on earlier versions of this manuscript. The conversations and dialogue with them about this chapter pushed me to deeper levels of awareness, understanding, and expression. I am especially indebted to Ruthellen Josselson for her constructive suggestions and support throughout this process.

Early Interests in Narrative and Worldview Explorations

My own research on the development of lives over time, and the concomitant exploration and classification of worldviews, has been in the works for the past 16 years (Miller, 1982, 1988, 1994). Its roots in spirit, however, stem from very early in my life.

Throughout most of my adolescence and young adulthood, I fancied myself as a philosopher in general and an existentialist in particular. I saw myself as one who struggled with the effort to make meaning in life, to find meaning in decisions and in relationships. I wondered if others struggled similarly. So, when the time came to choose a dissertation topic, I began a project that would permit me to explore the strivings, yearnings, influences, and existential meaning-making processes of adults. Somehow I must have taken Wilhelm Dilthey's (1926/1961) call to the "rediscovery of the I in the Thou" to heart. I accepted the challenge to do just that.

To explore the range and depths of people's meaning-making efforts, I developed an interview (Miller, 1994)[1] that would enable me to address questions such as, What are the similarities and differences in people's strivings? What are the drives, motives, and goals that push and pull lives over time? To what degree do people view their lives as stories? What are the "ultimate points of reference" (Kaufman, 1981, 1993) that people develop or construct for themselves? What do individuals experience as the "ground and/or aim of their being" (Tillich, 1963), and what influence does the conceptualization of ultimate points of reference and other guiding principles have on the way a particular life is lived?

My project became both an existential and a hermeneutic inquiry; the existential portion refers to the exploration of the basic meanings and "whys" of life, and the hermeneutic component refers to the process of teasing out and interpreting these meanings.

Ethical Considerations

When engaging in this work, we must ask ourselves some fundamental questions: Is it ethically appropriate to perform such research? What value is there, if any, to this kind of research? Who benefits from such projects? Does everyone involved, participant and researcher alike, receive some value from such endeavors? Do the researchers use the participants' responses to work on their own issues—to tell their own stories? If so, how might this dynamic affect the questions asked and the responses selected for discussion?

Sometimes interview work may be viewed as intrusive or invasive. Critics from this camp might argue that people do not want their private worlds explored: They may not want their inner lives exposed to public scrutiny; perhaps they would rather keep such matters to themselves.

On the other hand, I contend that this kind of research is the quintessential ethical project: It serves as an "aid to self-reflection" (Habermas, 1993, p. 23) and it addresses the perennial ethical concern and goal of sensitive, aware human beings—answering the existential question of the "wherefore of our lives" (Habermas, 1993, p. 118). Of course, even more central to this kind of interview project is the fact that it not only stimulates self-reflection but that it occurs in the interplay of the self and the other—in the dialogue of the I and Thou. Gadamer seems to take the position that ethics *is* dialogue (as cited in Crowell, 1990). Although this is a curious juxtaposition, I shall continue to develop this argument in the spirit of Gadamer's formulation. Perhaps we also need to claim that dialogue is ethics; true dialogue is ethical. I contend that it is in the dialogical, relational arena—in a symmetrical arena with a level playing field—that individual (and group) positions can be voiced, heard, and explored. In this light, then, the locus of ethical perspective and decision is in the interplay of self and other—in the dialogue. It is through the act of exploring within these parameters that ethical outcomes become possible. In fact, as I shall soon illustrate, it is the act of exploring the narrative that gives meaning, and it is in the act of exploring narrative that both meaningful and ethical consequences arise.

In this context, I decided to create an atmosphere that would permit explorations in meaningful, ethical dialogue. A critical first step was creating a situation in which people felt comfortable expressing themselves. I discovered that many simply needed to be, and wished to be, heard out—to have their stories listened to by an attentive other. This desire is not dissimilar to that which often motivates people to seek psychotherapy or psychoanalysis. Below is a response from one of my interviewees concerning the necessity of being heard:

> I believe that any time a person is allowed to ventilate his feelings to another person qualified to "hear" them, it has a healing, therapeutic effect. That has been the case with you and me. In our sessions, you helped me understand the processes of . . . development that I experienced over the years with regard to my early familial or/and especially seminary training, and helped me compare that past "indoctrination" with my ever-growing existential understanding of morality (God). (Participant 120)[2]

Listening to the stories and addressing the existential questions— working on the *whys* and *wherefores*—occurs in my project through an intersubjective, dialogical approach. It is the opportunity to be listened to and to communicate that people want and seem to need.

A principal value, then, of both interview research and the psychotherapeutic experience is in being heard. In addition to being heard, there also seems to be a coequal or even deeper wish of being understood. The necessity of being understood and the sense of joy experienced by people when they feel that some bit of understanding has come their way cannot be underestimated (cf. Kohut, 1984; Rogers, 1970). For example, a client recently remarked,

> I am feeling really known by you. I am feeling understood. This is so rare for me. Perhaps the first time in my life being known by anyone. It is wonderful and terrifying at the same time; it's exciting, wonderful, and terrifying.

Whether the understanding or interpretation offered to a research participant or client is accurate, experienced as veridical, or not—does not seem to be the primary issue. What seems to be central is the fact that someone is trying to understand. To find understanding and meaning in terms of one's present existential and emotional state—as a stepping-off place for where one might be, for where one might move to as one moves into the future—can be a remarkably enhancing, growth-producing experience.

From Participant 120 again:

> Our sessions have helped my worldview expand because your questions probed areas of my life that I simply did not consider looking into. I discovered some skeletons, some rubbish, some feelings, and much beauty of person that I had failed to integrate into my psyche. You did open up a new view of the world for me.

Interview-based research affords people the opportunity to explore themselves, to increase their awareness, to find meaning, to be understood, and to be understood within the context of a relationship. This work is fundamental and ethical in its own right. The dialogue that takes place is inherently ethical.

Narrative and Hermeneutics
in Dialogical Relationship

The current lifestyles of the latter part of the 20th century offer few avenues for the exploration of meaning making, for the pursuit of ethics and values, or for personal understanding (see Kegan, 1994; Lifton, 1993; Taylor, 1989). In my research, I wanted to provide an opportunity for meaningful, ethical dialogue and the explication of narrative that addressed questions of ultimate concern for my participants, my colleagues, and myself. I wanted to give myself a chance to follow my passion in these arenas and to create the occasion for further self-discovery—for both the I and the Thou.

In this light, I must say that I am in agreement with Buber's (1970) notion of the discovery of self in relationship (in dialogue) and, more recently, with Taylor's (1989, 1994) idea of the discovery of self and the enhancement of identity both occurring through dialogue and relationship. Martin Buber struggled to articulate his belief in the ontological primacy of relationship in his seminal and provocative treatise titled *I and Thou*. In this rare and rather poetic work, he also discusses how the individual learns of both self and other through a process of interrelating. Buber's position is both complex and compelling. These words are from Buber (1970), as translated by Walter Kaufmann:

> In the beginning is the relation—as the category of being, as a readiness, as a form that reaches out to be filled, as a model of the soul; the a priori of relation; the *innate You.*
>
> In the relationships through which we live, the innate You is realized in the You we encounter: that is, comprehended as a being we confront and accepted as exclusive, . . . ground[ed] in the a priori of relation. (pp. 78-79)

Buber discusses the innate human drive for both relationship and reciprocity. He posits that it begins as something instinctive—as an instinctive need or drive *to be with,* which eventually evolves into the need for conversation and dialogue. Buber (1970) continues:

> In the drive for contact (originally, a drive for tactile contact . . .) the innate You comes to the fore quite soon, and it becomes even clearer that the drive aims at reciprocity, at "tenderness." . . . [I]t also determines the inventive drive which emerges later (the drive to produce things . . .), and thus the product is personified and a conversation begins. The development of the child's soul is connected indissolubly with his craving for the You. . . . [It forms through] gradually entering into relationships. . . . [One] becomes an I through a You. (pp. 79-80)

Charles Taylor (1989, 1994), a contemporary scholar and philosopher of self, adopts a Buberesque position on relationship and dialogue and expands it for the postmodern condition. Both thinkers, it should be noted, take positions on the importance of relationship and interconnectedness that stand in opposition to the individualism so often associated with modern and certain postmodern descriptions of self. Taylor (1989) decries the "modern character forms of . . . highly independent individualism" and the philosophical stance that argues for the ontological nature of our independence and self-sufficiency (pp. 38-39). In contrast, he constructs a Buber-like foundational position on dialogue and relationship. He essentially takes Buber beyond himself as he integrates these themes with the core concepts of self development, identity, and dialogue. Taylor (1989) says the following:

> The crucial feature of human life is its fundamentally *dialogical* character. We become full human agents, capable of understanding ourselves, and hence of defining our identity, through our acquisition of rich human languages of expression. For my purposes here, I want to take language in a broad sense, covering not only the words we speak, but also other modes of expression whereby we define ourselves, including the "languages" of art, of gesture, of love, and the like. But we learn these modes of expression through exchanges with others. People do not acquire the languages needed for self-definition on their own. . . . The genesis of the human mind is in this sense not monological, not something each person accomplishes on his or her own, but dialogical. (p. 32)

I take Buber's and Taylor's positions together as substantiating both the ontological and ethical underpinnings of an interpersonal, intersubjective, and hermeneutic enterprise. Their clarification of the ontological primacy of relationship becomes the foundation for a hermeneutic effort of mutual understanding and self-development. Development and growth for both parts of the dyad derive from mutual dialogical exchanges.

Widdershoven (1993) expands on these ideas in the first volume of *The Narrative Study of Lives.* It seems that he agrees, from a hermeneutic point of view, that any dialogue might become a process of mutual self-exploration—whether it is friend to friend, researcher to research participant, patient to therapist, or, generally put, speaker to listener. Each benefits from the interaction. Each has the opportunity to be heard; each may have his or her life enriched and life's meanings deepened from the mutual exploration of perspective and truth. Such consequences follow from an inherently ethical process.

Habermas (1993) has remarked about the efficacy of this kind of discourse, and he relates it to both the development of the self and the development of the group or community. He contends that dialogue can lead to ethical self-reflection that forwards the developmental concerns of both the individual and the larger whole. Habermas notes that in dialogue,

> [people] can clarify who they are and who they want to be, whether as members of a family, . . . or as citizens of a state. The . . . evaluations that shape the self-understanding of the person . . . are here up for discussion. An individual life history or an intersubjectively shared form of life is the horizon within which participants can critically appropriate their past with a view to existing possibilities. . . . Such processes of self-understanding lead to conscious decisions that are judged according to the standard of an authentic way of life. (p. 23)

Perhaps we also can think about this and similar dialogical dynamics from the context of Gadamer's (1992) hermeneutic writings, in which he sees truth and understanding as the dual objectives of the hermeneutic process. In genuine dialogue, as in any effort to truly explore meanings, participants are taken to further levels of understanding and personal development. Crowell (1990) quotes Gadamer to clarify this point, as he refers to Plato's *Republic* for illustrative purposes:

> To understand Plato's *Republic* is not simply to reconstruct what Plato actually wrote, not *simply* to understand Plato as he understood himself, but to be brought to think further about the "issue(s)" by means of the encounter with Plato's text. (p. 342)

Of course, it is not being argued that one should not be interested in Plato's original meaning or that his original meanings are irrelevant. Rather, it is proposed that one must enter into a dialogue with Plato—with his writings; we should want to understand them as he understood them and perhaps better. Furthermore, I suggest that our efforts at interpretation might take us to more complex and deeper levels of meaning than those previously considered. We might come to understand what Plato meant, and more, as we enter a dialogue with him through his words. Gadamer's thinking is important with regard to this argument not because he and later hermeneutic writers take this position with respect to written text but because they have come to treat oral discourse and narrative in a similar fashion.

I have taken a position similar to Gadamer's (and some of the later hermeneutic writers) with respect to the narrative deriving from the dialogical relationships into which I have entered—both with my research participants and with my psychotherapy patients. My goal has been to understand the expressed meanings and to suggest possible deeper meanings embedded in the narrative. Thus understanding the participant (or client) as the participant understands himself or herself is what both the worldview interviews and the process of psycho-therapy strive toward. In both endeavors, we find that an opportunity for a deeper and more complex understanding is offered. Both the interviewer and the interviewee are presented with an opportunity to think further about the issues and to probe for deeper levels of meanings. How many varied levels of meaning there might be remains to be explored. As a case in point, I was struck by the recent musings of one of my clients as he wondered aloud, "How many more layers of meaning are we going to find here? We've been at this for a few years already and are only on Layer 7. Golly [said jokingly], there must be at least 10 more layers of meaning to go."

Dialogue by means of language is what unites people in relation-ship. It is the medium through which our differences and intersubjec-tive distance may be resolved. Language, then, serves relationship—it is in the service of dialogue. Dialogue in relationship, with an effort toward hermeneutic interpretations of the participant's narrative, is the central interpersonal and epistemological dynamic of narrative research.

Why we do this work and why anyone would volunteer for such studies may in part have been answered above. Participants' motives may not seem so unusual: the opportunity to be listened to, the chance to tell one's story, to have that story understood by another, and to explore the whys and wherefores of life.

But the researchers are changed as well. Wilhelm Dilthey's (1926/1961) notion of the rediscovery of the I in the Thou underlies the very powerful interaction between researcher and participant. In this research, the experimenter may evoke or provoke change in the other; the experimenter is also changed by the other—changed through the interaction (as shall be illustrated later). Both researcher and participant are on a search—engaged in a project of exploration and inquiry. In this context, it might be said that together they form the unit of inquiry. Each is attempting to both discover the other and rediscover the self in the other in a mutual process of understanding and interpretation.

The Worldview Project

My primary concern in this worldview research was to frame a set of questions[1] that would focus on the philosophical and personal trials and dilemmas encountered by individuals as they develop a workable ethic and a set of ideas and goals to live by. I wanted to investigate the major influences on their thinking. Who were the main people that influenced them? What were the most influential experiences of their lives? Was it important for them to view their lives as stories? How actively did they work at understanding their lives, its influences, and their worldviews? In short, how did each of them wrestle with philosophical issues to eventually arrive at an ever- evolving, ever-unfolding, philosophy of life? Did they or do they strive to grasp the "wherefore" of their lives?[3]

Participants in this longitudinal study have been 40 adult males[4] between the ages of 28 and 57 (mean age = 37). I set a minimum age of 28 years because I assumed at the time that an individual must live at least this long to develop the degree of maturity needed to arrive at a fairly consistent and expressible life and worldview. I have since reconsidered this assumption and have begun to use the worldview interview with a younger population.[5] Participants over 57 years were not recruited because of the projected 10-, 20-, and 30-year follow-up interviews (Miller, 1982, 1994; Miller & West, 1993).

To increase the likelihood of sampling diverse life experiences and worldviews, participants were chosen from five vocational and professional areas: physical scientists, social scientists, lawyers, military personnel, and ministers-priests (see Miller & West, 1993, for a further discussion of these professional groups). Participants were recruited through colleagues, family members, friends, and friends of friends, and, in general, by word of mouth. All participants were volunteers. No one was pressured to become involved; rather, most participants appeared to be pleased to participate. The project was explained thoroughly before they were again asked if they were willing to participate. Informal informed-consent procedures were followed in the early stages of the project. Confidentiality protocols were reviewed with each participant. In retrospect, I could have been more thorough with these procedures back then. I have become much more attentive to informed consent and confidentiality procedures since the early days of this project. Due to my concern for ethical considerations, I have begun to take more time with these matters and have continued to reaffirm the ongoing interest and commitment levels of my participants.

With such ethical concerns in mind, let us move to a discussion of findings that are related to the matters at hand, such as ethics and understanding, self-development, and the exploration of intimate and ultimate concerns—in and through dialogue.

Related Findings and Ethical Implications

At the broadest level, I found that people had worldviews they could articulate, that these worldviews could be categorized, and that participants' views were influenced by both life experiences and key people.[6] I also learned that people were changed by both the process of the interview and their relationship with me. Some participants even seemed to consciously attempt to change themselves as a result of the interview process. They thought about their answers as they listened to themselves engage in dialogue through the interview relationship. As a result, they found themselves paying more attention to their inner lives. They began to discern deeper layers of meaning as they heard themselves talk and as they felt understood. For some, it was as if their initial reason for participation had begun to yield fruit or pay dividends.

This complex, interactive process is aptly illustrated in the following comments from one of my participants:

> My major thought . . . is that as long as I am challenged by you to continually look into my psyche and ask myself who I am, where am I going, what are my feelings on any subject, what are my sources of physical, spiritual, and intellectual help, guided by the philosophies of the greatest teachers and thinkers of the ages, I must necessarily grow in all areas of human experience. (Participant 120)

Here are comments from another participant:

> Over the past several years, I've been more and more conscious and more and more consciously resisting things that are . . . not in line with [my] worldview. . . . I think I'm in the process now of taking an active sort of approach, . . . trying to have more discipline and more structure. . . . This is the first time I have attempted to actively change something that's fundamental about my personality. First time in a while, anyway. And, incidentally, I don't think it is a result of free will, either. I think that it's the result of a particular kind of social circumstance I'm in right now and guys like you asking me these kinds of questions. . . . I hope that 10 years from now, when you do this again, I'll have it. I'll have corrected that one and I'll be making other mistakes by then. (Participant 116)

This response highlights a potential ethical dilemma inherent in this kind of research. Does the interview itself place a demand to change on the participants? Does the interviewee assume that there is a "correct" worldview that he should strive to develop? Here the participant is stating that the process of the interviews has put pressure on him to be different. On the one hand, there is the sense that he wants to "work on it"—to develop, change, transform his worldview and way of thinking. On the other hand, one gets the sense that he is succumbing to pressure from without—that he feels pressured to "get it right." Nevertheless, a delightful sense of the participant's self-awareness and self-critical humor is apparent in the quote. It is as though he is using the interview process to do work that he would be less likely to do on his own. He seems to want the process to nudge him a little.

Another interviewee who denies any conscious attempt to change himself as a result of the interview process but who has tried to be more aware of his worldview and "to live up to its demands" on a day-to-day basis, had the following to say:

> No, I don't think I have actively changed [my worldview] as a result of this process except in the following way. An experience like that forces the serious participant to examine himself and his goals very closely—and critically; if anything, the experience has motivated me to try to live up to my worldview, even to validate it. Simply having articulated it out loud to another person had the effect of crystallizing it in my consciousness, which has sometimes had the effect of making it more available and accessible when I have had to make decisions or deal with crises or challenges.

This same participant also addressed the importance of narrative and the value of employing a storied approach to understanding his life:

> [It is] helpful to think of my life as a story. . . . If you don't think of it as a story, your chances of living the unexamined life are infinitely greater, at least in my worldview. I'm not sure, however, what the chicken or the egg is here; maybe people who examine their lives automatically think of them as stories. Maybe for the literary types, examination of one's life naturally falls into the pattern of analysis of narrative lines. . . . The study provides a neat framework—almost as would various literary techniques of narrative framework—in which such thought can be carried out, but I always thought of my life as a story—I have very specific memories

of doing so from a very early age, late single digits, I suppose—and probably always will. (Participant 101)

Both of the preceding quotations illustrate the use of storying and its effect on coherence—making a life make sense. Widdershoven's (1993) comments about storying come to mind: "By telling a story about our life, we change our life. As we do so, the story itself becomes richer, as it is filled with life experience. Thus experience and story are said to communicate with each other" (p. 13). This participant seems to use the interview and other storying experiences to examine his life, to understand it, and to frame it.

Another participant spoke specifically about the importance of thinking in terms of narrative:

> It seems to me that narrative is what gives life coherence and meaning—namely, the sense that there's a beginning, a middle, and an end—hence that there's a purpose which gives our life direction. Not to have this kind of narrative structure leads almost inexorably to incoherence of personality and the inability to make commitments and stick to them. . . . I would say that my own participation in . . . [this] project has certainly sensitized me to the connections between worldview and narrative. (Participant 129)

This participant's comments seem remarkably similar to those of White and Epston (1990) as they promote the need for storying and narrative in the psychotherapy process:

> The success of [the] storying of experience provides persons with a sense of continuity and meaning in their lives, and this is relied on for the ordering of daily lives and for the interpretation of further experiences. Since all stories have a beginning (or a history), a middle (or a present), and an ending (or a future), then the interpretation of current events is as much future shaped as it is past-determined. (p. 10)

In the above quotations, from both my participants and White and Epston, we find the authors talking about the structure and coherence offered lives—both by the interview process and from thinking about lives as narratives and stories. This sense of coherence and identity is similar to that addressed by Habermas (1993) and Gutmann (1994). Both have noted the positive effects deriving from the coherence that narrative explorations bring to a life—to a life story. Occasionally I found that some participants would struggle for coherence at any cost—as if the state of noncoherence was too confusing and disquieting.

The push for coherence, the need for coherence, in addition to the aforementioned need to be listened to and understood, have been major findings in this worldview project. For many participants, the narrative process helped them reauthor their lives—their life stories—as they became more creative creators of meanings.

Effects of Thou on Me

Perhaps one of the most noteworthy findings from my research relates to my own process—my own developing awareness. For instance, I found that I increasingly tended to approach each interview with a sense of respect and amazement, appreciative of the opportunity to explore such intimate and ultimate topics with my volunteers. There was a kind of anxiety and anticipation as I did so. What would I find? What might I find? How would these people, these individuals, engage in the meaning-making process? Would they relish it? Would they struggle with it? How hard would they struggle? How would they interact and interrelate with me?

I also found that I was (and I continue to be) changed by each interview. I left each interview, sometimes 5-hour interviews, inspired and in awe. To be with interviewees, to experience their struggle with such issues from moment to moment throughout the interview, was both humbling and enriching. Their efforts and strivings made my own more intelligible, and in a way, their courage in the struggle nourished my own ever-evolving courage.

I noticed that I left some interviews with a knot in my stomach—with an uneasy feeling. It was as if there was more going on in some interviews than either the speaker or listener could assimilate and consciously process. I can remember one interview session in particular when, on the way home, I began to realize just how important the interview process had been to this participant and the degree to which the interview was being used as a therapy session—perhaps even a confessional. After a while, I had begun to "get" what was going on and was upset with myself that I had missed it. This participant was talking about experiences of pain, loss, and trauma that were difficult for me to listen to or take in. It was as though I did not have access to the level of interpretation and understanding required at that moment, perhaps due to my own defenses and pain. It was hard for me to hear, to listen to his tragedy and the awful pain. Finally, it was as if someone threw a bucket of cold water in my face. I woke up in that moment. As a result, I began to experience an even greater respect for the necessity of carefully attending to and interpreting the narrative of the other; I also experienced greater appreciation for the power of this research and genuine hermeneutic explorations. My understanding of the need to relate in an ethical and respectful way with the material and participants was deepened. Not only did I develop an expanded awareness of their need for me to go to such difficult emotional places with them (perhaps places where my own defenses kept me from going), I also realized (and continue to do so) that I *am* able to visit these places along with them. Through the process of staying with such difficult experiences, I developed a greater capacity for more mutual exploration and deeper understanding. I continue to develop this ability to go to emotional levels and places that are not easy for me. As a result, I feel an even deeper degree of commitment to my participants, to the work, and to myself in the work.

I attribute some of this increased awareness on my part to my ever-growing experience as a psychotherapist. I acknowledge that when I started doing this work, I was, in my own mind, primarily a social science researcher. I was going after data, information—at least on a conscious level. Since those early years of doing the research, I have had significantly more training as a psychotherapist, and I have been practicing psychotherapy for a number of years now. In the process, over these years of training and practice, I think I have become much more in tune with the emotions of my participants and the general themes of their lived experiences. I also have become more aware of the psychotherapeutic value of this narrative interview process. I think I have become more in tune with the other and have developed a capacity for deeper empathy—and maybe, hopefully, a more genuine way of relating to the other. I also have begun to feel like a steward or caretaker of something very special. As a result, I am constantly asking myself, "Can I do justice to the preciousness of that which is being placed before me?"

I wonder if we must ask ourselves, in the context of this project and the above vignettes, if there is an ethical dilemma developing when participants get involved initially just as research participants and then find themselves opening up to the interviewer as they might with a psychotherapist. It comes to mind that formal training in psychotherapy may be necessary for a considered, ethical engagement in this work. Perhaps, at the very least, all narrative researchers should be encouraged to undergo supervision with a seasoned clinician. There is so much at stake and so much to learn. How far do we go with our research participants in their attempts to be known? Are there necessary limits, ethical limits, to the depths of the dialogue? In this light and without resolving this question, I at some point realized that I could not look at my involvement in this work as merely involvement in a research project. I developed an even greater sense of responsibility and commitment to the work and to my participants and found myself being changed ever more deeply through the process.

Throughout the interviews, I found myself taking in a little—sometimes more than a little—of the other. There was a taking in of their ideas; there was a being changed by their ideas—slowly and gradually by each interview, by each person with whom I spent time. It was (and is) as though each exchange of emotion, idea, or perspective added fertilizer to seeds of thought or feeling that had been lying dormant in me. It was a process similar to the one described by Gadamer (1992), in his reference to the reading of Plato, in which every encounter with Plato's text would take the reader, the listener, to new and often deeper levels of understanding. Of course, I had an advantage over the reader of Plato; I was engaged in an interactive dialogue with the other in which a continual refining of meanings was possible, in which the horizon between the I and the Thou, the self and the other, could be mutually and consistently encountered. In short, I was constantly being affected and influenced by the other. I, in turn, affected and influenced them. I can only stand in awe of such experiences.

Notes

1. For a transcript of the complete worldview interview, contact Melvin E. Miller, Department of Psychology, Norwich University, Northfield, Vermont 05663. Also see Miller (1994).

2. Participants' identification numbers have been recoded to enhance the level of confidentiality provided.

3. I also decided that as I explored worldview development from this perspective, I might look at the development of particular personality and cognitive variables along the way. For the most thorough discussion of these variables, see Miller (1994) and Miller and West (1993).

4. After much debate and with the advice of my dissertation committee, it was decided that only men would be used as participants in this research. Because my project was exploratory, hypothesis-generating research, I was advised not to complicate the results by using both genders. I recently have been involved in discussions with a doctoral student who is interested in performing a very similar study with women.

5. On two occasions, students from different universities were administered the worldview interview. Both times, these college-aged students seemed to enjoy the process of exploring worldviews and life stories, and they seemed quite capable of articulating their ideas, ideologies, and the factors that may have affected their development.

6. For the most thorough discussion of these findings, see Miller (1982, 1994).

References

Buber, M. (1970). *I and thou*. New York: Scribner.

Crowell, S. G. (1990). Dialogue and text: Re-marking the difference. In T. Maranhao (Ed.), *The interpretation of dialogue* (pp. 338-360). Chicago: University of Chicago Press.

Dilthey, W. (1961). *Meaning in history*. London: Allen & Unwin. (Original work published in 1926)

Gadamer, H.-G. (1992). The historicity of understanding. In K. Mueller-Vollmer (Ed.), *The hermeneutics reader* (pp. 256-292). New York: Continuum.

Gutmann, A. (1994). Introduction to multiculturalism. In A. Gutmann (Ed.), *Multiculturalism: Examining the politics of recognition* (pp. 3-24). Princeton, NJ: Princeton University Press.

Habermas, J. (1993). *Justification and application: Remarks on discourse ethics*. Cambridge: MIT Press.

Kaufman, G. D. (1981). *The theological imagination: Constructing the concept of God.* Philadelphia: Westminster.

Kaufman, G. D. (1993). *In face of mystery: A constructive theology.* Cambridge, MA: Harvard University Press.

Kegan, R. (1994). *In over our heads: The mental demands of modern life.* Cambridge, MA: Harvard University Press.

Kohut, H. (1984). *How does psychoanalysis cure?* Chicago: University of Chicago Press.

Lifton, R. J. (1993). *The protean self: Human resilience in an age of fragmentation.* New York: Basic Books.

Miller, M. E. (1982). World views and ego development in adulthood. *Dissertation Abstracts International, 42,* 3459-3460.

Miller, M. E. (1988). Developing a world view: The universal and the particular. *New England Psychological Association Newsletter, 5,* 3-4.

Miller, M. E. (1994). World views, ego development and epistemological changes from the conventional to the postformal: A longitudinal perspective. In M. E. Miller & S. Cook-Greuter (Eds.), *Transcendence and mature thought in adulthood* (pp. 147-179). Lanham, MD: Rowman & Littlefield.

Miller, M. E., & West, A. N. (1993). Influences of world view on personality, epistemology, and choice of profession. In J. Demick & P. Miller (Eds.), *Development in the workplace* (pp. 3-19). Hillsdale, NJ: Lawrence Erlbaum.

Rogers, C. R. (1970). *Carl Rogers on encounter groups.* New York: Harper & Row.

Taylor, C. (1989). *Sources of the self: The making of modern identity.* Cambridge, MA: Harvard University Press.

Taylor, C. (1994). The politics of recognition. In A. Gutmann (Ed.), *Multiculturalism: Examining the politics of recognition* (pp. 25-73). Princeton, NJ: Princeton University Press.

Tillich, P. (1963). *Morality and beyond.* New York: Harper & Row.

White, M., & Epston, D. (1990). *Narrative means to therapeutic ends.* New York: Norton.

Widdershoven, G. A. M. (1993). The story of life: Hermeneutic perspectives on the relationship between narrative and life history. In R. Josselson & A. Lieblich (Eds.), *The narrative study of lives* (Vol. 1, pp. 1-20). Newbury Park, CA: Sage.

PART III

❧ 11 ❧

Ethnography and Hagiography

The Dialectics of Life, Story, and Afterlife

Yoram Bilu

*P*ostmodern anthropology is informed by a social reality in which the boundaries between the ethnographer and the informant are being systematically eroded: the "native" as an object of analysis may become an analyzing subject (Rosaldo, 1989) and the "other" may appear as a critical reader of the ethnographic account (Clifford & Marcus, 1986; Marcus & Fischer, 1986). Under these circumstances, anthropologists have become more attentive to the reverberations of their fieldwork and particularly ethnographic writing in the lives and the social world of the people they study. The growing sensitivity to the effect of ethnographic accounts on the communities studied (and on other circles of readership beyond the relatively small professional group of colleagues and students) has recently given rise to two collections of insightful essays on the political and moral-ethical aspects of this subject matter (Blackman, 1992a; Brettell, 1993).

The essays in Brettel's edited volume, *When They Read What We Write,* discuss various dimensions of the complex relations between fieldwork, text, and audience (when the natives talk back, when native scholars object, and when the press intervenes). Blackman's (1992b) edited collection, which appeared as a special issue of the *Journal of Narrative and Life History*, was designated *The Afterlife of the Life History*. The articles subsumed under this title focus on the post-publication of what is written as life history.

> Afterlife makes the point that the life-history continues beyond the crystallization of the narrative into text to encompass audience response to the published work, reflections on its construction as text, as well as its impact on the lives of its narrator and collector. (p. 2)

Issues related to the afterlife of ethnographic accounts are particularly pertinent in Israel. On top of the fact that most Israeli anthropologists are studying their own society, the small size of the country, the relatively open avenues of communication, and the wide exposure to the same few mass media agencies create problems of involvement with which anthropologists working in remote milieus are less bothered. I believe that the case I narratively present here—the postpublication vicissitudes of the life story of a legendary rabbi-healer who died in Morocco in the early 1950s—sheds light on some of these problems of involvement. Beyond the ethical problems of the "politics of the life story," amply discussed in Blackman's (1992b) collection, the case to be presented raises an intriguing epistemological question concerning the interplay between the ethnographic text and the reality it is supposed to represent.

I first came across the name of Rabbi Ya'acov Wazana in 1975 when I was collecting data for my doctoral dissertation on Jewish Moroccan ethnopsychiatry in Israel. Focusing on two *moshavim* (smallholders' cooperative villages) of immigrants from southern Morocco near Jerusalem, I sought to study the traditional curing system through interviews with those inhabitants who turned to local rabbi-healers with all kinds of problems in living. The interviews were explicitly directed toward the current Israeli scene. But the informants often resorted to the Maghrebi chapters in their lives, basking in memories of an era in which the folk practices I was interested in were an integral part of the traditional ambiance. It was in this context of discussing episodes of illness and health-seeking behaviors in Morocco that some informants invoked, with awe and astonishment, the name of Rabbi Ya'acov. "In all Morocco, there was no healer like Wazana," they would reiterate wistfully. "At times when physicians were practically nonexistent, he was our only doctor."

Such admiring statements and the intriguing accounts of curing feats that usually followed them at once drew my attention to Wazana. But the urge to retrieve and explore his life story had to be weighed against three serious reservations. First, I soon found out that only a small number of the interviewees had known Wazana in Morocco. They all had come to Israel from the same circumscribed area in the Western High Atlas region, and this geographical boundedness accentuated Wazana's position as a provincial healer, a celebrity in a remote, peripheral place. His name was not known in the urban centers of the coastal zone, where most of the Jewish population has been concentrated since the establishment of the French Protectorate. Why bother, then, with the life story of a peripheral figure who, in terms of popularity and renown, was far behind many more centrally located, urban healers.

Second, the first recollections of Wazana already convinced me that he was a "deviant" type within the Jewish Moroccan curing system, given his antinomian personality and the audacious and extravagant manner in which he enacted the curing role. Hence Wazana's life story did not appear to be a good representation of the typical Jewish Moroccan rabbi-healer.

Third, in addition to his peripherality and atypicality, the fact that Wazana died in 1952 in Morocco, just before the massive wave of immigration to Israel eliminated the Jewish presence from most parts of the Maghreb, made him a mediated object of knowledge. His life could be examined only through texts elicited from people who knew him in other times and in other places rather than through straightforward facts of his life history. In other words, these texts were constructed of historically situated memories replete with retrospective evaluations and interpretations and imbued with personal meanings to the narrators. This epistemological concern, although common to most forms of investigation that rely on narrative accounts, could be mitigated to some extent by replacing Wazana, a shadowy figure from an elusive past, with a contemporary Jewish Moroccan rabbi-healer who could be addressed and studied directly.

That I remained engrossed with Wazana's figure despite these concerns attests to the compelling power of a dramatic life story. Yet beyond the immediacy and the emotional effect of a heroic-tragic narrative (to be unfolded presently), I felt that the selection of Wazana's life story as an object of study could also be defended on theoretical grounds. First, when seeking to portray a life as a totality in all its complexity and uniqueness yet without the presumption that it should serve as an exemplary model or a typical representation of some collectivity, then the life story of a provincial figure is worth telling no less than that of a central, more popular one. Moreover, this idiographic justification seems altogether superfluous when the question of Wazana's atypicality is at stake, because it was precisely Wazana's deviant dimension that could bring to the fore and highlight core elements of the symbolic universe and the cultural setting of the Jewish Maghrebi communities. In the audacious, boundless manner in which he enacted the healer role, Wazana traveled to the edge of the social order. He went further than any other Jewish healer I have heard of in exploiting the potentialities of the idioms of his culture and in challenging and eventually defying its constraints. Dialectically, then, these idioms could be explored most lucidly through the intricacies of his admittedly exceptional biography.

The epistemological concern about Wazana as a mediated object of knowledge can become a virtue when the investigation is conducted from a constructivist rather than an essentialist perspective. It may appear presumptuous and naive to launch a fact-finding expedition in a time machine to expose Wazana's "authentic" figure in the name of historical positivism. It is no less unfounded to directly embark on the motivational bases of such a mediated figure in the name of psychological essentialism. But if the diverse layers of mediation that separate Wazana from the investigator—the dialogue between the informants and Wazana in the past (as fashioned and refashioned in memory), their ongoing dialogue with his image in the present, and the dialogue between the investigator and the informants—are deconstructed rather than ignored, than we can draw nearer to the complex, multivocal process in which a figure from a growingly dim past is developed and mythologized. I espoused this multidialogic approach in dealing with Wazana's life story.

Before embarking on the repercussions or afterlife of Wazana's life story as promulgated in my work, which is the gist of this chapter, a brief sketch of his biography and my analysis of it is in order. My engagement with Wazana, which now spans two decades, gave rise to three written accounts of his life. The short section on his life in my dissertation (Bilu, 1978) was expanded into an article in Hebrew (Bilu, 1986) and later in English (Bilu, 1988), and then developed into a book in Hebrew (Bilu, 1993). The following account was abstracted from the book.

Wazana was born at the turn of the century in a small village nestled near the highest peaks of the Atlas mountains. He spent most of his life in this mountainous area, and his reputation barely exceeded it. The genealogy of his family was laced with pious rabbis acknowledged as saintly figures *(tsaddiqim)*, and this virtuous background was conducive to his assumption of the curing role. Most noted among these venerated forefathers was Wazana's great-grandfather, Rabbi Avraham el-Kebir ("the great"), the source of the family blessing, whose miraculous accomplishments made his tomb near the town of Ouarzazat a popular pilgrimage site.

Wazana's father, also called Avraham, a pious student of Jewish mysticism, was a worthy successor to the family legacy. His miracle-saturated death account (see Bilu, 1988) clearly resonates with similar episodes in the genre of saint legends. Young Ya'acov, still a child and away from home when his father passed away, could not resign himself to the loss. In a desperate attempt to catch another glimpse of his father's face, he dug up his tomb and exposed his body. When his mother died 30 years later, again in his absence, Wazana exhumed her body, too, for a last farewell. I interpreted these religiously forbidden acts in the narrated profile of Wazana as conveying his unrelieved pain and longing for his parents as well as his boldness and temerity. More specifically, they reflected his tenacious ambition to stare at what should be invisible and to retrieve what by all means is irretrievable. This passion would become the leitmotif for Wazana's curing activities in the future.

What made Wazana so unique in the Jewish Moroccan curing system was his profound involvement with Muslim practices—to the extent of dangerously blurring his Jewish identity. His passion for Muslim esoteric knowledge stemmed from his desire to gain control over the *jnun* (demons), the major source of affliction in Moroccan ethnomedicine. To that end, he studied under Muslim sages and went as far as absorbing himself in Muslim prayers and marrying a she-demon. It should be noted that a human-demon marriage was an option in the traditional Maghrebi setting. But it was considered an extreme act, dwelling on the limits of social conventions, because of its exclusively binding character: the husband of a she-demon could not marry a human. Although Wazana's demonic spouse and the children he begot remained invisible to his associates, no one doubted their existence. His demonic and Muslim leanings, which could easily bring about ostracism in bigger Jewish communities, were somehow tolerated in those peripheral areas where demons were givens in the culturally constituted reality and Muslims lived in close coexistence with Jews. Both groups, it should be remembered, amply enjoyed Wazana's therapeutic services, which were based on these eccentric leanings.

Wazana had an impressive appearance. Strong, tall, and good-looking, with his spotless white *jellaba* (gown) and red *tarboosh* (head cover) typical of Muslims, he gave the impression that age had no effect on him. The audacity with which he pursued his role was mitigated by the air of carelessness and lack of arrogance that surrounded him. His cheerful, Gargantuan character made him the center of any social gathering. On these occasions, he would resort to his conjuring tricks to bring forth, by sleight of hand, *arak* (an alcoholic beverage), mint tea, or tobacco. His associates believed that in these frivolous tricks, too, he was helped by his demonic kin. In seeking to epitomize Wazana's peculiar character, one of them stated that "he [Wazana] feared nothing, he cared about nothing, and he lacked nothing."

As an indefatigable healer, fortified by impressive Muslim-based curing devices, Wazana treated all kinds of life problems, but he was particularly renowned for his ability to expose sorcerers and to identify thieves. Other healers were reluctant to cope with these malefactors because of the potentially dire consequences of a confrontation with the identified offender—believed to be someone from the victim's close social circle. But for Wazana, unheedful of social conventions and fervently determined to unravel what should normally remain hidden and unknown, such intricacies were of negligible importance. It was this determination "to go all the way" in his therapeutic undertakings, coupled with his arrogant contempt of the social order, that brought on him a horrible, untimely death.

Wazana died in the summer of 1952 when he was in his early 50s. There is a consensus that his tragic demise was precipitated by a forbidden cure. He was called on to remedy the moribund daughter of a famous Muslim sheik who had fallen prey to the demons' wrath after she had killed their offspring in snake form. Haughtily ignoring the demonic admonitions not to treat her, Wazana succeeded in bringing the girl back to life. This therapeutic victory was Wazana's greatest achievement as a healer, but it proved short-lived as the demons hastened to take their revenge on their ally turned adversary. They attacked him vehemently, and Wazana underwent a rapid physical and mental deterioration. Confused and panic-stricken, he made desperate attempts to extricate himself from his fatal condition, but to no avail. He sank into a twilight state and died in agony and pain. The Jews of the village found his body fetid and swollen, soaked in buckets of vomit and blood, and hastened to bury him in the local cemetery. The tenor of Wazana's death account, sharply contrasted with the death legends of his saintly ancestors, seals the saga of the family with a tragic hue indicative, perhaps, of the ambivalence harbored in the community toward his anomalous lifestyle.

On the basis of Wazana's reconstructed biography, presented here in a very schematic form, I analyzed Wazana's calling, particularly the prodigious healing energies attributed to him, on two levels.

First, without denying the aforementioned epistemological concerns of studying a mediated object of knowledge, I nevertheless sought to explore Wazana's motivational structure. In doing this, I followed the informants who, although reluctant to articulate their impressions of Wazana within a psychological idiom, were quite intrigued by his strong attachment to his parents and by his inability to resign himself to their deaths. Without going into their detailed accounts here, I raised the possibility that his unrelieved grief and sense of loss were the generator underlying his inexhaustible healing energies. His unique style of work, characterized by temerity, audacity, perseverance, and resourcefulness, might have been molded by his desperate yearning to cure his parents and to bring them back to life. In this respect, the resuscitation of the daughter of the sheik constituted the ultimate cure that symbolically compensated for the death of his parents. Wazana's own death seems to reflect, beyond the culturally ingrained notion of restoring the equilibrium between the human and the demonic worlds, the extinction of that inner source of vitality once the mission of his life was completed.

Given the mediated process in which Wazana's figure has been constructed, I proposed a second perspective for analysis that moved the limelight from the protagonist's psychic reality to the dialogic reality of his encounter with the Jews of the High Atlas (symbolically maintained up to this day through memories and dreams). In this cultural-symbolic analysis, the ambivalence that Wazana's position at the edge of the social order had elicited in his community was taken as a starting point. The crux of the argument was that Wazana's liminal position was deemed threateningly dangerous and therefore discommendable, but at the same time, it presumably made him capable of unleashing endless amounts of healing energies.

The negative, condemning aspect of this ambivalence becomes all the more conspicuous when the respective death episodes of Wazana and his father (as well as other pious ancestors) are juxtaposed and compared. The comparison, too elaborate to be depicted here, puts Wazana in a very unflattering light. His death account, communicating impotence and incompleteness, appears as the mirror image of the idealized death episodes of his forefathers that, in keeping with the genre of saint legends, are replete with miraculous events and convey strength and complacent harmony. Thus a tacit but firm condemnation is launched at the profligate son who abused the powers of his ancestors by crossing and dissolving the boundaries they were so anxious to maintain.

Along with this harsh cultural verdict, Wazana's unique marginality and disregard for social norms also made him a vital therapeutic resource for his community. Presumably his image as a great healer in the eyes of Jews and Muslims was related to the fact that he integrated and personified in his figure a set of seemingly contrasting categories that normally are sharply differentiated. Viewed at once as human and demon-bound, Jew and Muslim, pure and profane, old and young, single and married, Wazana crossed and dissipated the major ontological, ethnic, social, religious, and moral boundaries that constituted the grid of the social order in traditional Morocco. This categorization-defying mobility is dangerous and unrestrained but also potent and creative because in crossing the conceptual boundaries recognized by the culture, it releases energies and modes of actions that those locked in social casts and rigid structural positions are not able to recruit or pursue.

In residing at the edge of the social order, Wazana appears as a liminal figure (Turner, 1974) or a symbolic type (Handelman, 1985), capable of employing the fluidity and disorder that were his essence to restore order and wholeness and to cure. It should be noted, in this vein, that the word *wazana* in Arabic means "to balance." In bridging oppositions in Maghrebi cosmology, Wazana balanced worlds as shamans often do (Myerhoff, 1976). His death account lucidly demonstrates what might happen when the shamanic gift of maintaining order, harmony, and equilibrium is abused.

Although I became engrossed with Wazana in the context of studying folk healing and ethnopsychiatry, his name kept accompanying me when my interest in the vicissitudes of the Maghrebi cultural traditions in Israel led me, in the early 1980s, to the related realm of the folk veneration of saints (see Bilu, 1991). Because the significance of the vicissitudes of Wazana's afterlife is couched in the renaissance of saint worship in Israel, the essence and main features of this cultural complex should be explicated.

Saint veneration, a hallmark of Moroccan Islam, was also a major constituent of the Jewish collective identity in traditional Morocco. The Jewish saints *(k'doshim* or *tsaddiqim)* were depicted as charismatic and pious sages, erudite in kabbalah (Jewish mysticism), who possessed a special spiritual force from which their adherents could benefit. Unlike their Muslim counterparts, most Jewish Moroccan saints were acknowledged as *tsaddiqim* only posthumously. Therefore, their tombs, densely distributed all over the country, were the foci of their cults. The high point in the veneration of the saints was the collective pilgrimage to their tombs on their death anniversaries and the celebrations (hillulah) there. In the case of the more popular saints, these pilgrimages involved thousands of followers in a formidable spectacle, several days long, which combined high spirituality and marked ecstasy with excessive self-indulgence (e.g., feasting on slaughtered cattle and consuming large quantities of arak). In addition to the hillulah day, supplicants frequented the sanctuaries of the saints throughout the year with a wide variety of human afflictions.

One did not have to go on collective or individual pilgrimages to enjoy the saints' bliss because their presence was also strongly felt in daily routine. People would utter their names and dream about them whenever facing a problem. At home, candles were lit and festive meals organized in honor of the saints, and male newborns were conferred their names in gratitude (and also to ensure the help of the sublime namesake). As a major cultural idiom for articulating a wide range of experiences, the pervasive and enduring relations with the saint often took a symbiotic form spanning the entire life course of the devotee.

The sociocultural fabric of Moroccan Jewry was ruptured following the massive aliyah (immigration) to Israel in the 1950s and 1960s. The folk veneration of saints was particularly vulnerable because it was associated with physical loci—tombs, shrines, and sanctuaries— which had been left behind. Indeed, the first harsh years after aliyah witnessed a rapid diminution and decentralization in the celebration of hillulot (plural of hillulah). But this attenuation process was stopped and reversed when the new immigrants gradually and pain- fully alleviated the cultural shock and the enormous economic difficul- ties that were their share after aliyah. Specifically, Moroccan Jews were able to resume their intimate bond with the saints by employing various compensatory substitutes for the deserted Maghrebi sanctu- aries. They annexed and "Moroccanized" old (local Israeli) pilgrimage sites attributed to various Biblical, Talmudic, and mystical luminaries and established new centers around the new tombs of charismatic contemporary rabbis.

My research on Maghrebi saint worship in Israel has focused on a third alternative, more daring and innovative than the former two, that was called for to restore the forsaken Maghrebi saints of childhood— not merely to compensate for their absence. This alternative involved the symbolic transfer of Jewish saints from Morocco to Israel and their reinstallation in the new country (Ben-Ari & Bilu, 1987). It was based on the spontaneous initiative of simple devotees of Moroccan background, men and women alike, who erected a shrine for a Maghrebi *tsaddiq* in their homes following an inspiring dream series in which the saint urged them to do so. They usually promulgated these dreams as "announcements to the public," which they circulated among Moroccan-born Israelis. I designated these individual entrepreneurs *saint impresarios* to convey their relentless efforts to develop their shrines and increase their popularity. Much of my work with the saint impresarios centered on their personal narratives and life stories (e.g., Bilu, 1990; Bilu & Hasan-Rokem, 1989). As articulated by them, these accounts, always ending with the appearance of the saint's apparition and an enduring liaison with him, are based on life events that pave the road for the transformative visitational dreams.

At this point, Wazana's position vis-à-vis the Maghrebi cult of the saints should be clarified. In traditional Morocco, the authority and renown of rabbi-healers were primarily based on "the virtue of the ancestors" *(zechut avot)*, that is, the divine powers enveloped in the blessing of sainted figures in the family, which worthy descendants were capable of inheriting. As we already know, Wazana's prodigious family background, saturated with many sainted figures, constituted a propitious ground for healing. Yet with his antinomian character and deviant lifestyle, Wazana appears as a negative template of the conventional *tsaddiq*. As I attempted to show in my analysis, he was the family's black sheep, the profligate son who, to gain extraordinary therapeutic powers, went so far as to embrace Muslim practices and demonic affiliations. Jewish saints were hardly made of this subversive stuff. Indeed in Israel, Wazana's memory was cherished by a relatively small group of associates and grateful ex-patients. He did not enjoy the popularity of his forebears and definitely remained outside the Jewish-Maghrebi pantheon of saints.

The Anthropologist, the Media, and the Afterlife

My book in Hebrew on Wazana appeared in March 1993. Although it was published in a small number of copies by an academic press, it received relatively high media coverage. I believe that the concatenation of events that ensued was triggered by this media exposure (the credit for which should go to Wazana's colorful and intriguing character) and particularly by two lengthy pieces that appeared simultaneously in the weekend supplements of the two leading Israeli daily newspapers. I found out that the book, no less than its protagonist, was a mediated object of knowledge. But this time, the filters through which Wazana's figure was conveyed to the public were newspaper and television reports in which his exotic and magical aspects were all the more accentuated.

In the beginning of April 1993, a 35-year-old man named Yoseph from the town of Beer Sheva, an ex-barber who now worked as a clerk in a local religious institution, called me in my office at the Hebrew University. Claiming that his parents had known Wazana in Morocco, he started to unfold, in a trembling voice burning with excitement, a series of dream encounters with the late rabbi-healer. Although it was impossible to rule out the possibility that some of the dreams had preceded the publication, it became evident at the outset that the book, and particularly the attention drawn to it by the media, precipitated Yoseph's decision to "go public" with the nightly messages from Rabbi Ya'acov. Needless to say, Yoseph's phone call engaged my attention instantly. I suggested a meeting in Beer Sheva so that I could record or write down verbatim Yoseph's dream accounts. He wholeheartedly agreed but said that to expedite matters, he would send me the written version of his nocturnal experiences with Wazana. One day later, a handwritten, six-page-long account of six dreams reached me through the department's fax machine. Only after I read the dream report did I start to realize the scope of Yoseph's vision and my expected role in it: as Wazana's biographer (or more akin to Yoseph's point of view, as his hagiographer), I was assigned the role of Yoseph's confidante and adviser in his attempts to promote and give publicity to the name of the legendary but relatively unknown healer in Israel.

In the introduction to the dream accounts, Yoseph praises the greatness of Rabbi Ya'acov and the holiness of his great forebears. Then he asks, "How did it turn out that precisely now, 51 years after the death of Rabbi Ya'acov Wazana [in fact, only 41 years had passed since Wazana's death], it was decided to erect this holy site, which bears the name of these tsaddiqim?" In his answer, he highlights the miraculous cures that Wazana lavished on his family but then moves on to give credit to my work:

> Professor Yoram Bilu . . . [here my academic title and
> position, as presented on the back cover of the book, are
> specified] traveled through the whole country in his attempts
> to inquire about the greatness of Rabbi Ya'acov Wazana.
> And he found out that many were the people who had
> known Wazana and his miraculous achievements. This
> journey in the footsteps of Wazana he described in a book
> (titled) *The Life and Death of Rabbi Ya'acov Wazana.*
> And he certainly deserves a credit for his wonderful work
> and commitment.

In an unmistakable allusion to Joseph, the great biblical dreamer, the dream series was titled "The dreams of Yoseph." It represents a coherent narrative sequence in which the drama of the multiple encounters with Wazana picks up until its final resolve. In the first dream report, Wazana reveals himself to Yoseph and asks him to erect a site for him and his forefathers for celebrating their *hillulot*. The pattern of the reported nocturnal interactions between the dreamer and the healer that ensues is indistinguishable from that reported by the saint impresarios I have studied in describing their emergent alliance with their patron *tsaddiq*. Like them, Yoseph initially assumes an ambivalent if not a reluctant position, doubting his ability to pursue the calling imposed on him by Wazana. But the latter, like the saints in the dreams of the impresarios, gradually disarms him of his resistance by showering him with messages of encouragement and promises for help.

In the fifth dream, Yoseph finally makes a solemn vow to erect the site and to celebrate the *hillulot* of Wazana and his ancestors. To this acquiescence, Wazana responds with a warm embrace and a blessing. In the sixth and last dream, these affectionate gestures are transformed into specific instructions: Yoseph is sent to the municipality to mobilize the resources for the project. The pursuit of these instructions represents the afterlife of the dream sequence. Against all odds, Yoseph was assisted by various functionaries in the municipality to achieve his goal. Some of them explicitly stated that they did what they did against their better judgment, as if activated by an external power. As a result of their compliance, Yoseph finally got hold of a huge public shelter not far from his home. His account ends with "a passionate appeal to the public" to make contributions for remodeling the shelter and transforming it into a shrine. In subsequent phone calls, he tried to recruit me to that end as well, begging me to look for benefactors for the site in Israel and abroad.

I soon found out, however, that Yoseph was concerned with remodeling Wazana's figure no less than with remodeling the shelter. Our first meeting took place in Beer Sheva at the end of May 1993, just a few days after I had discussed Wazana in a literary program on the Israeli television. Once again, Wazana's antinomian character was in the limelight, but this time, Yoseph could not disregard it. He was devastated by the idea that his idol, for whom he was seeking to establish a sacred site, was presented in the program as a deviant healer, partly Muslim and partly demonic. In his despair, he even suggested eliminating all the copies of the book from the bookstores and that we write a revised version together after gaining the proper rabbinical approval. He withdrew his suggestion only after I made it clear that it was precisely the subversive side of Wazana that made me write down his life story.

This was, in fact, our one and only confrontation. Still, Yoseph could not resign himself to the unorthodox aspects of Wazana and did all he could to decrease their salience. In his discourse, he was cautious not to mention Wazana's name without juxtaposing it to his pious forebears, thus seeking to envelop him, as it were, in their saintly aura. When Wazana's oddities nevertheless came to the fore, he was adamant to remove their sting by positive reframing. Thus he would often resort to mystical causes, presumably incomprehensible to ordinary people, in accounting for Wazana's alliance with the Muslims and the demons.

Yoseph's efforts to deprive Wazana of his uniqueness and to recast him in the mold of a stereotypical Jewish Moroccan saint added a measure of unrelieved tension to our relations. Nevertheless, the dialogue between us could be maintained because it was based on a certain degree of symmetry, reciprocity, and interdependence. As a university professor keenly interested in the figure Yoseph sought to idolize, I could serve as a source of legitimation and respectability for him in his efforts to popularize the new site.

But Yoseph was no less important to my work because I was determined to document and study the intriguing "resurrection" of Rabbi Ya'acov Wazana that he initiated. To some extent, my professional career was dependent on Israelis of Moroccan background like Yoseph—folk-healers, traditional patients, saint impresarios, and other devotees—whose knowledge, beliefs, visions, and misery I promulgated into scholarly work. In the case of Wazana, the taken-for-granted contribution to my academic standing was augmented by narcissistic gratification. The idea that my book was conducive to Wazana's re-emergence in a saintly guise was so captivating that I was resolute to investigate exhaustively the cultural phenomenon that I helped to create. In a curiously symmetrical way, each of us managed to overcome or contain the problems posed by the other side—for Yoseph, the deviant aspects of Wazana emphasized in my book; for me, Yoseph's attempt to replace these aspects with saintly ones—recognizing the potential contribution of the other to one's own goals.

The uneasy complicity between Yoseph and me had been tested already on my first visit to Beer Sheva. In fact, I scheduled the visit on the same day I was supposed to discuss my book on Wazana with students at Ben-Gurion University in Beer Sheva. In doing this, I was well aware of the two levels of discourse, pertaining to different epistemological realms, that I juxtaposed, yet I was confident, and even took delight in the fact, that I could maneuver between the two readings of Wazana—as object of enshrinement and veneration and as object of skeptical inquiry. Unlike the protagonist of my book with his shamanic power of bridging between worlds, I sought to maintain the two realms of discourse compartmentalized, but Yoseph interfered with my plan. When I tried to take my leave after visiting the shelter turned into a shrine, he insisted that I should stay overnight in his place, and I had to tell him about my other commitment. He immediately put forward his wish to join me and dismissed all my alarmed attempts to dissuade him from doing so. Even though I made it explicit to Yoseph that the students might be particularly interested in those antinomian aspects in Wazana's lifestyle that he sought to silence, I felt quite insecure when we entered together the lecture hall where the meeting took place.

Despite my apprehension, the evening was quite successful. Sitting quietly among the students, Yoseph followed attentively my introductory remarks and the lively discussion that ensued (in which, as I expected, the bizarre side of Wazana was a central topic). Toward the end of the meeting, one student raised the issue of relevance: Is it possible that people living in Israel in the 1990s are still moved by Wazana? To answer the question, I invited Yoseph to the podium, on the spur of the moment, to tell his story. Delighted to have the arena for himself, Yoseph unfolded the sequence of events that led him to erect the shrine to the Wazana family. I was amazed by his articulate and poised performance, which left the audience speechless. For one enchanted moment, the two realms of discourse mingled after all.

Elated by the effect he had had on the students, Yoseph felt very grateful to me for giving him the opportunity to tell his story in a setting he considered very prestigious. Much later, I was puzzled to find out that he had recorded the whole affair on a small tape recorder that he carried in his bag. I do not know how, if at all, he used the recorded material, but the measure he had taken further reduced the traditional gap between ethnographer and informant. The taken-for-granted prerogative of the researcher to isolate and objectify data extracted from the other, rendering it amenable for processing and analysis, was thus seized and employed by that other.

My turn to use a tape recorder (and a video camera) came several weeks later, in mid-July 1993, when Yoseph invited me to "the first *hillulah* of Rabbi Ya'acov Wazana in Israel, commemorating his 41th death anniversary," at his home in Beer Sheva. Because some members of the Wazana family were also among the guests, I was a bit concerned about possible negative reactions to the book, but to my relief, no one mentioned the anomalous aspects of Wazana. Moreover, from the compliments they bestowed on me for promulgating the life story of their kin, I came to the conclusion that none of them had read the book. From my perspective, the high point of the modest, domestic *hillulah* was an ornate speech delivered by a local rabbi, a remote kin of Rabbi Ya'acov and one of the most respected descendants of the Wazana family, which was sealed as follows: "Rabbi Ya'acov Wazana has made many wonders in his lifetime and in the afterworld, but his greatest miracle was to make a distinguished professor at the Hebrew University write this book."

Yoseph also delivered a speech in which he elaborated on my association with Wazana. He deconstructed my name, Bilu, an acronym for a Biblical verse, *Beit Ya'acov Lechu Venelcha* ("House of Jacob, let us go"), as indicating my eagerness to go from house to house (of would-be informants) in pursuit of Rabbi Ya'acov.

Note that in both speeches, the two realms of discourse on Wazana were combined again, but this time, it was the traditionally privileged social science perspective (Wazana as an object of investigation) that was appropriated and accounted for by the mystical perspective (Wazana as sainted figure). Of course, the process did not end here because my ongoing attempts to document it constituted some form of reappropriation, which was reflected, among other things, in this very presentation. The video camera, in particular, gave me an edge over Yoseph. Operated by a doctoral student of mine, it enabled me, by "freezing" the events of the *hillulah*, to transform them into an objectified topic of study amenable to multiple analyses and decon-structions. In the subsequent months, however, Yoseph added a video camera to the growingly advanced arsenal of tools he has been using in his attempts to promote his venture. The extent of his organization-al efforts and sophistication became evident to me in the next public event he initiated for promoting the shrine, which took place in May 1994.

This time, the celebration took place in a synagogue in Beer Sheva. From the invitation, I learned that the new shrine was designated, "The Glory of the Ancestors—The Wazana Dynasty." The gathering was depicted in the invitation as "an evening dedicated to the Torah" in which many religious functionaries and political figures, from the chief rabbi of Beer Sheva to two deputy mayors, were supposed to address the attendees. My name, too, appeared among the local dignitaries. I was surprised to find out that I was "a member of the presidential body of the Hebrew University" and, even more so, that

I was nominated "a member of the presidential body of (the sanctuary of) The Glory of the Ancestors—The Wazana Dynasty." The symmetry between the two designations, and particularly their juxtaposition, were a lucid demonstration of how deeply engulfed I had become in the "sacred discourse" about Wazana that Yoseph had cultivated. Aside from my name, my attention was also drawn to an enigmatic statement in the invitation announcing that "the sacred book of the saint Rabbi Ya'acov Wazana will be presented in the synagogue."

The evening was well organized. Food and beverages were distributed to the 150 congregants, and a local band played popular religious music. An articulate master of ceremonies presented the speakers, and a professional team of photographers with all types of cameras, including video, documented the affair, including the speech I was asked to deliver. Realizing the delicacy of the situation, I decided to circumvent the issue of Wazana's oddities in my address and limit myself to the genealogy of the Wazana family and the way in which I collected the material for the book. I was well aware that in so doing, I was acquiescing to Yoseph's attempts to sanctify Wazana, but in the ceremonial atmosphere that prevailed, I did not feel I could act otherwise. I comforted myself that my temporary betrayal of the protagonist of my book was a necessary price for maintaining the privilege to study a phenomenon that I had inadvertently helped set in motion. Moreover, there was something exciting, though at times upsetting, too, in documenting the very process into which I was drawn as a key participant.

Listening to the other speeches, I could witness once again how my academic involvement with Wazana was mobilized in the service of mythologically rearranging his figure. Thus I was amazed to hear that my voyage in the footsteps of Wazana was conducted in the remote areas of the Atlas mountains, where I withstood many a predicament. This way, the voyage (and by implication, the figure that propelled it) was made grander and more heroic. Another speaker informed the impressed audience that in 17(!) universities throughout the world, research on the Wazana family was currently being conducted. A common thread in many of the speeches was that my engrossment with Wazana could not be incidental. Rather, it was mystically informed and ought to be taken as another indication of Wazana's great stature.

Yoseph, respectfully designated "Rabbi Yoseph" by the master of ceremonies, was the last of the speakers. After unfolding the concatenation of events that led him to erect the shrine, he came to the highlight of the evening. He related how, following clues he received from Wazana in a recent dream message, he was able to secure, after an arduous odyssey, one of the healer's enigmatic books. To appreciate the excitement that this disclosure stirred in the audience, it should be noted that Wazana's ex-associates consistently referred to his old, hand-written books, replete with magical incantations and esoteric formulas, as a major source of his power. Most of them, however, also contended that Wazana's few possessions, including these precious books, have all mysteriously disappeared after his sudden death. Despite persistent rumors claiming that one or more of the books have found their way to Israel, no one admitted to having seen them.

Following the public auction of gigantic colorful candles designed to collect money for the shrine, an indispensable part of such celebrations, the book was presented by Yoseph to the congregants. As far as I could see, it was indeed a genuine book of medicine, handwritten in the distinctive Judeo-Maghrebi discursive writing. The unmistakably Jewish origin of the book was incongruent with the recurrent claim that Wazana was exclusively relying on Muslim traditions in his work, but the participants were not bothered with questions of authenticity. Bustling and swarming, they congregated around Yoseph trying to touch the book with their hands and kiss it. It was clear that in their eyes, the book—a kind of metonymic extension of the great healer—was endowed with great therapeutic powers that could be absorbed through physical contact. Having anticipated this enthusiastic response, Yoseph circulated special forms among the congregants in which they were asked to write down the names of relatives and friends "to be blessed by the book of the saint." This initiative proved very lucrative, as indicated by the pile of envelopes filled with forms and money that was aggregated on the podium at the end of the evening.

The celebration in the synagogue was the last public event associated with the shrine that I attended, but the story of the afterlife of Wazana (or, no less important, of his promulgated life story) is still being developed. Becoming more concerned about my reluctant yet growing participation in the authorship of this afterlife, I decided to distance myself a bit from the shrine and its builder. The time was ripe for some disengagement on both sides because Yoseph, having established himself a name as a saint impresario and a healer (due to the fast-spreading therapeutic appeal of Wazana's book), was less in need of respectable legitimators.

The discovery of the book adds an ironic twist and a sense of narrative closure to the story of Wazana's resurrection. The symmetry of the two realms of discourse between which I was precariously navigating had been extended to the domain of the text, heretofore the cherished prerogative of the researcher. I could not escape the egocentric notion that the book of healing attributed to Wazana was brought to the fore, among other things, as a counterweight to my own book. The ethnographic writing, an initial booster but also a potential obstacle to the sanctification of Wazana, has been replaced with a sacred text, more suited to the folk-religious idioms of the believers, that tangibly retains his healing power.

In the narrative of Wazana's afterlife, however, these two books appear complementary no less than antagonistic. The revival of Wazana as a sainted figure, which may have been precipitated by my book, gained momentum with the discovery of the book of healing attributed to him. With a committed agent actively and creatively seeking to publicize his name, a shrine to commemorate him and plead for his intercession, and a book that encapsulates his bliss, the transformation of Wazana from a peripheral and antinomian healer into a venerated *tsaddiq* seems to have come of age. As this presentation lucidly shows, I became inextricably involved in this process. What started as an attempt to document and present as reliably as possible a dynamic reality evolved into an intricate situation, epistemologically precarious, in which the ethnographic product became a building block in further constructing and enriching this reality. In this process, I have inadvertently become a popularizer and propagator of Wazana—an impresario of saint impresarios.

References

Ben-Ari, E., & Bilu, Y. (1987). Saint sanctuaries in Israeli development towns: On a mechanism of urban transformation. *Urban Anthropology, 16,* 243-272.

Bilu, Y. (1978). *Traditional psychiatry in Israel.* Unpublished doctoral dissertation, Hebrew University of Jerusalem.

Bilu, Y. (1986). Life history as text (in Hebrew). *Megamot, 29*(4), 349-371.

Bilu, Y. (1988). Rabbi Ya'acov Wazana: A Jewish healer in the Atlas mountains. *Culture, Medicine and Psychiatry, 12*(1), 113-135.

Bilu, Y. (1990). Jewish Moroccan "saint impresarios" in Israel: A stage-developmental perspective. *Psychoanalytic Study of Society, 15,* 247-270.

Bilu, Y. (1991). Personal motivation and social meaning in the revival of hagiolatric traditions among Moroccan Jews in Israel. In Z. Sobel & B. Beit-Hallahmi (Eds.), *Tradition, innovation, conflict* (pp. 47-70). Albany: State University of New York Press.

Bilu, Y. (1993). *Without bounds: The life and death of Rabbi Ya'acov Wazana* (in Hebrew). Jerusalem: Magnes.

Bilu, Y., & Hasan-Rokem, G. (1989). Cinderella and the saint. *Psychoanalytic Study of Society, 14,* 227-259.

Blackman, M. B. (Ed.). (1992a). The afterlife of the life history [Special issue]. *Journal of Narrative and Life History, 2*(1).

Blackman, M. B. (1992b). Introduction: The afterlife of the life history. *Journal of Narrative and Life History, 2*(1), 1-9.

Brettell, C. B. (Ed.). (1993). *When they read what we write: The politics of ethnography.* Westport, CT: Bergin & Garvey.

Clifford, J., & Marcus, G. (1986). *Writing culture: The poetics and politics of ethnography.* Berkeley: University of California Press.

Handelman, D. (1985). Charisma, liminality, and symbolic types. In E. Cohen, M. Lissak, & U. Almagor (Eds.), *Comparative social dynamics* (pp. 346-359). Boulder, CO: Westview.

Marcus, G. E., & Fischer, M. J. (1986). *Anthropology as cultural critique.* Chicago: University of Chicago Press.

Myerhoff, B. G. (1976). Balancing between worlds: The shaman's calling. *Parabola, 1*(1), 6-13.

Rosaldo, R. (1989). *Culture and truth.* Boston: Beacon.

Turner, V. W. (1974). *Dramas, fields and metaphors.* Ithaca, NY: Cornell University Press.

12

Some Unforeseen Outcomes of Conducting Narrative Research With People of One's Own Culture

Amia Lieblich

*E*arly in the morning, I enter the dining hall of the kibbutz that I had studied 16 years ago and, with my breakfast tray in hand, look for familiar faces. I am in Beit Hashita for a 2-day visit, having agreed to present a talk in the kibbutz about a recently published book of one of its members that had created a controversy. Dafna, a woman of about 50 years, approaches me urgently, "I am so glad to see you before you leave. My mother has cancer; we're afraid it's terminal. You must see her, it will be so meaningful for her!"

Indeed, I spent the next 2 hours in Hedva's tiny office, admiring her files of didactic materials for biology teachers. And it was so meaningful.

Both Dafna and Hedva (among 120 informants) were very useful interviewees in my old study of the kibbutz, and the book I wrote then (Lieblich, 1981) contributed a great deal to my career and reputation. In return, I have never fully disengaged myself from the community and some of its prominent members. What started as a research became a relationship. Similar processes have occurred with the four or five major qualitative research projects that I have conducted in the past 20 years (Lieblich, 1978, 1989, 1993, 1994).

The essence of the issue I would like to develop is that as I have asked my "subjects" to cooperate with me on deep and meaningful levels, I have become indebted to them in many ways, more than I had ever imagined. Many became friends. Is this good or bad? Could I anticipate this development?

In traditional psychology, we find research on the one hand and therapy on the other. Research, which is best exemplified in the psychological laboratory experiment, is impersonal. People are labeled *S*s and have no names. They are volunteers or students fulfilling their requirements for a degree; in many cases, they are paid for their cooperation. The aspects of their behavior that are evoked and measured are frequently marginal and irrelevant to their deeper concerns in real life. In dealing with their *S*s, experimenters are objective and follow strict instructions. If they "cheat" on their *S*s, they are doing it with the permission of ethics committees for the benefit of scientific knowledge. If they are kind and smiling—they are required to be that way to every *S*. *Debriefing,* which is the less formal interaction that may follow an experiment, is short and aims at prompt separation without hard feelings.

On the other hand, in therapy, the patient (unless a minor or under the ruling of a court) takes the initiative for the contact and pays for it. People are labeled *patients* or *clients*. They look for therapy because of some deep concerns or needs in their lives. Intimate matters are often revealed but, in most schools of psychotherapy, are out of the patient's free will. Norms of ethical behavior of the therapist are highly articulated in our culture and, among other things, require that the therapist maintain strict confidentiality, that no personal contact exist between the therapist and his or her patient outside of the "hour," and that the therapist does not accept any return for his or her expert help besides the payment agreed on. These ethical rules were developed because of the emotional, deep, and meaningful relationship that usually emerges between the two sides engaged in therapy.

Narrative studies have components of the two models outlined above but none of the clarity of their ethical regulations. I refer to narrative research that asks the individual to reveal important aspects of his or her personality—to tell his or her entire life story or report on a certain period (e.g., the war or childhood) or describe her or his areas of competence or relationships. In most cases, this is done out of the researcher's initiative and followed by the publication of the research in one form or another. Even if the participants are paid for their cooperation or thanked profusely in the introduction or footnotes of the final work, their stories are taken from them for the benefit of the researcher. Is this a fair transaction? And what does the researcher give in return?

In a small country such as Israel, whose population is highly literate, the ongoing contact of the researcher and his or her informants is almost unavoidable. My experience may illuminate general processes characteristic of narrative research even if they find their expression more subtly. In the following account, I will focus on my ongoing interactions with the participants of my kibbutz research (Lieblich, 1981), although I have experienced similar developments in other projects, such as in my continuing role in the lives of some of the ex-POWs I had studied (Lieblich, 1994) and their wives and children. What started out of my initiative as research takes on many forms.

The kibbutz is a living community whose members live communally and permanently in a village. Naturally, they know each other quite well and compare their lot and behavior with those of their neighbors. Conducting a narrative research within a kibbutz has, therefore, a social aspect in addition to the personal transaction of the researcher and her or his informant. This unique quality of the described project will come up in the following description.

It has been 16 years since my field study of Kibbutz Makom terminated. I am, however, still in contact with the kibbutz and its members. This ongoing contact almost always happens on their initiative. For the single time of my asking them to cooperate, I am forever in debt. This is perhaps a measure of the significance of their single cooperation, conforming to my request to share with me, and allow me to publish, the stories of their lives.

In 1978, I contacted a 50-year-old kibbutz known for its ideological commitment and its economic success and suggested to study their oral history via personal interviews with a great proportion of the adult membership. I had, at that time, been invited by Pantheon, New

York, to write such a book for their "village series" (e.g., *Akenfield, Portrait of an English Village,* by Blythe, 1969) so the proposed book was scheduled to appear in English first. Having an author write about one's life and community in a foreign language may be perceived as a special case of the expected exposure: It creates some distance be- tween the subject of the narrative and the readers of his or her life story. Two points should be made here, however: A great proportion of this kibbutz's adults were fluent in English, and it was understood that eventually the book would be published in Hebrew as well. This delay, however, played its part in preparing the members for their exposure.

I have never been a member of a kibbutz, and no one in this kibbutz knew me personally, but some had read my recent book on the psycho- logical effects of the 1973 war (Lieblich, 1978). I was a scholar of psychology and sociology from the Hebrew University, a respected institution. In a meeting with the kibbutz secretariat and its Social Affairs Committee, I explained my goal and method and answered questions regarding my attitude toward the kibbutz as an ideological form of communal life. Naturally, I attempted to sound unthreatening to the community. I tried to convey neutrality leaning toward a positive approach—namely, an a priori nonjudgmental attitude—combined with the common Israeli positive regard for the kibbutz and its contributions to Israeli society. It was understood that I would write only and precisely what I could attribute to individual members in the form of first-person monologues. At the same time, I explained that I would be selective in the choice of stories that I would finally include— some people would not appear in the book or parts of their stories would be omitted. I promised to show each individual what I proposed to write about him or her and to be willing to introduce changes according to his or her comments. I promised to consult with people if I saw the need to. I insisted, however, that no individual or committee would have censorship rights other than on their own quotations. The final outcome would be my sole responsibility.

The matter of naming was elaborately discussed. My initial pro- posal was to try and maintain anonymity—namely, to use pseudonyms for the kibbutz and for each one of the interviewees—which was the final decision adopted for the book. Even in the first discussion, however, some of the participants raised the point that it would be for the benefit of Beit Hashita to be known to the public by its own name. The majority, however, decided on anonymity. I derived great literary pleasure from the naming process: Beit Hashita was renamed *Makom,* "place" in Hebrew. Two other kibbutzim that had a great part in this oral history were Tel Yosef, renamed *Molad* (nativity), and Ayelet Hashachar, renamed *Adama* (earth). All individuals also received fictional names.

But the final outcome was well foreseen. Israeli gossip identified the kibbutz quite soon after publication, and the guess was validated by a smart reviewer in the daily paper. The personal identity of the protagonists was, then, a simple game for all interested. Members of Beit Hashita itself could naturally identify each other with almost no difficulty. Although most of the individuals were rather pleased with their sections, a few were distressed. I will discuss this matter later on.

Going back to the history, my project was approved by the appointed committee and then by the general assembly of the kibbutz. During my fieldwork in 1978 and 1979, I spent a long time in the kibbutz. I had a room, ate in the common dining hall, and participated in all social events, such as assembly meetings and weddings. My goal—writing an oral history of the kibbutz—was known to the public via the local weekly newsletter. The members were aware that I was conducting personal interviews and recording them on tape. My presence and visibility probably affected the members of the community in direct and subtle ways.

In the beginning, conducting the interviews was ethically quite straightforward. After a short period of collecting general impressions, I dropped notes in certain members' mailboxes asking them to come for an interview. I explained my aim, making clear that they were free not to reveal anything too delicate or painful. I turned on the tape recorder, explaining that this device frees my attention for listening, and found out, consistently, that people liked to tell their stories and tended to forget the possible price of their exposure. I promised to show them their transcripts and edited narratives; some wanted copies of the cassettes to save in their family archives. The book seemed a long way into the future, and anyway, it would be published in the United States.

Problems started to emerge very slowly. Although almost all the people that I had approached consented to be interviewed, I discovered that some who were not invited felt left out, even insulted. "Does my story mean nothing to the history of this community?" Although toward the end of the year I felt that my knowledge of the community was complete—the stories tended to repeat themselves, and all the types of people and periods of their history were covered with great care from many perspectives—I decided to dedicate my time to listen to all who expressed interest in sharing their stories. My message appeared in the newsletter, but I am sure that some of the most sensitive souls did not dare initiate a meeting with me, and they may have remained with a sense of alienation.

Similarly, during the interviews, I often encountered people who could not limit themselves to a concise story and flooded me with detail. Two of these informants chose to tell me in detail about their experience in the holocaust prior to their joining the kibbutz, a topic that was, at the end, entirely omitted from the book. So, generally, can you ask a person for a life story—and than limit his or her time? Do you judge some persons' stories as irrelevant? What happens when very painful memories come up, especially if another interviewee is scheduled to come? These and similar problems are frequently encountered by therapists, with a major difference—that the therapist is called to help, whereas the narrative researcher is collecting material for a study. I solved my dilemmas by adopting two rules of thumb: Sympathy and flexibility in interviewing always pays, and when people find a sincere listener, they profit from sharing their experience, even if painful. But perhaps these rules represent some rationalization on my part.

My role as an emotional catalyst in the community grew in direct proportion to the length of my stay. I became more and more aware that as I was asking my general opening question, "tell me about your life in this kibbutz," I seemed to open a Pandora's box: Out came old wounds, long forgotten or hidden from the public eye. The emotional tone of the interviewing sessions gradually escalated, and people often cried or expressed anger. I was constantly tormented with the sense of opening my interviewees' wounds and (as I thought then) leaving them with the pain.

The emotional escalation may have resulted from two intertwined processes: I gained a reputation as a good listener, and people who came to talk to me later in the year were those who had hesitated more, who needed more courage to come out against the norms of the community. Often, they said in the beginning, "I don't want you to end up with only the official version, told by the elite members. You have to hear about my marginal life, or my deviant experience, to get the complete picture." Sometimes these stories were focused on simple pain, such as that of a young widow or a bereaved parent. Others had some traumas to ventilate or unfinished business with another member or the entire community. For example, mothers of babies born in the kibbutz almost 50 years ago cried about their missed opportunity to take full responsibility for raising their children, about their conformity to what they later saw as strict, cruel, and stupid rules of child care practices. Members who had taken sides in the kibbutz division that had occurred in 1952 expressed deep regret about their behavior. The opportunity to tell one's life story was taken as an attempt to correct that story with the help of later wisdom. People revealed to me the secret of the frequent suicides among the young, hardworking, hunger-stricken members of the early kibbutz, expressing their shame and perplexity yet worried that I might attribute too much significance to this part of their history. And so on and on.

At this stage, I felt as if I was promoted to the role of a witness, and the distinct role of researcher became blended with that of a therapist. It was unexpected, exhilarating, and highly demanding at the same time. I was getting dramatic stories—but what else was I doing in these people's lives?

The significance of my listening, now promoted to witnessing, became clear to me at the end of my fieldwork. A public evening with refreshments was organized to which all the people that had talked to me during the year were invited. It was a kind of a termination ceremony planned to highlight the collective effort shared by all the interviewees and myself. I planned to thank them and to disengage myself from the community to write the book. My dominant feeling was gratitude bordering on guilt for "taking away their stories." How surprising it was, therefore, to hear the words of several of the members as well as the kibbutz secretary thanking me for being there to hear them, listen to their stories, and collect them for the sake of history! This, in itself, they said, had been a beneficial process.

It was strange to stop traveling weekly to the kibbutz for 2 or 3 days, but I concentrated on my writing. My assistant was working day and night on transcribing the tapes in her clear handwriting. "How did you get them to tell you such stories?" she marveled. During the summer, some kibbutz members came to Jerusalem for a vacation and visited my home. I sensed the anxiety behind their gentle questions regarding my progress. I had been pregnant with my third child during the last months of my fieldwork. People called to offer congratulations, and the kibbutz sent a big box of food preserves produced in Beit Hashita when my son was born. When I felt too tired to work, I sensed their waiting for the book and returned to my desk. I felt the pain of writing sad, angry stories and imagined their reactions. How much easier would it have been if they were illiterate! I envied my anthropologist colleagues.

At the end of the winter (one old member who had a good story had died by then), I was ready with a draft of the 61 personal narratives and mailed separate envelopes to these individuals whose stories were to be included in the book. Feeling bad for those who were left out, I sent them letters of explanation and apology, offering to return their transcripts to them. In my letter to the participants of the book, I asked them to review the material and call me if they had any comments or corrections. I wrote that if I heard nothing in 3 weeks, I would consider the draft approved.

The majority of the interviewed individuals did not respond. I came to the kibbutz to talk to about 10 people who had asked to see me about their stories. Two women asked me to withdraw their entire stories from the book. Anita was a middle-aged widow and a bitter person. She had been married to a central member from the founders' generation, but she herself was never popular. Anita was taken aback by her own anger and alienation as they came out in the story and insisted that if people would read it and identify her, she would have to leave the kibbutz. "I don't know what came over me, that I told you all these buried stories when we met that night," she commented. I reminded her that the tape recorder had been openly placed there, on the table between us. "I must have been too tired to think," she said.

I tried to convince her that if "bad" stories were extracted, the total picture would be completely biased. I told her that she had a very original and powerful perspective, being the first war widow in Beit Hashita. (Even today, as I am writing this paragraph for a professional readership, providing minimal details, I am concerned about violating her privacy.) But with all my regret, I saw her point and destroyed my copy of her story as she had asked. What would happen to the authenticity of the book if all the 10 people who have reservations about their chapters withdraw, I was pondering as I walked to face the next problem. The deletion of Anita's story, even though a single instance, tilted the delicate balance of the book, this "fair representation" I was desperately trying to reach and having no good measure for it but my own intuition. But I had no choice about it.

Of the other "problems" I had to deal with, only Gila (Lieblich, 1981), 54 years old, another female member, also asked me to withdraw her short profile from the book. She was ashamed, she said, about private matters that should not be exposed to the public eye. Gila also expressed her bewilderment that she had told me the story, in particular, her miserable childhood in another kibbutz, her unsuccessful marriage, and her craving for a child (too late, alas). Gila, being shy and nonassertive, enabled me to convince her that her special, delicate story, which represented single women in a highly family-oriented community, should remain in the book. She is still resentful about it, however, and has not come to terms with the book and her profile in it. It might have been fairer not to persuade her. The power balance between me, the author, and her, "just" a single woman in the kibbutz, did not give her enough courage to insist on her wish. (This is even more clearly the case when a therapist "persuades" a client to have her story published or lectured about!) Perhaps my concern for the outcome—namely, the book—took precedence over my personal concern for Gila and her place in her community.

Other members had only minor changes or omissions they asked to introduce, which I did. Several months later, I sent the entire manuscript to three people in the kibbutz whose opinions I highly valued and who I trusted to be open enough to sustain the negative parts as well as the positive ones. I felt very proud to hand in the outcome of my work, yet I was apprehensive of the reaction. The days of waiting were hard. "The book is multifaceted," they finally said, "it will take some time to sink in." "But is it a good picture of your community?" I wanted them to clarify. "It is the picture you saw, or that we have shown you, and in that sense it is truthful," was all they said. I felt that they approved of my work, although its consequence was hard to digest for a while. Perhaps they were perplexed. Perhaps they were considerate of my autonomy. Specifically, they had very few suggestions. (Years later, I realized that had they been immensely pleased with the book—I should have seen it as a warning about its validity.)

One of the demanded corrections voiced by the three readers was that I should introduce a change in the autobiography of Simon, who had claimed that he was the first teacher in the kibbutz. "He was not," they vehemently objected. "The first teacher was Reuven, who had died many years ago. It is unfair to take his place in the kibbutz's history." I reassured them that this is what Simon had told me, and we cannot correct facts in other people's life stories, but I failed to convince them. One of their arguments was that Simon himself (who had approved of the draft!) would be shamed by the reactions of other members to his (conscious or unconscious) distortion of the accepted historical facts. I introduced a variation, then, writing that Simon had been "among the first teachers." Simon never inquired about this change.

Another matter proved to be of far more significant consequence. An older woman, Genia, who also read the first draft, was the person I respected more than any other member of the kibbutz. After the joint meeting with all the "readers," Genia asked to see me in private. "I am shocked," she said, "I cried so much." There is no need to elaborate on my feelings, but I had no clue as to the source of her turmoil. Finally, she explained that what caused her all this pain were the stories of her two daughters, which were included in the book. I realized that both of them said in so many words that Genia had been a "bad mother." During their childhood, she dedicated all her time to the affairs of the kibbutz while they felt neglected and rejected. Although remorseful tears were shed again in our conversation, Genia did not ask me to change a word in her or her daughters' narratives because she accepted their authenticity. But the book provided her with a painful insight. I then suggested modestly that some things need to be talked about between her and her daughters, and perhaps the book is the opportunity for this process to start.

Only then did I realize the most profound ethical aspect of my work: People used the book for venting old grievances against others, and this seemed to be, sometimes, the first opening of painful subjects never before brought up between them. Whereas my concern was for protecting every individual separately and each one vis-à-vis the community, the dyadic complications were hard to fathom. As I discovered when the book was published and read by all members (and again when it appeared in Hebrew, about 3 years later), the most painful reaction was that of family members who became aware, through the pages of the book, of memories, opinions, and feelings that belonged to their family life and relationships and had never been discussed among them openly before. My presence in the community and the resulting book had become, then, a means for communicating between family members, breaking the taboo of secrets and silence. In other words, it became therapy-like but through my solicitation of the narratives.

In the case of Genia and her family, the book was indeed the beginning of a fruitful therapy process, which led to much greater harmony between the generations. But this is, of course, something a researcher cannot count on happening.

Gradually, I observed that how people appeared in the stories of others emerged as the most touchy matter in this long-term project. No anonymity concealed the identity of Beit Hashita members from each other. "What will my friends, children, parents think about me now," became the most sensitive issue. In other kibbutzim and in the small country, it was a matter of days or weeks before everybody knew who was who. Many trips and conversations, as well as all my clinical skills, were dedicated to my attempts to smooth and heal unpleasant outcomes of that kind. My major message was that the overall picture of the kibbutz and the individual members was authentic, meaningful, and human—because it was not totally positive. The book was widely reviewed and sold well, which I used as indicators of the worth and significance of the members' endeavor. To this very day, I am convinced that this is the case, and as the years go by, my conviction is shared by more and more people—but not all. I am not sure that the individual members who were hurt by their profiles found consolation in the fact that today *Kibbutz Makom* is a classic and, in a way, a tribute to a utopian attempt at its peak.

When this turmoil quieted down after a while, I gained another role in the community—that of an expert. I was called to counsel about academic education, about psychotherapy of different types, about youth unrest, and so on. I became a resource for the members, a referral agent, and felt that I could not refuse any call for help from this community. When they sent me a student to supervise in writing her final high school paper on child-rearing practices in the early kibbutz or another to help determine what to study in the university, I felt obliged to do so. Sometimes, I was requested to write recommendations for certain people when they applied for work in the city, "since you know us so well." I was regularly asked to present talks in the kibbutz (e.g., at the graduation of high school students or the anniversary holiday). I had the feeling that my presence at weddings or funerals, for example, somehow raised the level of the event from the familial-communal to the historical-literary, but this may be my own sensitivity. On my side, I enjoyed the opportunity to visit and see old friends and was proud that after writing the book, I was still welcomed by the kibbutz. At the same time, in the kibbutz, I often felt deprived of real spontaneity and autonomy and somewhat defensive.

It was very surprising that 10 years after the original field research, I was invited by a popular Hebrew paper to write a long article on "Kibbutz Makom—10 years later." At that time, writing became even more difficult because the ideological and economic crisis, which marks the kibbutz at present, had started to show its signs. After my article appeared, I got a letter from one of the founders asking, "Did you join the enemies of the kibbutz movement?" As I was pondering my answer, I received another letter, from his son, saying, "I heard what my father wrote to you. Do not lose your courage. You must go on and write the truth as you see it."

I was sure that my article would ruin the friendship as well as my (or my students') ability to go back to any kibbutz to do any research. Three years ago, when a movie producer proposed to make a film about Beit Hashita focusing on war casualties (they had many), the Day of Atonement, and the return of Jewish traditions into the kibbutz lifestyle, the kibbutz approved under one condition: that I would be invited to join the project and be a major participant in planning, filming, and editing. By that time, I had become "family," someone they trusted despite all the friction. In any case, I was better than the unknown producer all on his own. This third exposure of Beit Hashita with my active participation was, undoubtedly, the one best accepted. I believe we have finally gotten used to each other. Whatever way I might have chosen to tell this narrative, I have certainly been spared the fate of the fictional sociologist described by Cohen (1979), whose subjects finally drove him into psychiatric hospitalization.

Today, my contacts with the kibbutz are less frequent, yet the relationship is sound and solid. I am there for them in certain ways, as they are for me. Is it ethics or friendship? I believe that a researcher who resents this entanglement should not start a narrative research about people who belong to his or her own culture and society. Looking back on the entire project and its outcomes, I still consider *Kibbutz Makom* to be a fair and human picture of a community as well as a historically and psychologically worthwhile endeavor. Only this firm belief has sustained me through difficult moments in my relationship with the people from whose stories I composed my work.

References

Blythe, R. (1969). *Akenfield, portrait of an English village.* New York: Pantheon.

Cohen, S. (1979). The last seminar. *Sociological Review, 27*(1), 5-20.

Lieblich, A. (1978). *Tin soldiers on Jerusalem beach.* New York: Pantheon.

Lieblich, A. (1981). *Kibbutz Makom.* New York: Pantheon.

Lieblich, A. (1989). *Transitions to adulthood during military service—The case of Israel.* New York: State University of New York Press.

Lieblich, A. (1993). Looking at change: Natasha, 21: New immigrant from Russia to Israel. In R. Josselson & A. Lieblich (Eds.), *The narrative study of lives* (Vol. 1, pp. 92-129). Newbury Park, CA: Sage.

Lieblich, A. (1994). *Seasons of captivity: The experience of POWs in the Middle East.* New York: New York University Press.

PART IV

❧ 13 ❧

A Historian's Perspective on Interviewing

Scott W. Webster

*I*t is said that Theodore Roosevelt had the frightening experience of being in a Washington, D.C., hotel one evening when a fire alarm sounded. Hotel personnel quickly instructed occupants to leave their rooms and to assemble just outside of the establishment. The young Roosevelt had made his way downstairs when his recalcitrant nature overwhelmed him. He resolved that he was not going to be told what to do, turned around, and began to march back up the stairs to his room—fire or no fire. A clerk took note of this activity and shouted at him, "Hey, who are you and where are you going?" Surely offended at the query, Roosevelt retorted, "I'm the vice president and I'm going to my room." This reply initially satisfied the inquisitor, who merely muttered, "OK." After a moment's reflection, though, the clerk shouted again at Roosevelt, "Wait! Vice president of what?" "Of the United States!" came the angry answer. "Oh," said the clerk. "I thought you were the vice president of the hotel. You get back down here immediately."

Whether the particular facts of this story are apocryphal or genuine, the anecdote nonetheless effectively conveys one of the ubiquitous characteristics of human nature. Most of us recognize the dynamic at play between Roosevelt and the clerk because we often encounter it in our own lives. One individual takes to touting his own supposedly exalted position and another person is appreciably unimpressed.

Because we all like to think that we are "someone" and that we have done "something," tainted or inflated self-portraits can creep into even the most professional and urbane of settings. In the same way that human actions cannot ultimately be reduced to a science, neither can human utterances. Historians, sociologists, psychologists, news reporters, and even the little girl who had been promised a bicycle for her birthday but failed to receive it, all have one thing in common: They understand that the spoken word is not always the true word.

For scholars and for some other professionals, the spoken word is an integral part of their work. Ideally, the spoken word in the form of interviews—dubbed *oral history* by historians—provides information that advances understanding of the subject being examined. In some instances, interviews offer an author or a researcher the opportunity to color his or her work with some perspective; in other instances, the interviews are the lone perspective. But in all instances, interviews are neither consistently easy to obtain nor easy to evaluate.

As a graduate student in history, I offer this chapter both for the sake of ordering some of my own thoughts as well as for some perceived value these comments may hold for fellow graduate students or other novice interviewers. What I have written is meant as a quasi-practical guide to interviews, although I have surely omitted many important tips. Indeed, I have consciously done so. Enough step-by-step books presently exist on the topic for me to justify my decision to select a few areas and comment on them.

I propose to address two themes. First, I shall dismiss the myth of the difficulty of interviewing famous people and, concomitantly, suggest some practical steps to interviewing. Near the chapter's end, I intend to wrestle with the means whereby a researcher can evaluate the veracity of interview material.

Obtaining and Conducting the Interview

Since August 1994, I have served as a research assistant for two esteemed individuals: James MacGregor Burns and Georgia Jones Sorenson. The former is a Pulitzer Prize-winning historian and political scientist from Williams College and the latter is a former Carter

White House policy analyst who directs the University of Maryland's Center for Political Leadership and Participation. I stumbled into the position, I am convinced, through some combination of serendipity and divine grace. It's the kind of position that young historians dismiss as fantasy—something out of the too-good-to-be-true school. My research duties involve some reading, some writing, and much interviewing for a forthcoming book on leadership in the Clinton White House. Burns and Sorenson are the coauthors.

At present, I have conducted approximately 70 interviews, the majority of them one-on-one interactions. It is noteworthy that most of these conversations were performed via telephone as opposed to in person. Lack of sufficient time, money, and in some cases, any personal inclination on my part to fly all over the country, demanded as much. The project is on a painfully fast track that made it undesirable to make too many plans to travel to Bill Clinton's Arkansas, Al Gore's Tennessee, or Hillary Rodham's Illinois.

I and others were fully aware that in conducting interviews in this manner, I was violating an important rule. I had read the experts' dire predictions for the success of most telephone interviews. Indeed, I myself had reasoned that a personal encounter was likely to yield more and better results. In a one-on-one episode, someone could see my face, I could see his or hers, and chances were that some semblance of "chemistry" would develop whereby the interviewee would offer some revealing insights. Theoretically that's how it was to work, anyway. And even if state secrets were not divulged, I thought that I at least stood a better chance of learning such secrets in a face-to-face interview. And such possibilities, I thought, were what interviews were about.

So much for thinking. My telephone interviews proved remarkably productive. A sizable percentage of them lasted for close to 60 minutes, and some even more. Several individuals spoke with me on more than one occasion. I seldom had the sense that someone was inattentive or that I was an unwelcome intrusion. Many answers boasted those elusive characteristics of being both responsive to the actual question I posed as well as thoughtful.

Typically, I reached my sources at home or in their offices. A few of them even allowed me to call them on their car phones as they were driving. I am certain that I was accommodated in this manner because

I had established the always necessary rapport with my subjects'
assistants. If someone was snappy, I took it on the chin. I kept my eye
on my objective: I wanted the interview; I would not jeopardize that
by sinking into battle with a petulant secretary.

Many interviewees were terribly busy persons, and I have concluded that the telephone interview was the best means of talking with
them, even if a one-on-one interview were possible. One individual
was on the road for most hours of the day, and my sense is that if I
had caught him in an office for a personal conversation, he would have
been worried about where he had to be in 2 hours. Instead, by my
calling him as he zoomed down a Tennessee highway, he was relaxed.
He was meeting his own time schedule; I was not preventing him from
being elsewhere. It was a great interview.

This time element pervaded my interviews. I was constantly aware
that my talking with these people was infringing on their daily plans.
I am sure they were aware of it, too. And, in part, I think this is what
made my phone interviews productive. It might be said that I was
imposing, but yet I wasn't imposing. My voice was there but my body
was not. One individual at the Department of Energy made it clear
that he was listening to me through his speaker phone so that he could
move around his office as we spoke. I am sure that he performed some
mundane tasks during our conversation; occasionally, an aide would
interrupt us to confer with him.

I must admit that because I, too, directed the phone call through
my speaker phone for the sake of recording it, I occasionally ambled
away from my own desk to rearrange books on a shelf or to peer out
my window. I think that it granted a certain freedom to the interview
without diluting its seriousness. My recorded transcript of the few
interviewees whom I know for certain were occasionally interrupted
as we conversed reveals no significant loss in their train of thought,
no non sequiturs in their remarks. I hardly want to suggest that I
cultivated more information from these telephone interviews than I
might have obtained had I made a personal trip to someone's office,
but I do mean to convey that in many instances, I was also satisfied
that I reaped no less information.

Some contend that a phone interview is ultimately of little value
because one cannot properly evaluate the way an answer is given or

the way a story is told. In short, some question the truth factor in a phone inquiry. I say that if one is going to be duped by an interviewee, such misdirection can just as easily be accomplished in person as over the phone. In fact, the two interviews I conducted in which I know for certain that I was deliberately being provided consistently positive answers about the President (those interviews, that is, in which I was being "spun") occurred in person—not over the phone. No man may be a hero to his valet, but a sitting president is still highly regarded by many former staff members.

Anyway, a phone interview still enables one to discern an appreciable portion of the truth. Aside from posing the dummy question (to which one knows the real answer and merely wants to gauge the response against it) or authenticating a statement through someone else, a phone conversation can reveal inconsistencies in speech patterns, or pauses, or the occasional less-than-bold manner of speaking that might suggest an evasive answer. A telephone interview hardly leaves one resourceless. I shall return later to the issue of authenticating interview material.

But this still leaves the question, "Why did I get such sound information?" Sure, the lack of direct personal contact may have permitted some officials to jettison, or at least loosen, the proverbial ties that constrained their comments. But there is more to it. A phone call could easily be perceived by the interviewee as being indicative of a lack of serious interest on my part or as suggestive that I merely contacted him on a whim and without any strategic planning. The call might be regarded as insulting as opposed to inviting. Hence it was hardly the dynamics of a phone conversation alone that produced the largely positive results.

Undoubtedly, the most potent arrows in my quiver were James MacGregor Burns and Georgia Jones Sorenson. My own ego and fantasies notwithstanding, I had—and have—no real reputation in the "outside world." I was a graduate student. It was my good fortune, though, that Burns and Sorenson are known to others. My mission was considerably facilitated by the reputation of two individuals and the reputation of a university-based research center.

But not all graduate students seeking interviews for, say, their master's theses or doctoral dissertations have such resources. This does not render the proposed interview(s) out of reach but it clearly—and not unexpectedly—complicates the mission. Graduate students would do well to seek and cultivate a relationship with a reputable institution in addition to the university they attend. Sending letters that describe the research project to a well-known organization or even a notable scholar might bear fruit. Graduate students might then be able to communicate to a potential interviewee that Professor X or Institute Y believes that the research is sound. It may be lamentable that such are the politics of interview getting, but sad or not, it is the truth.

The quality of my phone interviews was also enhanced by my willingness to provide these persons with the opportunity to complain about me at the outset. I frequently asked, as a first question, their reaction to the way in which the president, first lady, or vice president had been treated by the press. I believed this to be a "safe" question and one for which they would surely have a passionate answer. I also hoped that by asking it, I was eroding any regard for me as "just another one of those reporters." I wanted to distinguish myself from others who may have called and asked for an interview.

On several occasions, as a good historian is wont to do anyway, I specifically asked certain individuals who had complained about being misquoted in past articles to set the record straight. Bob Woodward and Carl Bernstein, as cited in Brady (1977), admitted that they appeared at the homes of some persons during their 1974 Watergate investigation to demonstrate that they were

> well-dressed and civilized. And you convince them that
> you're interested in the truth and not in any preconceptions.
> You tell them that if you've been in error, they're in a posi-
> tion to show you where you went wrong. We didn't think
> we were in error very often, but it's an effective introduc-
> tion. (p. 7)

This type of approach, combined with my decided refusal to be antagonistic or impatient with anyone, worked well for me. "I don't know why I'm talking to you," said one interviewee. "I have been very hesitant with others, but you somehow created an atmosphere in a couple of words that seemed favorable to visit." I thoroughly understood that inasmuch as I was forming an impression of my telephone partner, he or she was doing likewise. Don't underestimate politeness.

After the interview, I sent thank-you letters to the most well-known persons and even occasionally to their assistants. This made it more likely that any call I might make in the future would be well received. Dr. Burns and I have even remained in contact with an erstwhile gubernatorial aide to Clinton who lives in Washington. We recently treated her to lunch to retain good relations.

During the time I was conducting many of these interviews, neither Burns nor Sorenson nor other members of the book team had decided on any particular angle for our project—no angle, that is, other than the idealistically objective one. Hence I listened carefully, if critically, to what my interviewees told me. I worked hard to refrain from formulating many preconceived notions. I wanted the story that developed to be informed by the facts and not by my sense of what the facts should be. That's not always an easy task, and I shall return to the issue later in this chapter.

Logistically, though, obtaining the interviews was relatively easy, if frequently circuitous. In the first 2 weeks alone of attempting to contact people, I arranged to talk with the chairman of the Arkansas State Democratic Party, a former Arkansas governor, a former U.S. congressman, and a former U.S. senator. I had established some rapport with ex-Arkansas Governor Orval Faubus's wife and it's likely I would have interviewed him, too, if he had not been in such failing health. I convey this information not as a braggart but rather as someone who wishes to indicate that a measure of confidence in one's own ability to get the interview can have positive results.

Determining where your interviewees live and work can be daunting. My task of reaching friends and past colleagues of the president, vice president, and first lady was considerably facilitated by who they are. That is, my subjects are hardly obscure. Beginning with the 1992 presidential campaign, the national press corps had done much digging into their respective backgrounds. Accordingly, the names of former aides, rivals, neighbors, and even old girlfriends or boyfriends had been printed in newspaper and magazine articles and some books, too. Some of my work was done for me.

I relied heavily on the Lexis-Nexis system. Carefully constructed word searches quickly brought 20 years of public life to my computer screen. I came to love those reporters who revealed where someone lived; I came to loathe those who did not. My eyes lit up when I saw phrases like, "John Doe, a boyhood friend of Al Gore's, who now works for the Seattle law firm of Smith & Smith, says that . . . " On a couple of occasions, if I desperately needed such information but nothing appeared in the article, I unashamedly called the appropriate newspaper and asked to be directed to the appropriate reporter. I explained my project and then asked the reporter if he could recall where so-and-so was living, for instance. Sometimes it worked—sometimes it did not.

When I encountered some difficulty in locating former elected officials, I sought help at the Democratic or Republican Party headquarters in a given state or county. When one woman in Little Rock complained that "I'd like to help, but I don't like how y'all are treating the President; we like him down here and we don't want to be a part of any disparaging book," my naturally slight southern twang became a bit more pronounced as I retorted that I was not necessarily a Northerner, not a reporter, and that my mind-set was purely to get at the truth. She paused and then obliged with some information.

But if reaching my interviewees was, with some ingenuity, generally easy, convincing them to talk to me was more of a chore. I indicated earlier a few tips that worked well for me, but I still encountered some resistance. In a brief and rather rude phone exchange with a former aide to then-Governor Clinton, I was told that he did not want to be interviewed. Miffed because I had not been able to fully explain either who was writing the book or that it was a scholarly project, I wrote this person a polite note and included both of these points. I admitted,

> In all honesty, I cannot claim that you were in any way
> unclear when we spoke about whether you would talk with
> me. You noted that you would not. Having said that, I
> can only hope that I do not offend you by writing this letter.
> I can imagine that I may seem pushy, but truly do not
> want to seem so.

I expected no reply. But one came—2 months later. This aide said that he appreciated my letter and the opportunity to reconsider his decision. He said he would talk.

But there was another reason for his decision. He may have appreciated my candor, but in the interim, he also learned that I had spoken to a former, fellow Clinton staff member. This apparently made me seem less threatening. One should not underestimate the value of interviewing many for the sake of interviewing one. This is where developing some semblance of a strategy can be helpful. One stands a better chance of obtaining interviews if one starts at the so-called bottom and works up. Begin with those persons who might be most accessible because they are not "big names" or because they are big names who "talk."

I discovered that if I was willing to concede to certain time or subject matter stipulations, once the interview was under way, those stipulations became less rigid. A well-known newspaper editor, for instance, who claimed to have 15 minutes for me ultimately ended up talking for over an hour. Similarly, Dr. Sorenson and I expected only an hour with the famous parents of a famous politician but quickly found ourselves being offered tea and spending much of the afternoon with them. Hence one should agree to whatever time one can get; one might get more. Moreover, even if those interview-getting conditions remain in place, one can still boast to one's next potential interviewee that one has already talked to Congressman X or President Y. If that then leads to an interview with that person, one can again call on the first and ask for a few follow-up questions because one has now interviewed Chairman Z. This strategy can lead to both more interviews and more revealing—not to mention accurate—bits of information.

Once I had completed even a single interview, I included the name of that person and the fact that I had interviewed him or her in subsequent mailings. My "standard" request letter was sent after I alerted someone via telephone to expect it. It was then either mailed or faxed on the same day, more often the latter than the former; I did not want folks to forget me in the intervening days it would take the U.S. mail to arrive. My letter was composed on official institutional letterhead and it identified the project in which I was engaged, the names of and an impressive fact about Drs. Burns and Sorenson (e.g., Pulitzer Prize winner), and the specific contribution that Interviewee X could make to the project. As more interviews were conducted, I included a paragraph or more of the names of well-known individuals to whom I had already talked.

To my surprise, I discovered that some less than well-known persons were more reluctant to be interviewed than famous ones. A professor at the University of Maryland, for instance, declined to speak to me, but I interviewed former presidential candidate George McGovern on two occasions, one of which was over a nice lunch. I speculated that part of the reason might be that public figures are accustomed to being, well, public. They are not as easily put off by someone hoping to interrogate them. By contrast, instead of being flattered, less prominent persons may be frightened, or certainly uneasy, at the prospect of being the subject in an interview. The lesson here is clear. If it's well-known persons you seek, then seek away. They are accustomed to the intrusion—you simply need to convince them that your intrusion is more worthy of their attention than someone else's.

With regard to the interview itself, whether it has been done via telephone or in person, I have consistently had several questions prepared in advance and written on a sheet of paper. To attempt to think of questions—good questions—while the interviewee is talking is near impossible for me. To do so also prevents me from paying close attention to what is being said: It makes it difficult to critically evaluate what is said, and that is what I want to do. I want to pepper my interview with tactful comments such as, "Yes, but what about . . ." or "No, that's not what you said in an article last month." To begin an interview without well-conceived, thoughtful questions is to fail to reap many benefits from the interview. One should not desire an interview merely to obtain any off-handed comment from a famous person; one should want the interview so as to engage in a meaningful discourse and then obtain a considered comment. Questions prepared in advance often allow for the latter to occur.

I have also learned that a know-it-all personality fares poorly in an interview. My zeal in my first few interviews overwhelmed me. I so wanted to demonstrate that I had "done my homework" that I was loath to admit that I did not understand something that was said. That was a mistake. These were not analogous to street corner interrogations with just anyone. I was talking to experts or decision makers or policy makers—or those close to the experts, decision makers, and policy makers. To feign intelligence when all I possessed was ignorance was probably as obvious to them as it was embarrassing to me. I had to admit that I was, after all, lost and ask the interviewee to provide me with more background information so I could comprehend the subject.

Confusion, however, is not the same as indolence. One must prepare as best one can for an interview. "Judge a man by his questions," said Voltaire, "rather than by his answers." To determine those questions means, at the very least, reading books, magazine articles, and newspaper articles about the interviewee. Famous people are busy and have been interviewed many, many times before. Hence it is important to develop interesting questions, although basic queries are occasionally worth asking because an unusual answer may result. Most people, though, will have little patience with someone who demands such rote information as "When were you born?" The limited time available in most interviews should not be consumed with such light matters, unless there is genuine confusion around the issue. It makes the interviewee feel as though he or she is wasting time and, accordingly, the responses to presumably more important questions might be more terse and less considered than if these more intriguing queries had been posed earlier.

Often, the two most significant episodes in an interview occur at any point in the middle and at the end. In interviews, as in everyday conversation, gaps exist in the verbal exchanges between two people. Among friends, such gaps are not noticed or seldom cause concern. Among strangers, though, these extended pauses can seem awkward. We often rush to fill them with words. Researchers would do well to refrain from breaking the silence: Indulge it. If one permits one's "subject" to talk first, he or she may reveal some interesting tidbit that otherwise would have been kept to himself or herself. Remember to exercise wise judgment here, too. The interviewer doesn't want to end up staring at the interviewee waiting for this jewel of information while the interviewee quizzically looks back, expecting to hear the next question.

Similarly, at the end of the interview when the tape recorder is no longer operating, the researcher should be mindful of what the subject says. If the recorder served to intimidate the interviewee, he or she may now feel liberated. I can recall one individual adhering to a generally laudatory pack of responses while the tape was running. Then, as I shook her hand to leave, she let go with the words, "But, you know, sometimes you really wonder if the folks in the White House know just what the hell they are doing." This forced me to regard the interview in an entirely different light than I otherwise would have done.

Although I have not taken to offering interviewees the opportunity to peruse our interview transcript, neither have I opposed the prospect. I have obliged the handful of persons who have asked to read it. I think it lends legitimacy to the project. It's courteous, too. Someone has agreed to surrender some of his or her time to me; I should respond by allowing him or her to review some tangible product of our meeting.

I confess that I may well have taken to excess my charge to conduct interviews. Seventy is a sizable number of interviews; it is also an abominable number of conversations to transcribe. I do not enjoy transcribing. It is laborious and dreadfully time-consuming. Even the merit of relegating the responsibility to a paid professional is diminished by the cost factor.

The time needed for me to convert taped words into written text reduced even further the time I had to carefully read the transcripts. I obsessed about seeking more information, occasionally to the exclusion of analyzing and appreciating the information I already possessed. Some may say that's an enviable predicament—having too many as opposed to too few interviews. But this assessment is ill-informed. In a way, too much information is but marginally better than too little. I learned to be more selective in those interviews I sought and I often took notes during them, despite knowing that the microcassette tape would be transcribed. "A reporter who has taken ten pages of notes is in a much better position to go to work than a reporter who must work from thirty to forty pages of transcript" (Sherwood, 1972, p. 69).

My microcassette recorder has been most useful, but I have periodically turned it off, when asked, for the sake of obtaining some material "on background" or "off the record." I reasoned that this was worth doing because the information may be worth having. Of course, I either took notes as this tidbit was being relayed to me or—if I sensed that this too would have made my subject uncomfortable—waited until after the interview and then went to a quiet spot to write down as much as I could faithfully recall. At some later point, I may be able to convince this same person to admit to it for attribution or some other interviewee may agree to being quoted on it.

Evaluating the Evidence

Obtaining the interview and even executing it flawlessly might all be for naught if the information gathered is tainted. This indeed is a consideration that underlies the use of any source—whether written or in some other form. Interviewing is "a very difficult business. Anyone who does it successfully is probably so successful that he should himself be interviewed" (Morrissey, 1970, p. 118).

I admit that I have no quick-fix answer on the matter of ensuring absolute accuracy from interviewees. But I also submit that no such answer exists. Historians and other researchers must in many instances simply resign themselves to working with imperfect documents. In fact, significant debate within the historical community has led many to conclude that, even with perfect sources, an objective rendering of the past remains impossible. Many believe the 19th-century German historian Leopold von Ranke's call for an account of the past *"wie es eigentlich gewesen"* ("as it actually happened") to be desirable in theory yet unattainable in practice. There are too many events, they claim, through which the historian must sift to compose his or her narrative. The decision to focus on one event over another is an individual choice and value judgment that might not be made by another historian evaluating the same events.

Furthermore, one's formative experiences or political philosophy can easily, whether consciously or unconsciously, guide one's interpretation of the past. Historian James Gilbert (1991) readily confessed in the preface to his *Perfect Cities* that he was, in part, inspired to study the 1893 Chicago World's Fair because of the many train trips he had taken into the city as a boy; summer fun on Lake Michigan was indelibly etched in his memory and he wanted to know more about such fairs and the culture that inspired them. Similarly, William E. Leuchtenburg (1989) conceded in *In the Shadow of FDR* that as a college student in the 1940s, he was aware of Roosevelt's mighty influence and explained how the President both directly and indirectly enabled him to attend Cornell University. Historians are scholars and approach their craft with some sophistication and rigor, but they are hardly disinterested parties. They are, above all else, as human as the objects of their study. Their passions and their prejudices not only motivate but often accompany their writing.

Still further, Hayden White (1978) has asserted in a provocative essay that inasmuch as history is narrative, historians necessarily select particular plots for their stories. White maintains that the four common types of stories are tragedies, comedies, romances, and satires. He writes that the best history is written when historians are conscious of these categories—because their work inevitably falls into one of the groups, anyway—and write their story from that vantage point. An example might be electing to tell the Vietnam episode as a romance, with the United States on a quest to contain communism. But Vietnam might just as easily be portrayed as a tragedy both because of the loss of life commanded by a war in which America mobilized only a portion of its military resources and because of the domestic strife the conflict engendered.

All of this affirms that there is no single existing past and that evaluating oral testimony is but one of the many hurdles facing professional historians. In some ways, historians must even contend with themselves. It is not unfair to note that history is the intersection of the past with the historian's own thoughts. Michael Oakeshott (1933) opined that "history is the historian's experience. It is 'made' by nobody save the historian: to write history is the only way of making it" (p. 99).

In practicing oral history—for that is what interviewing is to the historian—one can only weigh all of the variables in pursuit of describing what actually happened. One should not expect to arrive at *the* truth in interviewing; one can expect only to be provided with some version of it. "The informant's statement represents merely the perception of the informant, filtered and modified by his cognitive and emotional reactions and reported through his personal verbal usages" (Dean & Whyte, 1970, p. 120). In this sense, oral interviews are neither more nor less reliable than correspondence, diaries, or newspaper quotes.

To that end, interview material must necessarily be treated with the same degree of caution and scrutiny as other information sources. Merely because the historian happened to be involved in the creation of the interview document does not, perforce, grant that document more authenticity than others. A fine rapport might develop between interviewer and interviewee—the interviewee might joke and laugh and offer to talk longer than expected—but the interviewee might nonetheless misrepresent the past. As Shakespeare wrote in *Macbeth,* "One may smile a smile and be a villain."

My having sounded these cautionary notes, interviewing remains a valuable tool for historians. Truman biographer David McCullough (1993) admits that "There are elements of a story, aspects of character, situation, conflicts of interest, and the chemistry of personality that can only be found through conversation with people who were there" (p. 8). By their very nature, verbal exchanges with others are more spontaneous than written thoughts, and the oral historian can use this to his or her advantage (Hoopes, 1979, p. 17). The less-considered thought can frequently be the most honest. Interview material often highlights nuances and provides greater clarity to the contours of an event. Interviewing reveals the personal.

Interviews have been dubbed *conversations with a purpose.* Some researchers contend that during the exchange, the interviewee typically engages in two types of games. The first is the *information-giving* game. In this scenario, the subject reveals his or her own views on matters raised by the interrogator. The second scenario is the *ingratia-tion game,* in which the interviewee seeks to cultivate a friendly relationship with the researcher. If the latter game is played, "it will become very much harder—and often impossible—to get relevant data on any subjects except those bearing on the interviewee's notion of appropriateness, courtesy, [and] friendship" (Dexter, 1970, pp. 136-137). The information-giving game is clearly the more desirable of the two scenarios from the researcher's perspective.

Scholars must be concerned with the truthfulness of interview material. Social scientists and historians alike engage in relatively simple—if time consuming and necessary—means of authenticating information gleaned from interviews. Perhaps the most obvious of these methods is known as *triangulation*. As described by Staley and Shockley-Zalabak (1989), this term denotes

> the use of multiple and diverse data sources and collection techniques to study a single research question or understand complex phenomena. In other words, researchers should work to verify, verify, verify.
> The underlying assumption for using triangulation is that multiple sources and diverse data contribute better than single sources and methods to our understanding of research questions and their contexts. (p. 250)

Historian T. Harry Williams understood this relationship between different sources. In researching his biography of Huey Long, as cited by Hoopes (1979), he discovered that

> the politicians [whom he interviewed] were astonishingly frank in detailing their dealings, and often completely realistic in viewing themselves. But they had not trusted a word of these dealings to paper. . . . Anybody who heard them would have to conclude that the full and inside story of politics is not in any age committed to the [written] document. (pp. 11-12)

Oral history well complements more conventional, written sources. In making use of as many resources as possible, the researcher increases the likelihood that his or her portrait will be more accurate than not. In this sense, historians and social scientists would do well to indulge in what famed anthropologist Clifford Geertz (1973) has dubbed thick description. To arrive close to the truth, uncover as much detail as possible and convey it to the reader in an intelligible manner.

Pursuing triangulation on a practical level, one should work to interview as many friends as enemies of the person or subject being studied. It's also important to pose the same questions to different persons and evaluate the responses. Moreover, ask questions to which the answers are known and determine if the right answer is provided. In situations in which the response offered differs from other information, make that fact known to the interviewee. On a couple of occasions, I reported to my subjects that several other persons and most newspaper reports assessed a particular situation quite differently. One interviewee quickly regrouped and changed his story; another stuck to her original answer and proceeded to offer a compelling explanation as to why her version was the correct one. From the latter experience, I learned to refrain from adopting a particular interpretation simply because the majority of my interviewees "said so." The minority opinion, assessment, or rendering of fact occasionally won out. I also learned that wholly discarding those interviews that contained many inconsistencies—either within the interview itself or when compared with other interviews—was folly. As John Sparrow notes, as cited in Barzun and Graff (1985),

> Every lawyer knows that a witness . . . while wrong on a number of points may yet be right on others, perhaps including the essential one. Every lawyer knows that honest and truthful witnesses may contradict themselves, particularly on questions concerning their own and others' motives and states of mind, without thereby forfeiting credibility. (p. 169)

Another tool whereby the researcher can reduce the possibility that he might be misled is to consider what each person has to gain—or lose—by relaying X bit of information. It is not surprising that my experience revealed that persons who were no longer working at the White House were more candid—and more willing to provide details—

than those who remain in the Clinton Administration. Still, this hardly rendered their every utterance truthful. Part of their motivation for talking with me, as I noted earlier, must have been the reputations of Drs. Burns and Sorenson. Some persons were also doubtless motivated by their own hubris, by their desire to cast the president in a decidedly positive or negative light, and by their commitment to the work of historians and the importance of accurate records for posterity. Some interviewees were best characterized by just one of these assessments. Most, however, seemed motivated by varying degrees of each. My knowledge of an interviewee's relationship with the president prior to the interview facilitated my ability to determine which answers seemed more truthful and which seemed less so.

Surely one of the most difficult interview responses to evaluate is a subject's recollection of how he or she felt during a particular time. There are few barometers against which a researcher might gauge such feelings or internal facts. One might pay particular attention to the certainty (or uncertainty) with which such emotions are recalled, or one might ask others in a position to know if so-and-so's anger or happiness at X incident seems reasonable. But little else can be done. In fact, oral historians would do well to remember that these internal facts are generally far less likely to be accurately recalled than are external facts, as William Cutler III observed (as cited in Hoopes, 1979). A bit of logic also supports this notion "because our feelings, even more than our outer behavior, are extremely personal facts, potentially most damaging to our egos when confronted honestly" (Hoopes, 1979, p. 16).

Finally, one resource that cannot be underestimated in this enterprise of discerning the truth is the historian himself. Historians must possess significant confidence in their own ability to assess the material that has accumulated. The authors of *The Modern Researcher* label this "informed common sense" (Barzun & Graff, 1985, p. 168). Mounds of research demand an intelligent interpreter. Interviews and correspondence and other documents do not speak for themselves; often, historians must do the talking. Their intimate familiarity with the subject and, in many cases, their relative distance from the episode being examined render these researchers capable of asking and answering for themselves the question, "Given other evidence and what I know to be true about this person, is his or her statement on this matter a reasonable account of what transpired?"

A Final Word

Interviews are a wondrous resource, but they should seldom be the only source of information. They are useful and enlightening—and most closely approximate the truth—when critically examined alongside other documents. By themselves, interviews are more illuminating about the present than about the past. By themselves, interviews fail to provide any sense of the larger historical context (Hoopes, 1979, p. 14).

Interviews will always be valuable research tools if for no other reason than they are far too tempting to conduct. We humans are inquisitors; we want to know. And if we don't know, we want to ask others who do know. Moreover, for historians at least, interviews provide color and detail and emotion. The British scholar E. H. Carr (1961) opined that "the historian without his facts is rootless and futile; the facts without their historian are dead and meaningless" (p. 35). Some interviews are the facts; others contain the facts. The historian labors to assemble these and other facts in an order that ventures to recount and then explain what "really happened."

When Hillary Rodham Clinton's mother, Dorothy Rodham, declined my request for an interview this past March, she reasoned that "it never turns out the way you expect it to." I did my best to convince her otherwise, but she would have none of it. Defeated, I managed to mutter "thanks" and hung up the phone. "Thanks." I meant it but I didn't. She was kind, but I was kind of disappointed. Now, Mrs. Rodham, I really mean it. Thank you. You have provided the perfect capstone to this chapter. It is fitting that an interview "never turns out the way you expect it to." An interview is a slice of life. And who among us believes that life turns out just as you expect?

References

Barzun, J., & Graff, H. F. (1985). *The modern researcher.* New York: Harcourt, Brace, Jovanovich.

Brady, J. (1977). *The craft of interviewing.* New York: Vintage.

Carr, E. H. (1961). *What is history?* New York: Vintage.

Dean, J. P., & Whyte, W. F. (1970). How do you know if the informant is telling the truth? In L. A. Dexter (Ed.), *Elite and specialized interviewing* (pp. 119-138). Evanston, IL: Northwestern University Press.

Dexter, L. A. (1970). What kind of truth do you get? In L. A. Dexter (Ed.), Elite and specialized interviewing. Evanston, IL: Northwestern University Press.

Geertz, C. (1973). *The interpretation of culture: Selected essays.* New York: Basic Books.

Gilbert, J. (1991). *Perfect cities: Chicago's utopias of 1893.* Chicago: University of Chicago Press.

Hoopes, J. (1979). *Oral history: An introduction for students.* Chapel Hill: University of North Carolina Press.

Leuchtenburg, W. E. (1989). *In the shadow of FDR: From Harry Truman to Ronald Reagan.* Ithaca, NY: Cornell University Press.

McCullough, D. (1993, Spring). Writing Truman. *Prologue, 25*(1), 7-15.

Morrissey, C. (1970). On oral history interviewing. In L. A. Dexter (Ed.), *Elite and specialized interviewing* (pp. 109-118). Evanston, IL: Northwestern University Press.

Oakeshott, M. (1933). *Experience and its modes.* New York: Cambridge University Press.

Sherwood, H. C. (1972). *The journalistic interview.* New York: Harper & Row.

Staley, C. C., & Shockley-Zalabak, P. (1989). Triangulation in gender research: The need for converging methodologies. In K. Carter & C. Spitzack (Eds.), *Doing research on women's communication: Perspectives on theory and method* (pp. 242-261). Norwood, NJ: Ablex.

White, H. (1978). *Topics of discourse: Essays in cultural criticism.* Baltimore: Johns Hopkins University Press.

❦ 14 ❦

Snakes in the Swamp

Ethical Issues in Qualitative Research

June Price

The Swamp

During the past 2 years, I have been studying the life history of personal relationships in women reported for child abuse. This topic has been fraught with ethical dilemmas from its inception, and as the study progressed, additional issues emerged like snakes from a swamp. I began to tread this territory with caution.

As a neophyte researcher, I sought advice and direction in the standard texts of the literature. Although a number of ethical issues and pitfalls were identified, and some guidance was offered, one was often left with the strategy of "trust in our own gut feelings about what is right in the immediate situation" (Lipson, 1994, p. 353). Punch (1994) likens this naive entrée into the field to an "unguided projectile" (p. 83), but to me, falling into Lewis Carroll's rabbit hole seemed a more apt analogy. Surely I was not the first researcher to encounter these problems! As I continued to search, part of the mystery became clear: The failures, regrets, and mistakes of qualitative research are rarely, if ever, published (Punch, 1994, p. 85).

My work has focused on a particularly vulnerable population: poor, minority women who have themselves been abused emotionally, physically, and sexually, and then reported for child abuse. They are the *Other,* marginalized, silenced, and oppressed. To further complicate the study, I am also a mandated reporter of child abuse; if a participant spoke of an abusive situation during an interview, I would have to report it.

General Guidelines

An excellent overview of ethical issues in qualitative research is provided by Miles and Huberman (1994). Brief theoretical models are described as a conceptual basis for decision making, and the authors enumerate many of the questions to be raised throughout the research process. Ethical issues are generally illustrated with anecdotes from actual fieldwork and an extensive bibliography is provided. The authors state, however, that "there is still no well-formulated set of ethical guidelines usable by qualitative researchers across a range of disciplines" (p. 289).

Lincoln and Guba (1985) describe additional circumstances that require serious reflection prior to conducting a study. These include the difficulty of predicting risk "since the design of a naturalistic study is emergent" (p. 254), that anonymity is not realistic "since inquiry records have no privileged status under the law" (p. 255), and that agreeing to participate is not necessarily agreement to be quoted.

Some texts are very general, only briefly outlining the prevalent standards: protect confidentiality, protect participants from harm, and provide informed consent (a conundrum when using a research method designed for discovery rather than validation). The advice begins to echo "to your own self be true" (Bogdan & Biklen, 1992; Fontana & Frey, 1994; Janesick, 1994; Smith, 1994; Wolcott, 1994). Practical suggestions and guidelines are limited. As I continued to encounter situations that demanded resolution, my "own self" warned me not to publish problematic data—to compromise the research rather than compromise the participant.

Consent

An initial dilemma in my study was the university's requirement for signed informed consent. My argument that signed consents actually jeopardized the confidentiality of participants, making them identifiable, was not heeded. Human Subject Review Committees in participating agencies insisted on them as well. I was caught between being ethical and being compliant; compliance won out. Mitchell (1993) recognizes this problem, stating that "signed informed consent forms may even pose a potential liability when those forms are unprotected from subpoena and can be used to link individuals to illegal or otherwise stigmatizing activities" (p. 25).

Trustworthiness

Lincoln and Guba's (1985) *Naturalistic Inquiry* fails to list ethics in the index but briefly mentions ethical issues in discussions of the "trustworthiness" (p. 290) of the study. Peer debriefing (p. 308) and member checks (p. 314) are advised as measures for ensuring honesty and in identifying researcher bias that might skew the interpretation (Stake, 1994). There is no discussion, however, of choosing which peers to debrief with, or which members to check with, or of choosing what to show them when each decision is potentially biased in itself. Member checking is a loaded issue; I continue to fear, despite contrary evidence, a participant's anger or pain in hearing my interpretation of their experience. And I'm not sure what Lincoln and Guba (1985) would say of the trustworthiness of interviewing someone strung out on drugs.

Lincoln and Guba (1985) advise leaving out "hot" issues (pp. 255, 372) that might not be highly relevant, but do not address how one might leave them in and still protect the confidentiality of a source. Illegal deeds or sensitive data may be highly relevant to the participant's motivations, actions, and lifestyles. Lipson (1994) suggests avoiding any identification of a specific participant in records, notes, or published reports, but this provides no relief when signed informed consents exist.

Feminist Perspectives

One is frequently referred to the moral high ground of the feminist perspective, striving for mutually empathetic and respectful relationships between researcher and participant (Denzin & Lincoln, 1994; Ely, 1991; Fine, 1994; Fontana & Frey, 1994; Punch, 1994). But in my study, clinical experience precluded such a relationship. I refused to give my home phone number and address to participants; I have had enough encounters with the irate boyfriends of battered women. Some participants wanted and needed more than a coparticipant relationship, which I was emotionally unable to fill. I had entered this field of study with empathy, not knowing the overwhelming horror I would encounter in their lives.

Participants were warned repeatedly not to discuss any incident of abuse during the interview that was not already known to authorities. This "power" invested in me as a mandated reporter hardly equalized our relationship; at the least, it compromised the data in ways that I will never know.

Secrecy

Much of the literature focuses on the ethical misconduct in infamous studies such as the Tuskegee Syphilis Study, Milgram's (1963) obedience to authority study, and Humphreys's (1970) study of homosexuals, all designed with purposeful deception (Adler & Adler, 1994; Mitchell, 1993; Punch, 1994). These tales of ethical violations are repeated and repeated. Yet there is very little published beyond these oft-cited examples (Mitchell, 1993), suggesting layers of secrets about the secrets of researcher conduct.

As I researched the related literature for my own study, I found transgressions that have been apparently ignored. In an extensive review of the child abuse literature, I found no mention of a researcher's obligation to report or intervene in the ongoing abusive practices that are the focus of the study. Researching voodoo practices in the United States, I stumbled onto Hurston's (1935/1995) pioneering work, where she knowingly participated in voodoo practices that led to the death of designated victims.

An opposing view is provided by Mitchell (1993), who speaks of the potential of the "researcher as prey" (p. 15), subject to deceit and con jobs by participants. He describes human subjects committee requirements as a "significant inhibition to qualitative fieldwork" (p. 24) and refers to informed consent as a power ploy of the "gate-keepers and elite to deny . . . access to the social settings they control" (p. 28). There is a danger that human subjects committees, institutional review boards, and professional codes of ethics can become self-serving watch dogs protecting their turf in the name of morality.

Mitchell (1993) argues that in research, all the participants conceal and that disclosure of purpose, motive, and practice is partial at best. He argues against the positivist position that "behavior and attitudes must be known, discovered, or controlled" (p. 31). He expounds the need for covert research, using examples from his own work on underground paramilitary organizations. Mitchell (1993) advocates for secrecy, for the need to explore powerful, possibly hostile cultures, and for the need to confront "privileged, and cohesive groups that wish to obscure their own actions and interests from public scrutiny" (p. 54).

Gatekeepers

As a doctoral candidate, I am subject to the power structure of the university setting and institutional review boards, as is anyone seeking to obtain access to participants through agencies, or to obtain funding. In an attempt to secure funding for my study, reviewers were concerned with the protection of confidentiality of participants. It was suggested that I obtain a certificate of confidentiality. Lipson (1994) also recommended this maneuver to protect "those who have 'secrets' that could hurt them or those who 'break the law' . . . those with stigmatized identities . . . or those who lack resources" (p. 348). However, this option was unavailable to me because there is no exemption in my state from the requirements of mandated reporting.

Subpoenas are a serious consideration, particularly in a conservative, "family values" political climate. The daily life survival skills of a "deviant" population may be subject to investigation (Mitchell, 1993). In one agency where I sought access, I experienced frequent requests for revisions and eventually was rejected. After repeated efforts to clarify the reasoning of the institutional review board, the agency lawyer explained that the reason for rejection was fear of "what ifs" based on this population: What if a participant spoke of abusing a child and sued for being reported? What if a custody suit was jeopardized? At first, I experienced this rejection as an attempt of the established power structure to silence this population. Finally, I recognized that the players tend to equate and confuse legal issues with ethical issues, as if rules guaranteed character. Wolcott (1994) identifies this confusion of rules versus moral principles, stating that " 'institutional ethics' have become little more than a bureaucratic hurdle. . . . 'Genuine' ethics' . . . are at risk of giving way completely to meeting the letter of the countless regulations promulgated by institutional review boards" (p. 403).

Conflict Resolution

Most authors speak to "issues of harm, consent, deception, privacy, and confidentiality of data" (Punch, 1994, p. 89). But it is unusual to find detailed descriptions of actual ethical conflict and resolution. An exception can be found in Sutton and Rafaeli's (1992) account of the decision-making process they experienced when their data did not support their hypotheses. Initially, they considered the alternatives of dumping the project or changing their hypotheses to fit their data. Their final resolution involved expanding their database with qualitative methods and publishing an account of the process as well as the results. Sutton and Rafaeli's (1992) account is a refreshing portrayal of a research experience "where the reality of the field setting may feel far removed from the refinements of scholarly debate and ethical niceties" (Punch, 1994, p. 89).

Due to the nature of qualitative research, it would seem likely that ethical conflicts occur frequently in the field. Yet examples in the social science literature are rare. In my search, I found one in an interview of anthropologist Clifford Geertz. Doing research in Bali, he was once forced to decide on how to provide medical care for a severely ill child: "If I take him to the curer, and he dies, I feel bad. If I take him to the doctor, and he dies, they think I killed him" (as quoted in Berreby, 1995, p. 44). Geertz finally takes the child to both: "But if both'd been impossible, I would've taken him to the foreign doctor and taken the heat. There are times when you stop being an anthropologist" (as quoted in Berreby, 1995, p. 47).

Interpretation and Ownership

In my study, I also had to confront the reality of interpreting the experience of poor, minority women as a privileged, white, middle-class professional. Fine's (1994) work provides an excellent discussion of the problem of trying to reflect, rather than distort, another's experience. In quoting bell hooks, Fine (1994) provides a chilling warning to those who attempt to analyze through the academic mirror:

> No need to hear your voice when I can talk about you better than you can speak about yourself . . . only tell me about your pain. I want to know your story. And then I will tell it back to you in a new way. . . . I am still author, authority. I am still the colonizer. (p. 70)

The specific method of my study, phenomenology, encouraged seeking references outside the scientific literature—to look to the arts, media, fiction, and biography, in order to gain a better grasp of the data. This is where I have gained analytical insight. An honest account of this process of interpretation is stated by Wolcott (1994): ". . . it is I who put the themes there. I did not find them, discover them, or uncover them; I imposed them" (p. 108). This acknowledgment of ownership is the foundation for an ethical study when accompanied by the recognition of one's own biases and prejudices (Ely, 1991).

Fine (1994) and Ely (1991) propose research for the purpose of social action as the antidote to the inevitable "act of betrayal" (Miles

214THE NARRATIVE STUDY OF LIVES

& Huberman, 1984, p. 233) that is qualitative research. They take the stance that research for the purpose of building a knowledge base or building a career is an inadequate justification for the intrusion of the researcher. Yet who is to judge what is in the best interest of the research participant? Who is to judge the goodness of social action?

These snakes, these ethical dilemmas, will remain and flourish in the swamp, a metaphor for the field. Punch (1994) admits to providing "no map" (p. 94) for the swamp; Ely (1991, p. 231) quotes Schön (1983): "In the swampy lowland, messy, confusing problems defy technical solutions . . . however . . . in the swamp lie the problems of greatest human concern" (p. 3).

References

Adler, P. A., & Adler, P. (1994). Observational techniques. In N. K. Denzin & Y. S. Lincoln (Eds.), *Handbook of qualitative research* (pp. 377-392). Thousand Oaks, CA: Sage.

Berreby, D. (1995, April 9). Unabsolute truths: Clifford Geertz. *New York Times Magazine*, pp. 44-47.

Bogdan, R. C., & Biklen, S. K. (1992). *Qualitative research for education* (2nd ed.). Boston: Allyn & Bacon.

Denzin, N. K., & Lincoln, Y. S. (1994). *Handbook of qualitative research*. Thousand Oaks, CA: Sage.

Ely, M. (1991). *Doing qualitative research: Circles within circles*. London: Falmer.

Fine, M. (1994). Working the hyphens: Reinventing self and other in qualitative research. In N. K. Denzin & Y. S. Lincoln (Eds.), *Handbook of qualitative research* (pp. 70-82). Thousand Oaks, CA: Sage.

Fontana, A., & Frey, J. H. (1994). Interviewing: The art of science. In N. K. Denzin & Y. S. Lincoln (Eds.), *Handbook of qualitative research* (pp. 361-376). Thousand Oaks, CA: Sage.

hooks, b. (1989). *Yearning: Race, gender and cultural politics*. Boston: South End.

Humphreys, L. (1970). *Tearoom trade: Impersonal sex in public places*. Chicago: Aldine.

Hurston, N. (1995). Mules and men. In C. A. Wall (Ed.), *Hurston: Folklore, memoirs, & other writings* (pp. 1-267). New York: The Library of America. (Original work published 1935)

Janesick, V. J. (1994). The dance of qualitative research design: Metaphor, methodolatry, and meaning. In N. K. Denzin & Y. S. Lincoln (Eds.), *Handbook of qualitative research* (pp. 209-219). Thousand Oaks, CA: Sage.

Lincoln, Y. S., & Guba, E. G. (1985). *Naturalistic inquiry*. Newbury Park, CA: Sage.

Lipson, J. G. (1994). Ethical issues in ethnography. In J. M. Morse (Ed.), *Critical issues in qualitative research methods* (pp. 333-355). Thousand Oaks, CA: Sage.

Miles, M. B., & Huberman, A. M. (1984). *Qualitative data analysis*. Beverly Hills, CA: Sage.

Miles, M. B., & Huberman, A. M. (1994). *Qualitative data analysis* (2nd ed.). Thousand Oaks, CA: Sage.

Milgram, S. (1963). Behavioral study of obedience. *Journal of Abnormal and Social Psychology, 67*, 371-378.

Mitchell, R. G., Jr. (1993). *Secrecy and fieldwork*. Newbury Park, CA: Sage.

Punch, M. (1994). Politics and ethics in qualitative research. In N. K. Denzin & Y. S. Lincoln (Eds.), *Handbook of qualitative research* (pp. 83-97). Thousand Oaks, CA: Sage.

Schön, D. A. (1983). *The reflective practitioner: How professionals think in action*. New York: Basic Books.

Smith, L. M. (1994). Biographical method. In N. K. Denzin & Y. S. Lincoln (Eds.), *Handbook of qualitative research* (pp. 286-305). Thousand Oaks, CA: Sage.

Stake, R. E. (1994). Case studies. In N. K. Denzin & Y. S. Lincoln (Eds.), *Handbook of qualitative research* (pp. 236-247). Thousand Oaks, CA: Sage.

Sutton, R. I., & Rafaeli, A. (1992). How we untangled the relationship between displayed emotion and organizational sales: A tale of bickering and optimism. In P. Frost & R. Stablein (Eds.), *Doing exemplary research* (pp. 115-128). Newbury Park, CA: Sage.

Wolcott, H. F. (1994). *Transforming qualitative data*. Thousand Oaks: Sage.

15

The Tale of the Anthropologist and the Kumina Queen

Two Voices in an Ethnographic Interview

Emanuela Guano

$\mathcal{T}$his is the story of an ethnographic interview that took place in Waterloo, Sligoville, Jamaica, during the summer of 1992. I, the interviewer (and now the author of this chapter), was a graduate student at my first experience in the field. I wanted to collect data on Kumina, an Afro-Jamaican religion with highly "African" (Moore, 1953, pp. 1-2) traits, such as drumming, dancing and singing, spirit possession, sacrifice of the goat, and ritual use of an African language. The interviewee was Queenie, Jamaica's most famous Kumina queen. The third person participating in the event was a man who acted as a mediator between the anthropologist and Queenie; I will call him the "salesman" because this is the role he eventually took on. During the interview, these three characters got involved in a more or less unsuccessful negotiation of their respective roles. In fact, if it is generally assumed that in an interview situation the interviewer is the one who controls the interaction, it is also true that the interviewee can more or less easily take over by subverting the frame of the interview (Briggs, 1986). This is exactly what happened to the anthropologist of this story:[1]

Queenie (also known as "Miss Queenie") is not only a Kumina queen but also a celebrity in Jamaica (and abroad, as she immediately explains to her visitors). Everything in her behavior constantly radiates this awareness. Whatever she is doing, whatever the context is, she *is* a queen even when she is sweeping a yard, and her attitude is always proud, sometimes disdainful.

As I have already mentioned, this interview represented my very first experience in the field. During the days I spent in the African-Caribbean Institute of Jamaica, I had been reading about Queenie, watching her dance in videotapes, and listening to her songs. Her imposing queenlike demeanor had already impressed me. Now that I had, at last, a chance to meet her, I felt really anxious about it. What if she wouldn't consent to talk to me? This uneasiness made my position in the interaction particularly vulnerable. In addition, my youth, my sex, and my appearance did not really confer on me the imposing aura of the scientist. Hence it became clear that to the interviewee, I was not so much the one who was asking questions as the one who had come begging for knowledge (and acceptance as an anthropologist). Due to my skin color (more or less white) and to the intervention of the salesman, the perception of my role shifted further to that of the one who was there to buy information, and to my disappointment it remained such until the end of the interview.

Of course, at first I was quite unhappy with the outcome of this interview. Only later, after turning the taped material into written form, I realized the lesson it had taught me: a lesson on the negotiation of roles in ethnographic interviews as well as on the paradoxes involved in creating an anthropological narrative.

The Kumina Queen, the Anthropologist, and the Salesman

Miss Queenie, whose real name is Imogene Parker, is a woman in her 60s who lives in a small cottage not far from Spanish Town. She is well known throughout Jamaica as the best Kumina performer and her skills also received broad acknowledgment overseas: in Great Britain, where she was invited to dance for Queen Elizabeth, and in the United States, where the Smithsonian granted her an award, which she proudly shows to her visitors.

In 1977, Maureen Warner Lewis published a book on Queenie; since then, the Kumina queen has frequently been visited by anthropologists and local authorities, and the recordings of a couple of interviews with her are available in the African-Caribbean Institute of Jamaica. As a result, Queenie is aware of her importance that reaches far out of the small Kumina community attending her services. She is a real queen and as such she behaves. To her, the presence of a researcher coming from overseas just to interview her is not a special occasion—and even if it is, it is not for her to show it.

The anthropologist had been gathering information about Queenie for a while; when she decided to actually interview the Queen, it turned out that this was not possible without a contact person because Queenie would not talk to strangers. At last, after a number of phone calls and visits to university departments and cultural institutes, the only person available to establish the contact turned out to be a functionary of a little governmental office in Spanish Town—the salesman.

It was a hot early afternoon; when we arrived at her cottage, Queenie was sweeping the yard. At the sight of the intruder and of the salesman himself—who apparently had not paid her a visit for 2 years, probably since the last interview—she declared she would not talk to these people. This statement immediately asserted her gatekeeping role by proving who was making the real decisions. The anthropologist, who had been eagerly waiting for this occasion, was worried; her situation was far from ideal: She was there to ask, she was young and female (which did not really improve her status), and she was white in a place where white skin sometimes arouses suspicion. Eventually, by mentioning that the visitor was willing to pay her a "*likkle* donation," the salesman got Queenie to accept being interviewed.

In the following few minutes, Queenie took up the role of the queen. As soon as everybody had squeezed into the little wooden cottage, she disappeared into her bedroom. I had time to observe the room where we sat; it was small, with pieces of old furniture piled along the walls. In the center of the room was a table covered with a plastic cloth with some dirty glasses on it; there I set my tape recorder and the notebook, nervously waiting for my interviewee. Goats and chickens could be heard through the door opened on the backyard.

And here she came: That tiny woman was now wearing a long, flowered, fancy dress; on her short, thick braids she had an embroidered crown of golden fabric. This was the Queen, the imposing priestess venerated by both *African*[2] people and overseas anthropologists.

With a broad smile, she explained that some people would even kill her for that crown. Then she pointed to a cupboard covered with parchments and photographs and proudly exhibited an award she had received from the Smithsonian Institute. The crown might have been the symbol of her importance within her community, but the Smithsonian certificate was a bridge between her world and the world of the visitor from overseas. Through this bridge, she could convey messages meant to establish her role in the eyes of the interviewer. That is why, whenever I tried to take a picture of her, this certificate was in her hands. Finally, after the display of the awards and a few minutes of small talk between Queenie and the salesman (the anthropologist was growing impatient, but there was nothing she could do), the queen declared she was ready to be interviewed.

I started with a question that was part of my own ritual: How were you initiated to Kumina? I already knew the story of Queenie's initiation from Warner Lewis's (1977) book, but my question was meant to mediate the passage from everyday reality to a reality haunted by Kumina spirits. Unconsciously, I was tracing an imaginary link between the beginning of Queenie's story and the beginning of the anthropologist's story: the interview. Queenie perceived the ritual quality of the question and enhanced it in her answer:

> When I was 7 years old, I plant seven wood of lily, and one Sunday morning when I wake up, I walk to the lily and find the lily[3] blow. All of them blows, I just find myself going backward. I go right down until . . . we have a cotton tree down a gully and in there I find myself at 21 days. After that, I was there the 21 days, and dumb. I couldn't talk. And then, I have an uncle, my mother sent for him . . . Him no see me, but I couldn't call him and him circle and circle until he find me. And at the 21 days I was there I don't eat, you

understand? And there I was, at that place you have five
grave, tombs, down there, you understand? I was there
getting sturdy at night, I get falling in trance, and from there
. . . I saw a light, and them build a table, and when it
touched 12 o'clock I talk, and from there on I started to
travel right home and do all dancing, until them test me at
Morant Bay parade. And them take me from there to town,
and when I came in town now I was there until Mr. Seaga
[came and talked to me]. By this time he was not a—him no
going up in the politics, him was still in the university. . . .
And then him took up his work and then started a festival.
The first festival in Jamaica I went there and then I carried
on until now.

As in Warner Lewis's account, Queenie's story evokes symbols such
as the image of the lilies, the downward movement, the teaching by
the dead, and the 21-day fasting (Warner Lewis, 1977). But this time,
something has changed. In contrast to the version she presented to
Warner Lewis, this time she does not spend much time talking about
the spirits: She still mentions the tombs, but she does not even specify
that they are the burials of "some ho'time Africans" (Warner Lewis,
1977, p. 63). Now that she has been telling this story to many a visitor,
everybody is supposed to know, and she can well skip the unessential
parts of it. Her story has become shorter, and from the stylized and
enchanted atmosphere of the initiation, she suddenly jumps into the
story of her career: her performance at the parade in Morant Bay;
then her meeting with the sociologist Seaga, former prime minister
and now leader of the opposition party; and eventually, her participation in the prestigious first Festival of Jamaica. The esoteric turns into
the exoteric within a few sentences, and with the telling of her first
possession, or as she says, *trance* (whereas the usual Jamaican way of
defining possession is "to get in the spirit"), her first performance
through the dead turns now into the performance for the living. If it
is true that the dead taught her how to dance and sing, whenever she
sings and dances she does it for the living: to entertain them, to give
them a message from the spirits, or maybe even to set a *duppy*[4] on
them. The borderline between the worlds of the dead and of the living
is blurred, but the performance element is omnipresent. As soon as I

realize this, I develop a feeling that performance is also the nature of what was going on now, during this strange interview. Each of the three characters has taken up a role and is trying to play it in the most proper way. Only, maybe the reciprocal expectations are different: From time to time, the interaction we are negotiating gets difficult, and we have to start it all over again. When a boy who has been hanging around us grabs my hair and vigorously pulls it, I, sticking to my role of anthropologist, try to keep as calm as possible. Queenie, on the other hand, promptly reaches for a stick and chases the boy away. The frame of interaction that had been created is now broken. Queenie starts talking again, but now her intonation is no longer so hieratic, no pauses stress her sentences any more, and even her facial expressiveness is less intense. It takes a few minutes to renegotiate our roles. The anthropologist, slightly angered, pretends that nothing has happened, whereas the queen still keeps her stick on the table where she can easily grab it. The salesman, who did not take part in the action, laughs in the yard.

The other problem that arises is the clash of reciprocal expectations. As soon as Queenie begins her exhibition of parchments, the anthropologist starts feeling annoyed by this display. What the anthropologist was longing for was not an informant waving a Smithsonian certificate but some piece of original information that no other member of the scientific community had ever come across. On the other hand, by that time, Queenie was probably a little disappointed that this Yankee girl (who is actually Italian) was not as impressed by her awards as by her stories about spirits. To Queenie, unlike Smithsonian certificates, duppies are to be found everywhere: "Oh, Lowd! There are lots of them, you know?"

But the anthropologist does not give up, and she goes on and on asking about the spirits. Fragments of what she considers the "real" information now emerge:

> You have a lot of them [spirits] who died, and come . . .
> [when you are] playing the drum now, all of them get up
> and come to you. And you must know all, how to handle
> them. You feed them, and everything, and then them talk to
> you and you speak back. [When I get in the spirit] I feel a

whole lot of different sensation of the whole body. When the spirit is up . . . you must feel a difference in your body . . . until gradually you return back out, and when you come back out you are different.

When I'm down there I get teachment, and a lot of teachment, from the messengers, and I recall it in the brains when I come up again. I see the spirits all the while, as soon as they turn on, I see them.

We call them *nkuyu,* at graveyard they call them *nkuyu nzwandi.* If them want to have dinner[5] them come and them dream you, and them tell you. And you build something for them. If you don't build it the right and proper way they don't accept it, and you have to go back over it.

Anytime them come and them should decide to do anything you can get them off of you. You can do a table and feed them, and get them off. [You need to offer them] rice, rum, cream soda, bread, wine, some of them eat *roti* (you take flour and make it how Indian make it) and *calalu,* and you use plain water put aside from the sugar and water.

You are supposed to have spirits that they come from God, you know? 'Cause you have Miriam and Gabriel that come from God. The true and living God. They are messengers.[6] You just talk to them in the way you talk to the dead.

It is not only that there are a lot of them; the relationship between humans and spirits is complex and partly articulated by a spatial metaphor. When you play the Kumina drums, the spirits "come up" (from their grave?); it is at this point that you "go down" in a trance. To return to the world of the living, you have to "come back out." You can "set" a duppy on somebody to kill them. In general, the relationship between the living and the dead is so tightly knit that when the dead want something from you, they communicate with you through your dreams. Only, it is not you dreaming of the dead but they who "come and dream you."

Even the living have a duppy, says Queenie. In fact,

the body and the spirit can't mix together, one live and one
dead, the two of them have to separate. At night time you
are sleeping and your spirit is living. It's two messengers you
have, you know, you've two shadows: One is short and one
tall, the short one he do not make too much problem, but you
see, the long one will make all worries when him dead. At
night when you sleep him stray, and the short one stay with
you, and when him return you wake, 'cause the short one is
with you so nothing can come and hurt you. So I am going
to teach you something that you don't know. You see, when
you die, that tall shadow don't go down in the grave, only
the short one, and him stand out there and make worries. If
you walking now, you going out there, you see you've two
shadows, look if you don't see one tall and one short![7]

I decline the invitation to go and check my shadows out in the yard:
I want to know more about Kumina possession.

[People at Kumina services] fall in a trance. Sometimes you
are gone, man, and you are pure spirit, and then you come
back again. When them just get in a Kumina then them mad.
Me do all that when me was young: climb trees[8] and do all
those things. At that time you have nothing but spirits
amongst you, but if the whole of them condemn you dead
then them just pierce you and you get mad, and you just
look right at my eye and you'll see a whole lot of pus over it.
When me there on the tree, when me want some rum I just
make them throw some rum in a glass and throw it up and
me catch it up there, and just wash my face with that.

As when she goes down in the spirit during trance, Queenie is
penetrating into the depth of her knowledge. The passage from
everyday reality to the world of the spirits is marked by the use of
words in the *African* language, the ritual language of Kumina.[9]

Suppose you wanted now to call me, me no a young lady,
me is a old lady, you call *yaya* in the African language; you
call a young person *kento,* you call a young man now *yakalà.*

All that I'm telling you is just coming down from the spirits teaching me. You know we have the African spirits, we call them *mondongo*, 'cause them want no catching from you. Suppose anything is going to happen to you sometimes them tell you, them will come to you and dream you and them tell you. And suppose you don't want to hear, you just not hear until it happens to you.

I ask about *obeah*.[10] To my surprise, Queenie talks about the devil. The Christian influence of Revivalism on Kumina[11] becomes particularly evident:

The spirit of the devil . . . him try to tempt you all the while, but you must know you have a spirit with you which is a conscious spirit. You don't link with the devil . . . because you will find yourself in devilment all the while.

I no say [obeah and the devil] connect, you see, the people is two types of obeah. The one that they connect to the devil will kill you now, because when him set for him judgment, he will kill you. But you have another one where you can just trick a person, don't dead him, just smash you up and put you down to suffer. I tell you, what him Satan do all the while is pure badness.

You can use Kumina against obeah. Man, that good! You can take the same in Kumina and lick away a man, too. And you take it and fight against anything which is bad, and you can take it and hurt anybody.

Many diseases, I am told, are caused by a supernatural intervention:

Some of [the diseases] is *duppies,* some of them is from God. That's God putting him hands on you. It's not easy for you to get into that. All those who cry duppy, you get off the duppy off of them. But sometimes you disobey God, you know? Them don't do what God tells you to do and then him put regiment on you. And when put you have to ask him God for deliverance, and him deliver you, him wipe the prison seal from your heart.

Though seemingly revivalist in origin, this God has African names. I expect Queenie to talk about *Zaambi* or *Nzaambi Mpungu,* as reported by Ryman (1984, p. 82), but she prefers to use a somewhat poetic circumlocution:

> When you have rainfall, you say *metaligyatu vulaku,* that means to say God falled rain 'pon the land. *Vulakukwele:* the rain is falling on the land.

To God and to the anthropologist, Queenie now sings an Our Father in the African language:

> *Kwali kwali n, n'den den de*
> *Beli ko lo mawa kisalaya*
> *Pem legele*
> *Len legele*
> *Luwi za'kwe n'da'kwe so*
> *Belam m'pese m'bambe*[12]

As the talk becomes more esoteric, Queenie's English gets more and more obscured by shades of Jamaican patois. From time to time, the anthropologist, who is not even a native English speaker, feels lost. Slightly offended (why the hell does the Yankee visitor claim she does not understand English?), the queen refuses to repeat herself. The anthropologist, pretending to sketch a few hectic notes, hopes that the tape recorder is working properly. Luckily it is, and later on, the anthropologist will be able to excerpt a passage about Kumina rituals.

> You do African dance work for sickness, you do it for uplifting, you do it for deliverance, you do it for peace, but you have to know how to do it. You can't do it like an idiot because the thing will turn over back on you and kill you, you see? The same thing that you do, them [the spirits] do you back. So, you have to know what you are doing.

> When you kill the goat at 12 o'clock [during a Kumina service] you feed the spirit. You throw a likkle rum in it and you can use it and bathe anybody that is sick. You throw a

likkle rum in it and wine, you mix it and bathe the person with the rum and the wine, and all who in the dance take a little of the blood, just tip it so and do some 'pon the person right round, everybody gets a part of it. You cook the meat with the rice and then you share it and take out the spirit's own. You don't cook it with a whole heap of salt.[13] Food is to cook fresh; you can tip one likkle drop of salt in the meat, but you see, the rice no salt. If the spirit is not taking a part of it you go back over it again but you see, the rice no salt. Spirits no eat no salt. You share the meat and you give all in the dance, but you take out the spirits' first and you put it with his rum and his sugar and water—we call it *swikidi lango*. Plain water, we call it *soso lango*.

You keep the ritual all night until daylight. [You start at] 7 o'clock or 8 o'clock, and you don't stop until the light of the morning. Because you cannot stop the dance when you are making dinner. If you stop the dance . . . you are going to get a lick. So you keep it straight along until daylight, everybody satisfied . . . and everybody find them yard. Spirit going *nzwandi*: spirit going back burial ground.

[When somebody dies] you just play drum right through until they bury him. When you go put out the dead, that ninth night. You put him out and you don't play [the drum]. Before a marriage I have 1 week of [Kumina]. All night, until the day breaks Thursday morning, and we end up with that. That time we have a long table laid with everything on it: fruits, drinks, wedding cake, everything that you have. Candles, everything . . .

Now the salesman, who was chatting in the yard with the drummers, feels that his presence is needed. As soon as he joins us, the roles switch again. The salesman realizes that the anthropologist is having problems with Jamaican patois, and he decides to act as a translator between her and the somewhat irritated Queen. Though sometimes helpful, his mediation increases the distance between interviewer and interviewee: The directness is lost; to the anthropologist, the presence of the salesman quickly becomes intrusive. The rhythm of the interview slows down. Now Queenie's answers tend to be short, and she does not expand her explanations unless she is asked. This gives the salesman plenty of opportunities to "contribute" to the interview. If Queenie talks about the food of the spirits—water and unsalted rice—the salesman assumes the visitor might misunderstand and adds some absolutely redundant details. Hence I am informed that the pure water Queenie offers to her spirits is "not a tea, just plain water." To the salesman, the visitor probably comes from too far away to be able to know something about Kumina. But she does not come from far enough away as to understand by herself that the rice offered to Kumina spirits is "just rice, not rice and peas," the latter being a popular dish in Jamaican cuisine.

At some point, I will be told that the information I am receiving is a teaching about the real Kumina, not the commercial one, the one that "is performed on the stage." This is the signal: The obeah-salesman is about to turn the anthropologist into the customer. To sell his merchandise at a higher price, the salesman elicits Queenie's narrations about the most spectacular aspects of Kumina. Blood sacrifice, people "in the spirit" climbing trees. Unexpectedly, a story about poison emerges:

> You know, them poisoned me, too? They poisoned me at
> Two Miles, they took water and then them throw the poison
> at it. Any time, you see, you are more than them, they will
> try to kill you.[14] So, if you don't know what you are doing
> they will kill you. Your own missionaries will do it.
>
> When I am in the spirit—I was in the spirit, fallen in
> trance—and ask for some water, and my own people them
> know the African language, 'cause when I speak I don't say
> "I beg a likkle water," I want *soso lango,* that means it's pure
> water I want, and then they took the cup and threw the
> poison in that, and then some of them had to hold me this
> way (me in the spirit) and feed me with the water and then
> them throw the poison but when the poison get down in the
> belly I feel a different feeling, and I just kick away anybody
> and kick them down, way down. Mad, now! Then I talk to
> them and then I get up and then I run straight to my yard,
> and when I run to my yard I feel like something is coming

up and I have some *bissy*.[15] And I just grate a little bit of it,
and I boil it up and drink it. And I vomit up.

But, apart from this anecdote, now Queenie is not a queen anymore.
She now embodies some kind of commercial sorcerer, and she diligent-
ly replies to all the questions the salesman is asking her. Obviously the
man already knows all the answers. Sometimes he even interrupts
Queenie when he thinks she has forgotten some interesting detail. By
this time, the customer is supposed to be deeply impressed.

The interview is quickly moving to its end: Soon I am offered herbal
baths for "the bad belly," and, in case I want to see a real Kumina
dance, I am told I can have one organized just for myself—provided
I pay in U.S. dollars. No, visitors are not allowed to attend Kumina
rituals performed by and for Jamaicans, but I still have a cheaper
alternative: I can listen to some Kumina songs under payment of
another "likkle donation." I accept.

The drums (*kbandu* and *playin' drum*) are pulled out. They are
oblong in shape and covered with goat skins (a male and a female) on
the top; one is a little bigger than the other. Queenie sits on one of
them and starts beating it; as soon as I take the camera and ask her for
a picture, she casts a worried glance at me. A queen is not supposed
to be photographed without her crown, and her head is bare now. She
puts on her crown again, and I am free to take a picture.

Eventually, the drummers come. The two elderly men take their
positions on the drums while Queenie sings and plays the scraper and
a girl is in charge of the shakers (the *shakkah*). The songs are in patois
and African language. It is hard if not impossible for me to understand
the words, but I devotedly record everything. The music has a syn-
copated, hypnotizing rhythm, and I regret nobody is dancing.

Now the music has been played, the rum has been ritually sacrificed
to both drums and anthropologist, and the salesman has collected all
the *likkle* donations due. It is not without relief that I return to the
taxi that will take me back to Spanish Town. In the next few minutes,
I will still have to decline a visit to "the most famous Jamaican artist"
and a stop at a local craft market—no, I am not interested in buying
Jamaican souvenirs. After all, didn't I get what I wanted? I am carrying

in my bag a tape that the salesman triumphantly says is "like gold."
Or like U.S. currency.

The Author's Conclusion

Until not long ago, most anthropologists used to believe that they
could present their readers with pieces of ultimate ethnographic truth.
The legitimacy of these little monuments of scientific objectivity was
often sanctioned by the use of technical devices (Rosenau, 1992). Like
many of my optimistic colleagues of the past, I, the inexperienced
anthropologist of this tale, turned to my tape recorder in the hope of
reifying the fluid and temporary nature of an interview I believed
would lead to a disclosure of important aspects of Kumina religion.
In so doing, I was not fully aware of a number of paradoxes I was
being trapped in.

I did not realize that Queenie's role as a Kumina queen (and my
own role as an anthropologist) was subjected to continuous negotiation. By attaching to Queenie the authoritative and somewhat stiff
label of "Kumina queen," I was unconsciously trying to turn her
interview into an ideally aseptic, booklike relationship between an
informant who carried an immutable knowledge (and was obviously
willing to share it) and the ethnographer who investigated it. None of
these roles turned out to be true, as I realized when trying to grasp
some pieces of information amidst what had turned into a baffling
interactional game.

Back to the tape recorder: Sure enough, this blessed technical
device had helped preserve all the details about a talk I could not
always master. After working long hours on my "Queenie tape," I
succeeded in turning the conversation with Queenie into a more or
less coherent written text.

At that point, however, I found that a strange alchemy had taken
place. Despite my good will, the interactional nature of the discourse
had been frozen into one of those rigid things Fabian (1990) once
labeled as *ethnographic corpses*. In addition, it soon became clear that,
although reported literally, Queenie's words were organized on the

basis of my own criteria and categories. It was almost as if I had disguised my own discourse through the authority of Queenie's patois (Clifford, 1988).

At the end of the process, however, I as the positivistic-minded anthropologist had turned into an author at least partly aware of my hermeneutical function. Despite the paradoxes I still perceived in the narrative, I thought this effort might be a little contribution to anthropology, and I decided to publish it.

Yet now the reader might legitimately ask: What kind of knowledge can be drawn from just another piece of ethnographic fiction? To this question, I can only answer tentatively: knowledge about how an anthropologist would describe Queenie's Kumina through Queenie's words—and maybe also, knowledge about what might happen during an ethnographic interview.

Notes

1. In telling the story of the interview, I will switch from time to time to the first person when referring to the anthropologist, yet I am aware of the distinction between the role of the anthropologist and that of the author.

2. The term *African* is used by Kumina practitioners to refer to all the features that are more strictly related to the esoteric part of this religion (African people, in this case, are the Kumina practitioners themselves).

3. According to Warner Lewis (1977), lilies in this context are probably a symbol of purity meaning that the neophyte is ready for the initiation. This symbol might have been borrowed by Queenie from her revivalist background.

4. *Duppy* is the Jamaican term for the spirit of the dead (Leach, 1961, p. 74).

5. *Dinner* refers to the table laid with food, drinks, and flowers as offerings for the spirit. This ritual seems to have originated in Revivalism and then spread to Kumina through the influence of Queenie herself (Ryman, 1984).

6. Miriam and Gabriel and the term *messenger* are borrowed from Revivalism.

7. The belief in the multiple souls of the humans is reported also in Haitian voodoo, where each individual is thought to have a *gwo bonanj* (big good angel) and a *ti bonanj* (little good angel) (Desmangles, 1992).

8. Climbing trees is part of one of the most spectacular patterns of possession dance in Kumina (Moore, 1953).

9. Kumina's African language is actually Kikongo, a Kongo language (Bilby & Bunseki, 1983). Queenie's excellent Kikongo (Brathwaite, 1978) might be due to the teaching of her maternal grandparents, who probably came to Jamaica from the Kongo region as indentured laborers (Warner Lewis, 1977).

10. *Obeah* is the sorcery tradition carried on by specialists (obeahmen) who manipulate evil powers and duppies through charms and rituals. Often associated with the evil power of obeah is *science*: a complex of magic beliefs of European origin (Barrett, 1976).

11. Queenie's mother was a revivalist. To her influence on Queenie is due the introduction of Christian concepts (such as the existence of God and the devil) in Kumina (Ryman, 1984).

12. As Brathwaite (1978) reports, this song is not a literal Kikongo translation of the Christian prayer.

13. Also in Kongo traditions, ancestors would reject any food containing salt (Ryman, 1984).

14. It seems that in Jamaican rural society, the manipulation and use of poisons, associated with obeah, might still be a means of social control.

15. A *bissy* is a small fruit, probably a berry.

References

Barrett, L. E. (1976). *The sun and the drum*. Kingston, Jamaica: Sangsters.

Bilby, K., & Bunseki, F.-K. (1983). *Kumina: A Kongo-based tradition in the New World.* Unpublished master thesis, University of the West Indies, Kingston, Jamaica.

Brathwaite, E. K. (1978, September). The spirit of African survival in Jamaica. *Jamaica Journal, 42,* 45-63.

Briggs, C. L. (1986). *Learning how to ask.* Cambridge, MA: Cambridge University Press.

Clifford, J. (1988). *The predicament of culture: The 20th century ethnography, literature and art.* Cambridge, MA: Harvard University Press.

Desmangles, L. G. (1992). *The faces of the gods: Vodou and Roman Catholicism in Haiti.* Chapel Hill: University of North Carolina Press.

Fabian, J. (1990). *Power and performance: Ethnographic explorations through proverbial wisdom and theater in Shaba, Zaire.* Madison: University of Wisconsin Press.

Leach, M. (1961). Jamaican duppy lore. *Journal of American Folklore, 74,* 207-215.

Moore, J. G. (1953). *Religion of Jamaican Negroes: A study of Afro-Jamaican acculturation.* Unpublished doctoral dissertation, Department of Anthropology, Northwestern University.

Rosenau, P. M. (1992). *Post-modernism and the social sciences: Insights, inroads, and intrusions.* Princeton, NJ: Princeton University Press.

Ryman, C. (1984). Kumina: Stability and change. *African-Caribbean Institute of Jamaica Research Review, 1,* 81-128.

Warner Lewis, M. (1977). *The nkuyu: Spirit messengers of the Kumina.* Kingston, Jamaica: Savacou.

16

A Woman Studies War

Stranger in a Man's World

Edna Lomsky-Feder

*B*etween the years 1988 and 1990, I interviewed 63 men about their experiences in the 1973 Yom Kippur War and the war's effect on their lives. These encounters were part of a research project that drew on the way Israeli men told their personal biographies to examine the process by which they normalize the war experience into their lives. The interviewees were all my peers from a similar socioeconomic background to my own; I had even been acquainted with some of them prior to the interviews. And yet the series of interviews proved to be a journey into a foreign land. In this chapter, I shall analyze the dialogue that developed between my interviewees and myself from the perspective of a stranger in a man's world.

One might suggest that I am exaggerating when I describe my encounters with the interviewees in terms of a stranger, as one of my colleagues claimed when I discussed the matter with him. How could Israeli women possibly be strangers to the war experience? After all, they are an inseparable part of the military culture in Israeli society. I would argue that even if my approach may include an element of dramatization, it emphasizes the problematic task facing a woman studying the war experience. The problems are anchored paradoxically in the fact that she is indeed part of the culture of war—a culture that defines war as one of the main characteristics of the male world and as one of the cultural elements that construct gender relationships.

The Researcher as Stranger

A researcher entering a new field is always something of a stranger, seeking to decode and understand an unknown culture. The need to observe things from the outside, from a marginal position, is an essential part of the "sociological consciousness" (Berger, 1963). According to Ager (1980), this strangeness is inherent in the role of the researcher, whom he dubs "the professional stranger." A researcher engaged in examining his or her own culture finds the passage to the status of professional stranger harder than the researcher investigating distant and alien cultures. Examining your own culture as a professional stranger is difficult precisely because you are part of this culture and you are embedded in its taken-for-granted assumptions (Ben-Ari, 1989, 1992). To engage in research, you have to make the subjects of your research strange so that you may examine them from a distance and in a new light (Gurevitch, 1988). I would argue that this process has a unique quality when the researcher is, from the outset, defined as a stranger by the members of the group he or she wants to study although they share the same culture. It is problematic when this status of stranger derives not from his or her research role but from one of the components of his or her personal identity (e.g., sex, religion, ethnicity) defined according to sociocultural norms common to both the researcher and the subjects. The problematic nature of this situation lies in the social hierarchy that accompanies these definitions, which affect the nature of the encounter between researcher and subjects.

My situation as a woman interviewing soldiers is therefore particularly complicated due to the deep-seated perception found in Israeli society that war is male-owned territory in which women have no claim (e.g., see Lieblich, 1978).

Women and War in Israeli
Society—Structural Strangeness

War is one of the main arenas in which differences between the genders are defined in human society. The role of the warrior is the epitome and realization of male strength (Elshtain, 1987; Gilmore, 1990; Mosse, 1990). A semantic reflection of this link can be found in Hebrew, in which the words for *man* and *hero* derive from the same root, which means "to overcome." Israeli society shows in a particularly marked way the function of war as a basic experience in defining gender relationships. An ongoing state of war is one of the main reasons for preserving the traditional model of the protecting, strong, and dominant man as opposed to the passive and dependent woman. This pattern is reflected in the family (Peres & Katz, 1991) and in the status of women and their patterns of political participation (Etzioni-Halevy & Illy, 1993).[1] The same pattern is also characteristic of gender relations inside the armed forces. Although Israeli society prides itself on the fact that women are drafted for compulsory army service, the reality is that half of all women do not in fact join the army and those who do usually fulfill traditional female roles (various forms of service positions). Although the Israeli army may have made an effort to recruit more women to technical and professional roles in recent years, they are still prevented from serving on the front line, not to mention as combatants.

The position of women vis-à-vis the world of warriors is consistent with Simmel's (1950) definition of the social status of the stranger. According to Simmel, the stranger is a constant element in a group whose position is determined by the fact that he or she is a priori defined as not being part of this group and yet close to it—touching the group's boundaries and, to a considerable degree, even defining them. This status of stranger is rooted in social structure and is therefore termed *structural strangeness*. The stranger has contacts with others, and these contacts may be intensive and even intimate, but he or she cannot penetrate the group itself or blur his or her separate position. Simmel argues that in any encounter between two people, there is a tension between closeness and distance, between belonging and separateness; but the encounter with the stranger maximizes this tension because it is socially determined (Simmel, 1950).

The definition of structural strangeness applies to the position of women vis-à-vis the warrior society. Their stranger status lies in the sociocultural definition that excludes women from the arena of war. Woman is and always will be a stranger because she "was not there"— she did not participate in the war.[2]

Structural Strangeness and Dialogue With the Subjects

As for myself, my motivation to explore this subject was undoubtedly whetted—both consciously and subconsciously—by my curiosity to understand this world from which I am excluded.[3] But my desire to research soldiers required me to break through a cultural barrier. Women's structural strangeness from the world of war has been internalized into the collective and individual consciences of men and women alike. This characteristic was therefore central in my encounter with the subjects because they and I share the same culture and are members of the Israeli society.

The unique social status of the stranger, according to Simmel, gives him or her special qualities in his or her contacts with the members of a group: "He is freer practically and theoretically; he surveys conditions with less prejudice; his criteria for them are more general and more objective ideals; he is not tied down in his action by habit, piety, and precedent" (Simmel, 1950, p. 405).

The marginal position attributed to the stranger also leads to a tendency among the group, in their contacts with him or her, to be open and honest to an almost confessional degree. In his analysis, Simmel emphasizes the degree of freedom and the advantages that the stranger's social status provides in his or her contacts with the members of the group, but he fails to discuss the other side of this position—the dependence, sensitivity, and vulnerability that result from the power relationship between the stranger and the dominant group. This is particularly problematic when the stranger intends to study this same group. These power relationships may impair his or her ability to act in an exploratory and critical manner. The researcher is required to be attentive, open, and nonpatronizing to his or her subjects but also to be independent, active, and questioning in his or her search for knowledge. In my own case—that of a woman researching war—my desire to penetrate this "foreign land" exposed me to the power relationship between the stranger and the dominant group. This was manifest in addition to the existing power differentials that pertain between men and women even when they meet on common ground.

I believe an analysis of the interrelations that developed between myself and my interviewees from the theoretical standpoint of strangeness could serve as a useful perspective from which to examine the problems faced by women who research men's worlds—an issue that has been neglected in the literature.

This analysis is based on materials from the interviews and on a diary that I kept during the course of my research. This diary can hardly be described as a field note in the classic sense of the word in anthropological circles. Most of the entries describe the interview and its characteristics, interpretative comments, and my comments and deliberations concerning the fieldwork. In the dialogue that developed between myself and the interviewees, a process emerged that can be described schematically in three stages: (a) denial of strangeness, (b) acceptance of strangeness, and (c) presence of strangeness.

Denial of Strangeness

At the beginning of the research, my contacts with the subjects evinced a clear denial on my part of the fact that I was not a part of their world. The penetration of the world of war involved my attempting to disguise my stranger status. Thus, for example, in the first interviews, there are obvious attempts to gloss over ignorance concerning military matters that are taken for granted by soldiers. This reflected a fear that my ignorance would reveal the fact that I was not an organic part of their world. When, in their stories, the interviewees mentioned technical terms of which I had no knowledge or used unfamiliar army slang, I refrained from asking them for clarification and would return home and consult my husband (who serves as a fighter). As well as attempting to disguise and camouflage my strangeness in the military world, I emphasized my points of contact with the subjects, stressing my own army service and not infrequently recruiting my involvement in my husband's military biography, as though the mere fact of my proximity to him granted me legitimacy in and knowledge of their world.

A reflexive analysis of the dialogue at this stage would seem to show that I was attempting to deny the fact that I was a stranger to the world of fighters. This was, to an extent, a denial of my own personal and social identity. At the time, I was unaware of my difficulty in meeting the fighters. As a direct result, I largely glossed over my presence as a woman and a researcher, which impaired my functioning as an interviewer. The attempt to hide the fact that I was a stranger to the world of the military focused much of my attention on myself rather than on my subject. The attempt to appear to be part of my interviewees' world made it difficult to listen attentively to them and prevented me from functioning fully, smoothly, and freely in the interaction. This is reflected in an entry in the diary that I kept at the time:

> During the interview with Adi, who spoke about the army and its significance as a primarily male society, I began to feel like an stranger invading a world that did not belong to me. At the same time, as I wrote up Ofir's interview, I noticed that there are some concepts, such as *rabbit house,* which I do not understand and do not know what they mean, and I need help from Yon [my husband] in order to make them out. Recently I have felt more and more that I am a stranger and to an extent an intruder into a different world. I think I have to deal with this point—what impact does it have on my interviewees? Or on me? For example: When Adi told me about how he was injured, I didn't completely understand what the "mistake" was that he made during the training accident (he was injured himself and also caused others to be hurt), but I felt uneasy about asking him. He must have sensed my question and tried to explain, but I still didn't get it. He didn't really understand that concepts

that are second nature to him, such as what a mortar is or what you can and can't do with it, are totally alien to me as a woman—I don't understand them and they are not part of my life.

Acceptance of Strangeness

In my later interviews, it is clear that I came to accept the fact that I am a stranger to the subject of war. This acceptance actually led me to strengthen my defensive position in my interactions with the interviewees. It is true that I allowed myself to release more of my ignorance and to ask about matters that I didn't understand. But the feeling of, "What do I know about this? He [the subject] is the one who knows," reinforced my image of the subject as the superior partner and restricted my freedom to show doubts and demonstrate incisiveness in my contacts with the subjects and in my analysis of the material. In the interviews held during this stage, it is evident that I tended to diminish my own worth in the presence of the interviewee, which sometimes led me to uncritically accept everything I was being told. This stage of the interviews is marked by a certain passivity in my dialogues with the subjects and by a lack of any real demand on my part for them to involve me in their world. Comments by interviewees along the lines that "only those who have been there can understand it" paralyzed me ("Can I really understand?"), and the claim that "the war didn't affect me at all, why do you assume that it did?" impaired my confidence ("He must be right, I guess—after all, it's his world, not mine").

My acknowledgment of being a stranger at this stage would appear to be the product of accepted social definitions that see war as a territory on which women have no bearing, which led me to believe that I could not really share the men's experiences. My personal experience in the army service was not much of a help: I was not part of a combat unit, and I did not have day-to-day contact with combat soldiers. I was released from the army before the war, and none of my immediate family was injured. All these factors strengthened my feeling of strangeness vis-à-vis war and my relative passivity and defensiveness in my contacts with the subjects. At this stage, I was more of a listener than an initiator, and my potential advantages as a stranger—such as the subject's willingness to confess to the stranger—were realized only on the subject's initiative. At this stage, I did not feel entitled to challenge the interviewees or to insist on a point as I should have done to improve my own understanding of the phenomenon. In the deepest sense, control of the interaction still lay with the storyteller—the subject—and I acted in accordance with the accepted definition of a woman's role in the context of war. At this stage of my research, I was an observer of war from my position of structural strangeness rather than a researcher investigating and questioning her surroundings. I was aware of the distress caused by this situation, writing at one point, "Again I feel that I'm not getting the most out of the interview. I must be more direct and straightforward, and more probing about the war." This awareness, and my disquiet at my passive and defensive position to my subjects, pushed me toward the next stage.

Presence of Strangeness

This stage is characterized by a rejection of my former lack of confidence. Through working with the subjects and analyzing the interviews, I became aware of my passive and defensive behavior and of the reasons for this. I began to be more active in the interviews and to take greater control of the emerging process. This was reflected in more active and incisive behavior—I asked more questions when they were called for and was more skeptical when there was reason to be so. I was less inclined to accept things at face value and more determined in my desire to understand. The need to function as an active, challenging, and inquisitive researcher required me to overcome the structural social definitions of woman's strangeness in the field of war, definitions that consolidate her status as dependent and submissive in her relationships with men. The goal was to understand the world of men at war despite my marginality to this world. At this stage, my strangeness as a woman was internalized as another aspect of my identity as a researcher and it appeared in my self-presentation. It is true that I had not "been there," but it does not mean that I couldn't study this world and approach it through my dialogue with those who were there. I wasn't "one of the guys," but this fact could be used to my advantage. This stage is marked not only by acceptance of my strangeness but by making it present—the desire to understand and know from the position of strangeness. This did not impair my attempt to encounter the subject's world. On the contrary, I made more active use at this stage of the qualities inherent in my role as a stranger. Strangeness became a resource in interaction. Presenting my strangeness, and sometimes even demonstrating it, was one of the tactics I used in the interviews to prod my subjects. From here on, my interviews include statements such as, "As a woman, I can't understand this—could you explain it more for someone who wasn't there?" Or "As a woman who's heard about war from secondary sources, what you're saying is the opposite of what I would have expected. Could you explain it a bit more?" By accepting my strangeness not only as part of my identity as a woman but also as part of my identity as a researcher, I was able to use it when necessary to motivate the interviewee to interpret, comment on, and explain the war experience. Thus the interviewee lost his domination of the dialogue and ceased to have sole control of the war story and its meaning.

Summary: From Structural Strangeness to Professional Strangeness

A reflexive analysis of the material shows that the process of coping with strangeness during the research work can be seen as a process of growth and maturing in my role as a researcher. This process reflects a transition from a situation in which my strangeness as a woman dominated my encounters with the subjects—structural strangeness— to one where my strangeness as a researcher was the prevalent aspect— professional strangeness. In the early stage of the interviews, it is clear that I denied my strangeness to the world of war and attempted to hide this from the interviewees. In the second stage, I accepted my strangeness but submitted to the dominance of the interviewees. In both these stages, the structural strangeness that derived from my status as a woman in Israeli society was the dominant factor in my dialogue with the interviewees; largely suppressing the professional strangeness inherent in my role as a researcher, I acted not as an analyst who questions and probes her subjects but from a more passive and submissive stance. My conduct in the interviews was largely in compliance with the cultural definition that grants men mastery of this situation. Only in the third stage was this strangeness presented and presented as a tool in understanding the interviewees. Only in this stage did my strangeness as a woman interviewing fighters become a significant component of my role as a researcher—a contributing aspect rather than one that inhibited my dialogue with the subjects.

Epilogue

I completed the research and began presenting my work. At this stage, too, my encounters with male colleagues led to ambivalent reactions to my status as a woman discussing their experiences. This point erupted overtly and stridently in one of the seminars where I presented my research project. At the end of my lecture, one of those present claimed that as a woman I could not ask the right questions because I hadn't been there and couldn't understand what war is. He then went on to describe in detail his exploits in the Sinai desert during the 1973 war. The need to cope with my status as a woman researching a man's world would not, therefore, appear to have ended but merely to have relocated to a different setting. This article is in small measure one more stage in this process of coping.

Notes

1. A conference on the subject of Female Identity and National Discourse in Israel was held at the Van Leer Institute in Jerusalem in November 1993. The conference devoted much time to the place of war in this context: for example, the lectures by A. Shademi on "Women in Black," H. Herzog on "Women in the Discourse on the Collective's Boundaries," A. Lieblich on "The Captive Wife," H. Hever on "Women's Poetry during the War of Independence," and A. Zinger on "Image of Women in Israeli Movies."

2. Within male society, too, there are differing levels of relating to the warrior society. A home front soldier is naturally more of a stranger to war than a soldier in a

combat unit. In general, however, Jewish men in Israeli society are closer to the war experience than women. Men also have a greater measure of freedom of choice concerning the extent of their attachment to war, whereas for women, the social barrier is dictated and not negotiable. For Israeli men, whether they themselves have fought or not, army service is a dominant and significant part of their sexual and social identity (Ben-Ari, 1989, 1992; Helman, 1993; Lieblich, 1989).

3. In this context, it is interesting to note that among Israeli researchers, there is a particularly strong presence of women who examine war from the soldier's viewpoints (Helman, 1993; Lieblich, 1987, 1989; Syna-Desivilya, 1991; Yarom, 1983).

References

Ager, M. H. (1980). *The professional stranger*. New York: Academic Press.

Ben-Ari, E. (1989). Masks and soldiering: The Israeli army and the Palestinian uprising. *Cultural Anthropology, 4*(4), 372-389.

Ben-Ari, E. (1992). *Conflict in the military world view: An ethnography of an Israeli infantry battalion*. Jerusalem: H. S. Truman Research Institute & Hebrew University of Jerusalem, Shain Center of the Department of Sociology and Anthropology.

Berger, P. L. (1963). *Invitation to sociology—A humanistic perspective*. New York: Doubleday.

Elshtain, J. B. (1987). *Women and war*. New York: Basic Books.

Etzioni-Halevy, E., & Illy, A. (1993). Women in legislatures: Israel in a comparative perspective. In Y. Azmon & D. N. Israeli (Eds.), *Women in Israel* (pp. 237-251). New Brunswick, NJ: Transaction Publications.

Gilmore, D. (1990). *Manhood in the making*. New Haven, CT: Yale University Press.

Gurevitch, Z. D. (1988). The other side of dialogue: On making the other strange and the experience of otherness. *American Journal of Sociology, 93*(5), 1179-1199.

Helman, S. (1993). *Refusal to serve in the army as a redefinition of citizenship* (in Hebrew). Unpublished doctoral dissertation, Hebrew University, Jerusalem.

Lieblich, A. (1978). *Tin soldiers on Jerusalem beach*. New York: Pantheon.

Lieblich, A. (1989). *Transition to adulthood during military service: The Israeli case*. New York: State University of New York Press.

Mosse, G. L. (1990). *Fallen soldiers: Reshaping the memory of world wars*. Oxford, UK: Oxford University Press.

Peres, Y., & Katz, R. (1991). The family in Israel: Change and continuity. In L. Shamgar-Hendelman & R. Ben-Yosef (Eds.), Family in Israel, (pp. 9-32). Academon: Jerusalem.

Simmel, G. (1950). The stranger. In K. H. Wolff (Ed.), *The sociology of George Simmel* (pp. 402-408). New York: Free Press.

Syna-Desivilya, H. (1991). *War experiences in the Israeli veterans' lives: A life course perspective*. Zikhron Ya'akov: The Israeli Institute for Military Studies.

Yarom, N. (1983). Facing death in war: An existential crisis. In S. Brezniz (Ed.), *Stress in Israel*, (pp. 3-38). New York: Van Nostrand Reinhold.

PART V

Making Whole

Method and Ethics in Mainstream and Narrative Psychology

George C. Rosenwald

*E*thical questions in contemporary psychological research usually deal with matters of deception, confidentiality, or direct harm to the individuals serving as subjects—in short, with *safety* broadly defined. Methodological questions usually deal with matters of procedure or statistical inference—in short, with the conclusiveness of research broadly defined. In this chapter, I show some grave limitations in the concepts underlying the traditional ethical code and discuss the methodological characteristics of the newer narrative approach to life histories, arguing for its distinctive and valuable ethical contribution.

Ethics as Damage Control

"Since you are psychoanalytically oriented, aren't you concerned," he asked, "that in extracting a subject's life story during a series of interviews, you might confront her with memories and connections that she had repressed and that you might thereby cause some . . . upset?" He later made clear he meant *trauma*.

The audience directing questions at the colloquium speaker consisted mostly of graduate students of psychology who had been taught to carry out research by enlisting so-called naive subjects, administering various questionnaires and tasks to them, and then discharging them with a brief explanation of the study's purpose. Even though the student's worry reflects a vastly distorted view of what goes on in life-historical studies, it is of interest because it expresses values widely shared by mainstream psychologists.[1]

As is well known, socializing and other pressures brought to bear on the developing individual may cause discontinuities in experience and memory. In some cases, these pressures are so powerful and persistent that sizable spans of life become permanently unavailable for the individual's recall, leaving behind only the scars of excision. It is, however, not only the explicit recall but also the implicit stock of past experience, potentially relevant to the conduct of one's life, that becomes impoverished. What is noteworthy, then, about the student's question is that it concerned the harm arising not from the fragmentation of life experience but from the effort to put the splinters back together. It is fair to say that the psychological researcher's code of ethics is less immediately concerned with the abatement of mundane misery, however widespread, than with the prevention of situational stresses in the laboratory.

We may be doing the student an injustice; perhaps he would not raise this concern if he knew that the narrator would be helped gradually and painlessly to a new set of realizations about herself. Perhaps it is only the supposedly explosive effect of the retrieval that alarms him. If he indeed meant to encourage researchers to strive for the reduction of gaps and obscurities in individuals' self-knowledge, but to do so in a safe manner, he would be hard put to find guidance in psychology's handbooks on research method. For scientific psychology has never striven for such goals, has devised no relevant methods, and has opened no discussion about the gains and risks arising from such methods.

In the social sciences, ethics and method are closely connected to each other and to larger philosophical commitments. In the case of 20th-century U.S. psychology, these commitments refer prominently to the kind of knowledge considered worth pursuing. They create the vantage point from which deviant approaches to research are evaluated—both in the name of acceptable logic (method) and in that of acceptable practice (ethics). If we wish to evaluate the mainstream's ethical and methodological concerns about heterodox approaches to knowledge, we should begin with some clarifying observations about what the mainstream regards as unproblematic in its own practice.

In the conduct of traditional research, it is considered important as well as sufficient to leave the human subjects of an investigation in no worse condition at the end than they were at the start. Neither their physical nor their psychological well-being is to be impaired in any respect. No investigator is blamed, however, for failing to improve the subject's condition. Even the so-called debriefing at the end, brief and quasi-technical as it often is, commonly amounts to a "cooling the mark out" rather than a step toward fostering personally useful insights (Goffman, 1952). This is not a mere matter of short-term improvisation. Even after the results have been processed, subjects rarely become direct beneficiaries of the knowledge they helped produce or even readers of the printed version. This is treated as ethically unremarkable as long as the production of the knowledge involved no damage to the subjects.

Two sets of questions arise here: First, why does psychology, with its inherent potential for improving the human condition, not envision positive goals? Whence this ethical minimalism? Practitioners in the various applied subfields of psychology are explicitly dedicated to the alleviation of individual suffering and to the improvement of group functioning. Why is the same value not foremost in the ethical code of academic-psychological scholarship? Perhaps applied psychology would serve its legitimate goals more effectively if the pure research it draws on were oriented to the same values. It is surely tempting to dismiss this first set of questions as naive or antiscientific. However, precisely because it turns the light on disciplinary commitments taken for granted by the mainstream, we must guard against a premature dismissal of the issue.

The second set of questions takes us from ethics to the history of method: Why is psychological research potentially harmful to the human subjects of investigation? Why must committees be set up in research institutions to rein in the pursuit of knowledge at the expense of the subjects' welfare?

The answers to these two sets of questions are related. The natural sciences, which mainstream psychology has long emulated, lend it not only their methods but their concentration on the factual. The natural sciences seek not to enhance nature but to capture it in concepts and thus make it more serviceable. As to the methods of natural science, psychology has long followed the strategy of analysis and reconstruction. This strategy is well illustrated by the physiologist's approach to the conceptualization of any complex or chained process—for instance, sensation or digestion. Such processes are sectioned into their finest dimensions and components, and only human ingenuity and technical resources limit the degree of fineness achieved. The resulting causal accounts, linking each component with the next, can then be gathered into a comprehensive conception.

Beginning with the 18th century and continuing to this day, it has been held that scientific reason's

> most important function consists in its power to bind and
> dissolve. It dissolves everything merely factual, all simple
> data of experience . . . and it does not rest content until it
> has analyzed all the things into their simplest component
> parts. . . . Following this work begins the work of construc-
> tion. Reason cannot stop with the dispersed parts; it has to
> build from them a new structure. . . . Reason understands
> this structure because it can reproduce it in its totality and in
> the ordered sequence of its individual elements. (Cassirer,
> 1951, pp. 13-14)

It is not hard to see that the social sciences proceed in a similar manner. In psychology, analysis and reconstruction have always been applied to the phenomena and processes actually given in the experience and behavior of people in our world. Seeking to improve these—to negotiate between the actual and the possible—has not been recognized as serving the advancement of knowledge, however praiseworthy it might be from other viewpoints. Furthermore, the mainstream[2] consigns efforts to improve the world to an ethical limbo; after all, who is to decide what constitutes an improvement? Improving the world, in short, is regarded as neither an epistemically nor an ethically compelling mission.

Although it seems that method and ethics have the identical thrust, limiting disciplinary attention to what is rather than what might be, I shall show that in another respect, method and ethics have opposite implications. The antagonism between the two is necessary. The strategy of analysis and reconstruction requires the code of ethics as a restraint on its own inherent excesses. Concern for the dignity of the human subject, which runs through the *Ethical Standards of Psychologists* (American Psychological Association [APA], 1953), represents a mandate directly opposed to that of analysis and reconstruction.

One can grasp this opposition if one recalls that in the days before research plans had to be approved by institutional committees on the use of human subjects, it was common for experimenters in psychology to use insults and threats to increase subjects' drive levels. Concepts of human motivation were modeled on physiological drives, which could be manipulated directly and without significant side effects on the rest of the organism.[3] But in human beings, it is realized today, the effects of threats and insults cannot be confined to the domain of motivation; they are bound to affect others of the subject's psychological functions, including his or her self-regard. An insult may be effective in increasing a subject's level of aggression; unfortunately, it has the unintended side effect of injuring his or her dignity. Similarly, to ask someone to address an audience with remarks running counter to his or her own genuine convictions, as was often done by social psychologists studying attitude change, is an exercise that is apt to affect not only the speaker's belief system but his or her moral self-concept and hence dignity.

Even though research psychologists mean to address only those functions or processes that are of theoretical interest to them at the moment, the human subject remains sentient and reflectively aware. Theoretical interest may impel one to break down the organized assembly of the subject's living wholeness into component parts and ever finer elements and to submit these to various pressures and provocations.[4] But the person's reflective awareness resists these efforts at segmentation and isolation. The common complaint is, then, that the investigator is objectifying the subject, treating it as an entity reflectively unaware of its parts. Radical analysis is therefore rarely successful either in the phenomenological or in the theoretical sense. That is why one cannot discharge a subject who has been insulted or humiliated with even the profoundest apologies and most thorough explanations of the purpose of the experiment. Apologies and explanations cannot make up for a deliberate assault on the subject's dignity. Respect for the infrangible integrity of the individual is in fact what we mean when we speak of preserving human dignity.

Milgram's (1974) well-known studies of obedience to authority illustrate the role that may be insistently played by personality factors other than those the investigator or authority wishes to address. Milgram asked his subjects to carry out his instructions without regard to the consequences, which he declared himself ready to take on. This was an effort to isolate one personality function—the capacity for mechanical compliance—from others—conscience, compassion, and the like. Some subjects refused to accept this segmentation, insisting that they remained responsible for their actions whether these were mandated or not. To various degrees, they expressed indignation over Milgram's presumption. Others seemed to accept the segmentation and complied without demur.

A person's sense of dignity represents his or her personal wholeness in subjective awareness and functions like a pain signal in the sphere of human relations. Evidently, the sense of personal dignity varies from one individual to the next and from setting to setting. In reaction to a felt violation, people complain, at the extremes of intensity, of feeling insulted or merely bored. In either case, we may assume that the investigator did not take the subject's complex integrity into sufficient account.

It has been speculated that some college students complied with Milgram's instructions because they felt themselves to be serving science, helping out in an experiment. This suggests a correlation between one's role perception and one's resistance to segmentation. Milgram made the most of this correlation by addressing his subjects as "teacher" throughout,[5] rather than by their names, thus impressing on them the role they were supposedly playing in the experiment. In doing so, he imitated a stratagem of enforced specialization-deindividuation commonly employed in many corporate and totalistic organizations. We may speculate that subjects first had to escape from the constraints of this assigned role into the larger accustomed frame of their person-hood before they could realize the indignity done to them.

Considering how the *Ethical Standards* (APA, 1953) are applied today (and how some of Milgram's critics wanted to apply them at the time), the fact that some of Milgram's subjects did not object to his request for blind compliance reflects only on their tolerant sense of dignity and not on what the discipline accepts as right or wrong. Committees on the use of human subjects do not conduct referenda among prospective subjects to determine whether human integrity is apt to be infringed. Rather, they follow their own assumptions, and these must be seen as historically conditioned rather than as deduced from timeless principles.[6]

Fifty years ago, Gestalt psychologists and others tried, on theoreti-cal grounds, to dissuade behaviorists from segmenting the indi-vidual. Human beings were too complex, they held, and segmentation would produce falsehoods. Today, an ethical demand reinforces that theoretical warning: Segmentation will damage the human interest in integrity.

The APA's ethical standards restrain researchers from damaging subjects' welfare. Yet they do not recommend ethically relevant topics any more than do the canons of science direct us to worthwhile projects. To the lay public's astonishment, psychology attaches ethical significance to methods but not to topics. What researchers choose to investigate appears to be determined by various agendas, among them theoretical fashion, governmental policy, institutional traditions, and the like. But explicit, widely shared consensus about the society's or community's interest is not one of them.

It is not surprising therefore that, as a rule, ordinary people pay only slight attention to psychological research. What matters to them does not matter to the researchers. Subjects and readers expect no personal benefit. Whatever questions and confusions about them-selves, about other people, or about institutional life subjects might have brought into the investigation, these are not likely to be ad-dressed. Instead, the subjects of investigation are usually compensated with money or academic course credit. That is to say, in regard to neither method nor to topics do the *Standards* prevent the frustration of subjects' interests in self-enhancement. In psychological research, the subjects are usually presumed sound of mind and body so that no positive obligation falls to the researcher. What, after all, could an experimental social or developmental psychologist do to improve his volunteer subjects' condition?

But is the presumption justified? Do college sophomores not have many unfulfilled needs, which a dedicated psychological discipline might wish to address? In a later section of this chapter, I shall discuss such needs in greater detail. For the moment, however, it may be concluded that the ethical code, by its agnosticism about ordinary people's unmet needs, prevents only damaging acts of commission but not of omission.

I have discussed the active role of the *Standards* (APA, 1953) in restraining scientific analysis from damaging human wholeness, as signaled by the sense of personal dignity, and its passivity in articulating the link between research and human interests. This discussion is offered here not as an indictment or to take up reform but to specify from what baseline any ethical debate in psychology begins. The question facing us now is what consequences the restraints in the *Standards* have for the theoretical tasks taken up by the mainstream. As I shall show, the *Standards* lead investigators into a characteristic set of dilemmas, especially when they pursue ethically and politically compelling topics.

The Enlightenment and Human Wholeness

My purpose in this section is to reconsider the concept of human wholeness underlying the *Standards*. An exemplary mainstream investigation will help in this critique. To begin with, however, I contrast two fundamentally different portrayals of human subjectivity and of the inquiring mind in particular. The comparison of these two portraits will raise the question of whether the subject's felt vital wholeness, as contingently represented in the personal sense of dignity and in whose name the *Standards* protect individuals, is as whole as presumed. I will argue that the concept of wholeness implicit in the *Standards* is—strange as it sounds—a partial and incomplete concept. The subjectivities we can expect to encounter in our subjects are not as whole as the *Standards* presume, and what they presume may not be comprehensive enough to satisfy human interests as commonly conceived. The standard of wholeness guiding the discipline is, in other words, too high as well as too low. Furthermore, without a thoroughly elaborated conception of human wholeness, the mainstream cannot give adequate representation to human interests when formulating its theoretical programs. That is, the ethical code curtails not only the mainstream's methods but also its theories.

We have seen that investigators and subjects do not place the same values on the knowledge they produce together. The mainstream regards this divergence as merely temporary. The investigative impulse, it is believed, will in time search out all that is to be found, provided inquiry is given free rein. All that is found will eventually fit together as a model of our world, and this knowledge will set us free. This view of scientific curiosity features the inquiring mind as restless, expansive, and robust; the whole world will eventually come under its sway.

The thirst for new knowledge often tends to be regarded as a human universal—as a desire serving the maintenance of life itself and as part of the larger natural transaction by which we seek to transform a less satisfactory into a more satisfactory situation. Now if the investigative impulse is natural, so continues the chain of assumptions, then we ought not to interfere with it; strong directives might spoil its spontaneity. Many legends support this faith in the natural energy of the creative mind and in the spontaneous, even aleatory, processes of human invention. The sheer unpredictability of scholarly genius is celebrated in our culture and documented in countless innovators' biographies.

In assuming the inquiring mind's natural expansiveness and its necessary attachment to the method of analysis and reconstruction, the modern age has fashioned an image of the scientist that calls for constraints in the interest of human dignity. To put it bluntly, the scientific spirit is regarded as a Hobbesian menace, and the ethics of science are the restraining sovereign.

There is, however, another tradition in portraying inquiry. Here the natural expansiveness of the mind is seen as slowed or stalled by other tendencies. For instance, Bacon was pessimistic about human curiosity. He thought minds had to be distracted from their languid and sterile attachment to traditional knowledge and urged to exert themselves "for the relief of man's estate" (Bacon, 1826, p. 39). Minds were naturally conservative. More recently still, Kant (1949) put before us the portrait of natural reason socially broken:

> Enlightenment is man's release from his self-incurred tutelage.[7] Tutelage is man's inability to make use of his understanding without direction from another. This tutelage is self-incurred when its cause lies not in lack of reason but in lack of resolution and courage to use it without direction from another. *Sapere aude!* "Have courage to use your own reason!"—that is the motto of enlightenment.
>
> Laziness and cowardice are the reasons why so great a portion of mankind, after nature has long since discharged them from external direction, nevertheless remains under lifelong tutelage and why it is so easy for others to set themselves up as their guardians. It is so easy not to be of age. If I have a book which understands for me, a pastor who has a conscience for me, a physician who decides my diet, and so forth, I need not trouble myself. I need not think, if I can only pay—others will readily undertake the irksome work for me. (p. 286).

With these sentences, Kant extolled each individual's reappropriation of natural capacities split off from the rest, surrendered to authority, and thus stunted. Only by reclaiming human wholeness could we achieve self-determination, he continued. He had his eye on institutional and political deterrents to growth, mediated as they were by anxieties at the individual level. Whatever tendencies to laziness and cowardice keep us from deploying our natural gifts, we are further discouraged by those in authority. Although he prophesied that enlightenment would follow if freedom were granted, he also recognized that people, like cattle, often love their state of servitude and fear liberative projects (Kant, 1949).

By linking political unfreedom with psychological stunting, Kant acknowledged the social and historical context from which a social science might derive its emancipative goals. What this might mean for the theoretical program of psychology can, at this point in history, be envisioned in general terms. It means the confrontation of human fragmentation as a social artifact.

This second tradition in the portraiture of human reason calls psychologists' attention to rather different perils than those envisioned by the Hobbesian metaphor. Human subjects are not seen as wholenesses to be preserved against cracking but as casualties in need of repair. No longer can we presume that investigator and subject must above all respect each other's sturdiness. Instead, investigators must beware lest their own blinders prevent them from seeing their subjects' blinders.

The restoration of human wholeness is of course an ancient ideal, not a device recently installed to restrain the rapacious mainstreamer. Authors as diverse as Allport and Piaget, and Jung and Freud, have considered the integration of personality as the hallmark of maturity. The various functions of the personality become increasingly organized, interconnected, and mutually regulative when the individual achieves self-mastery. Human autonomy rests further on the attainment of thoroughgoing self-knowledge and self-understanding, the more inclusive the better. Later in this chapter, I shall refer to this notion as *transfunctional wholeness*, intending not merely the comprehensiveness of the inventory but its internal connectedness.

It should be kept in mind throughout that the attainment of transfunctional wholeness is not exclusively or chiefly a cognitive accomplishment. The ideal has two complexly interacting aspects—one operative, the other reflective. For example, in the moral domain, transfunctional wholeness is manifest to the degree that individuals can reflectively summon and weigh the moral and other dimensions of their life experience in evaluating an action and can yet act reflexively, that is, without reflection, in a manner that reflection would sustain. I shall assume that the operative and reflective aspects of wholeness can support each other mutually and that both are vulnerable to scientific analysis in the manner described earlier.

Investigators who proceed as though the various domains of a personality—motives, beliefs, concepts, feelings—were not only ontologically separate and distinct but isolable from one another are occasionally brought up short by the remonstrations of indignant subjects as we have seen in Milgram's studies.

The reconciliation of wholeness and analysis has proved elusive and has generated an unending debate in psychology. For how can one restore and preserve the wholeness of the person—in theory and in practice—if one's methods steer one again and again to dissect the individual into segmental, isolated functions and to trim complexity for the sake of better control (Rosenwald, 1986)? This contradiction is most clearly manifest in the work of research psychologists who have dedicated themselves to tasks of social or individual reconstruction and empowerment. Commonly, they encumber progress by their allegiance to the empiricist program's reductive method. Filled with concerns about impairing the subject's human wholeness and dignity, the mainstream may fail to discern that this wholeness is yet to be created. This amounts to a fetter on theory itself.

Knowledge is always pursued to satisfy specific interests. Whatever tends to satisfy these is regarded as theoretically significant. But interests in knowledge rest on assumptions—psychological or anthropological assumptions—about what humanity requires, what injures, and what restores it. Rather than to formulate abstractly how the notion of human wholeness underlying the traditional code of ethics is deficient—it is deficient in several ways—I shall illustrate one neglected aspect of human wholeness by reference to a mainstream investigation and its public consequences. *I shall argue that, restrained by only a limited notion of human wholeness, the strategy of analysis tolerates and encourages the pursuit of a kind of knowledge that is apt to neglect or injure ethically more demanding versions of human dignity and wholeness.*

A recent article by Sandra Scarr (1988) exhibits how a truncated conception of human wholeness may limit the scope of psychological theory. Scarr scolds colleagues who decline to undertake the forthright investigation of differences between ethnic and gender groups with respect to critical psychological dimensions. She considers this kind of hedging a craven yielding to our political climate in which anyone setting out to establish differences between gender or ethnic groups is suspected of reactionary tendencies. Only if we look courageously into differences and the sources of these differences can we ever hope to remedy social disadvantage, she argues, and only then will we have a chance to discover the hidden strengths as well as frailties of under-represented groups. The choice Scarr offers us is between pursuing and suppressing group differences. The first is considered politically courageous, the second cowardly. In short, Scarr advocates the study of ethnic and gender differences on ethical grounds.

In doing so, she seems to ignore that the members of such groups and even their learned representatives are not nearly unanimous in calling for the exploration of the kind of differences that interest Scarr. There appears to be a roughly even split between those who welcome such findings and those who disavow them (Akbar, 1991; Lykes & Stewart, 1986). If this difference of opinion did not shake Scarr's conviction regarding the relevance of group difference studies to sociopolitical progress, a personal experience of her own might have done so.

In a transracial adoption study, she discovered that black adolescents reared in white middle-class families performed rather well on IQ and school achievement tests. Soon, this finding was condemned by critics as a slur on black parenting. Now anyone familiar with the history of adoption studies must recognize how paradoxical this reaction is; such studies were launched decades ago to refute biological racism and to raise hopes for the sociopolitical reversibility of ethnic disadvantage. But the reaction is paradoxical only from an academic viewpoint; in the political perspective, it manifests a certain practical rationality. Perhaps the critics recognized that a documentation of socially created disadvantage would not, by itself, lead to the social reversal of these disadvantages. More likely, in the given sociopolitical context, such documentation would tend to entrench discrimination.

Psychologists may, of course, study any topic that strikes them as interesting. But confusions are introduced into the discipline when improbable pragmatic claims are raised on behalf of such investigations. The question Scarr pursued was apparently not well enough informed by considerations of the actual political process she hoped to facilitate. Indeed, it appears that some people whom Scarr expected eventually to benefit from her contribution felt offended by it instead. This is the paradox that must interest us: A mainstream methodological commitment made on ethical grounds is rejected by readers on political grounds—mainly because the supposedly advantageous knowledge it yields about a group is found by the group's members to be injurious to them.

To avoid such an outcome, the scholarly consideration of the individual adoptee's situation would have had to include consideration of the collective situation of African Americans in contemporary U.S. society. The inclusion of this larger sociopolitical condition within the study of individuals would reflect what Erikson (1980) might have called a commitment to the *psychosocial wholeness* of subjects. It would "act back" on the formulation of research questions and forestall the exploration of pointless and injurious ones.

Scarr's study illustrates the predicaments into which the existing ethical code is bound to lead even those scientists most deeply concerned with the invigoration of enfeebled groups and individuals. Unfortunately, Scarr could hardly have avoided walking into this hornet's nest, given the gerrymandered concept of wholeness in our ethical code. "One cannot be said to be individually damaged," she wrote, "by research that exposes one's group to criticism or denigration, however psychologically painful the implications might seem to be" (Scarr, 1988, p. 58). That is, we cannot complain if the group to which we belong is shown to be defective. Uttered in the second half of the 20th century as a self-evident truth, this assertion is simply breathtaking. Yet it reflects a tacit understanding within the mainstream.

As a matter of routine, we study the domain of personality with the use of statistical group comparisons. Individuals are held to define the groups to which their characteristics assign them. However, while members are recognized as part of the group, group membership is not taken to be constitutive of the individuals. That is to say, the idea of internalization has little stability or conceptual influence in mainstream psychology. If it did, we would take for granted that research denigrating a group injures its members.

The *Ethical Standards* (APA, 1953) protect individuals only against damage and only against damage inflicted directly and pointedly. On this ethical view, the study of ethnic and gender group differences continues to flourish in human psychology despite the fact that, in addressing issues of social concern, it inevitably produces odious comparisons—odious differences, odious equalities. Because there is nothing in the *Standards* to prevent injuring a tolerant individual through the depreciation of his or her group, there is also little impetus for researchers to exercise their ingenuity in the devising of research that would be beneficial to the groups about whom they are concerned.

What does it mean to be made whole, and in what particular ways can psychology contribute to such enhancement? I take these questions up in the remainder of this article. So far, I have briefly alluded to psychosocial wholeness. I leave a fuller discussion of this for another occasion and, instead, take up three other facets of wholeness and fragmentation.

Varieties of Fragmentation

When Kant wrote about the obstacles to our release from tutelage, as he defines the quest of the Enlightenment, he referred to the books and experts to whom we like to delegate our powers of inquiry and reflection and to those guardians who fill the majority of people with panic at the very notion of beginning to think for themselves. We, too, can ask about the historically specific debilities that individuals and groups present to us social scientists (and to which we ourselves are not immune) and about the correlated varieties of knowledge production that might contribute to the mitigation of these debilities. In what ways are we not whole, and how might we become so?

There is no generally accepted diagnostic manual specifying the types of subjective fragmentation most common in our age. But a few of these may be considered here in quite schematic form. Perhaps most obvious is the atomization of individuals in a mass society (Kornhauser, 1959). The prevalent sense of community is tenuous. This has consequences not only on the collective but also on the individual level: If one cannot fathom any but the grossest features of others' experience of life, then one cannot conceptualize one's own any more finely. In an abstract sense, college students—the putatively normal subjects in mainstream research—know that people differ from one another and that one can study individual differences. But in the application to their own concrete life experiences, they often seem to believe that everyone experiences things as they do because they regard themselves as sane and because reality is what it so obviously is. At other times, they seem to believe that no one experiences what they do because they are, each of them, unquestionably unique. They lack the notions of a variegated whole and of comparability—that others, differently situated in the world, experience the shared reality in determinate, consistent ways reflective of their personal and social situation and background and that each of these individual experiences informs us about the nature of the whole as well as about these personal and social situations. This lack of a sense of the social whole as variegated may well be the direct reflection of social institutions and cultural forms that place obstructions around anyone seeking insights into self and others deeper than those granted by the mass media.

The mysteries surrounding experts, the secretiveness mandated by the culture of competition, the stolidity deriving from educational and occupational specialization—all of these prevent a secure grasp of one's own and others' distinctiveness as both individuals and members of a group. All undermine the quest for better comprehension of life and world and thereby limit autonomy. The impoverished appreciation of the self as one among many is accompanied by an uneasiness with subjectivity itself. When college students are confronted with the personal and life-historical distinctiveness of their own responses to the world around them, they commonly squirm and feel "trapped" by their own personalities! It is as though they sensed the resistance that subjectivity presents to the imperative of boundless adaptability.

A second type of debility commonly afflicts individuals' developmental self-understanding. How did one become what one is? How did one acquire one's passions, sensitivities, revulsions? More elusive still: How did one come to take this or that form of pain or pleasure for granted as an inevitable fixture of existence? Once again, college students often voice discomfort when such questions are asked. The idea of continuity strikes them as coercive, as robbing them of choice and "transcendence." Sometimes they let slip that they are headed for the corporate world and want no fetters on their ambitions. They know that organizational life tends to place the highest value on what people do and can do, not on how they came to their abilities and limitations. Resumés of one's education matter as predictors of future performance more than as personal histories.

Psychological theories, too, emphasize functionalist conceptions of the person. The desuetude of the narrative study of lives reflects how exotic or irrelevant the notion of persons as expressions and producers of their histories appears to the mainstream. It is important, however, that developmental self-understanding concerns not only the grasp of one's sameness over time but also the reflective awareness of the transformations, reversals, complementarities, and discontinuities that are so common in lives.

A third and related debility concerns the sense of personal coherence. Psychologists tend to attribute the self-limitations under which people labor to the exigencies of largely private intrapsychic conflicts mandating the repression of some motives, skills, awarenesses, or interests. The extent to which such self-sacrifices are channeled and fortified by external forces and authorities, resulting in what Marcuse (1969) called *surplus-repression,* is often not recognized.

Erikson's (1980) positing of ego identity as a more or less normal achievement of personal coherence chiefly accomplished in adolescence and the dramatically opposite contemporary postmodernist tendency to debunk the notion of a unified self as a mere social-linguistic convention are but two moments in the dialectic of denial. The first supposes a greater ease of attaining what is in fact granted to few, whereas the second complacently and categorically declares its sheer will-o'-the-wisp impossibility. It seems much nearer the truth to point out the dependence of reflective, internally coordinated lives on socially guaranteed opportunities—not the discursive opportunities stressed by social constructionists but practical opportunities for the construction and cultivation of rewarding lives, lives that do not require a great deal of self-deception or self-stultification.

The debility to which I refer in regard to personal coherence is therefore not the simple failure to grasp one's transfunctional wholeness. On the contrary, it is rather the unawareness of one's fragmentation, asynchrony, and contradictoriness in comparison with greater potential coordination. The questions to be asked of oneself are, How do my avowed values accord with my own (suppressed) yearnings? How are my preferences to be reconciled with my own, perhaps unexplored, interests? How is my loyalty to significant (or not so significant) others at play in the development of my life commitments? And so on.

These three conceptual fragmentations—the stunting of variegated, developmental, and transfunctional wholeness—impose an enormous psychological burden on individuals. People are bound to feel unworthy and incompetent if they expect to find convergence among their values and a synergic purposefulness in their strivings. Instead, they are apt to discover contradictoriness, asynchrony, and sheer futility. For how could a person attain the vaunted standards decreed by our brand of individualism—sturdy, coordinated selves—given the inconsistencies among the norms specific to the various domains of ordinary life? It is implausible, for instance, that the contradictory roles recommended to or imposed on individuals in the many contexts of private and public life should coalesce into streamlined, harmonious lives. Illusions of coherence and continuity enfeeble individuals in their actual dealings with reality, leaving them perplexed about the lacks they discover in themselves. Once again, these lacks may be evident in the operative or in the reflective aspects or in both. Some people falter in comprehending the significance of their past, others in living out its implications.

Narrative Whole Making

I have vivified the debilities suffered by many young people in our society—the same ordinary people who serve as subjects in the investigations of scientific psychology and who are generally considered to be intact. I described their debilities to highlight the limitations of the concept of human dignity underlying the *Ethical Standards* (APA, 1953).

I shall argue that certain kinds of life-historical narratives can play a role in the whole-making process called for by the prevalent forms of human fragmentation. In doing so, I offer no claims of exclusivity. The point is not to tout narratives as the only aid in such restorative undertakings—though we might consider them of outstanding value. Rather, it is to relate the production of specific kinds of knowledge to a specific goal, the goal of making whole those who gain access to the knowledge. Among these, I include the active participants who offer their own life narratives as well as those who as readers or listeners attend the unfolding of such accounts. It is clear that distinctions can be drawn between these two groups as well as among the members of each, depending on their predispositions and sensitivities. But this is not my present purpose and would contribute nothing to the main argument. To put it simply, life narratives excel in featuring the kinds of wholeness and fragmentation discussed in the previous sections of the article.

It is certainly no solution for most of the ills described to present people with material illustrating and clarifying how shared social realities are refracted by subjective factors; how life stories embody potential, often unrealized; how sameness can be deciphered within change; or how lives may balance or be rent by contradictions. It is no solution, but it is a beginning. Without such demonstrations, the relevant questions cannot be asked and the reflection of individuals on their own social existence remains in the doldrums.

On the assumption that the reflective aspect of wholeness supports the operative, we may expect that the cognitive stretching stimulated by participation in life history narratives will, in general, launch more highly integrated living action. Certainly such translations of insight into acting and being must not be taken for granted, given the complexity of the interaction and the intervention of many other factors. Neither must it be dismissed out of hand in this discussion of the ethical implications of method. On the basis of this conception, *the documentation of human wholeness and fragmentation is the neglected ethical charge on the social sciences.* In general, mainstream psychology not only disregards this but even strengthens the hand of segmentation over wholeness. We ask more often how a particular capacity or skill can be strengthened or trained than how the person could become more coherent or continuous with himself or herself. We are more concerned with personal effectiveness than with reflectiveness and self-transparence.

The assertion that a certain kind of knowledge, say, narrative knowledge, can contribute to making socially debilitated subjects whole, thereby emancipating them from contemporary forms of tutelage, is a large claim. Mainstream skeptics will ask how we can be sure of this effect, whether we have studied it systematically and acquired sufficient evidence to reject the null hypothesis. If not, they will ask whether we can even be sure that the constructions of exemplary lives presented to readers are free enough from the notorious ambiguities of text interpretation to be credible. Restrictions of space do not allow me to take up these questions in full.[8] It can be pointed out, however, that emancipating processes, to which psychological research can contribute only in concert with other disciplines, cannot be conveniently "operationalized" (Rosenwald, 1986). Insofar as life narratives repair damaged or stunted subjectivities, their effects on different readers will be comparable but not identical; identical effects would in fact be alarming. Making whole is a developmental process, extended in time, without scheduled end, and variously transacted. Documenting such a process is to evaluate a certain quality of living, both outward and inward (Rosenwald, 1992). It is a process that presents the reader with other possible worlds and lives than those he or she had taken for granted. To put it simply, narrative psychology is a psychology of the possible—possible continuity, possible coherence, and possible group and ego identity (Rosenwald, 1985, 1988a, 1988b).

Another way of describing the ethical import of narrative life study is to say that it is a *hygienic* discipline, somewhat like gymnastics, in that it improves the person who practices it. If immersion in other lives refines, be it only a little, the conduct of one's own, then the knowledge in question carries ethical weight. In this, it differs most radically from mainstream scientific psychology, which tends to canonize the status quo. As has been argued, it is the mainstream's fervor with respect to analyzing the actual into its ingredients that has steered ethical discussion away from the restorative concerns highlighted in this article. The possible, however, especially where it is recognized as the stimulus for a reflective, self-formative process, cannot be captured by research methods that were designed to entrench the actual.

The investigation on which I now draw for illustrative purposes bears on what we might call the human use of religion, to distinguish it from theological or sociological investigations (Barreto, 1990). I have selected this study as an object lesson because it highlights the resources of narrative life study relevant to the types of debility discussed earlier. Although the study does not purport to tell us anything about matters of faith or the demographic characteristics of churchgoers, it seeks to relate individuals' lives to their own religiosity. The participants in this study all emphasized the benefits they drew from their religious commitments. In this topical sense, Barreto's (1990) study belongs to a body of research relating religiosity to adjustment and mental health.

Several correlational studies are reported in the mainstream research literature relating religiosity or religious orientation to measures of mental health, further broken down to self-esteem, the presence of mood disorder, adjustment, feelings of guilt, sense of one's own sinfulness, self-actualization, psychological well-being, and so on (Schumaker, 1992; Wulff, 1991). Taken together, these findings are no more and no less clear or consistent than those from other correlational investigations in social science. For instance, a lay reader in search of a contented and fulfilled life might be discouraged on discovering negative correlations between religiosity and what has been referred to as self-actualization and never realize the reason for this finding, namely that the measure of self-actualization commonly employed gauges the "tendency to be guided by one's own principles and motives, independent of external social constraints, yet not simply out of rebelliousness" (Hood, as quoted by Tamney, 1992, p. 134). Once one realizes that religious orthodoxy involves submission to an independent authority, the negative correlation is no longer astonishing. Such misunderstandings are a common hazard of the operationalist approach to segmental analysis.

Most readers with a personal interest in a given topic of this kind are probably less intent than the professional scholar on having dimensions pure enough to maximize prediction. Rather, they want to gain a foothold within their own experience of life in all its necessary burgeoning confusion and to organize their thought fragments into a manageable whole. The remainder of this chapter is intended to sketch in as vividly as possible how and why narrative material may provide a purchase on this experience.

I begin with a brief survey of Barreto's five cases,[9] showing the variety of ways in which the interviewed individuals make use of religion. Each has constructed and appropriated it in keeping with his or her situation, and each succeeds to a greater or lesser extent in resolving tensions inherent in that situation by means of the appropriations.

> For *Barbara,* religion represents, above all, protection against emotional turmoil caused by the rampant materialism of our culture. By leading a life of simple pleasures and offering up the occasional setbacks as her gifts to God, she avoids the maelstrom of avarice and ambition. She pities others, such as her mother and ex-husband, who have been swept away by it and cast down into frustration and depression.

> *Jesse* is thankful for his religious code's restraints on his base, unruly passions. Lust, gluttony, and vengeance are held in check by his religion. He has suffered much injustice in his life and come close to acting on murderous impulses.

> *Catherine* had spent a childhood in terror of her alcoholic, sexually threatening father who drove a wedge between her and her mother. She lost all faith in benevolence. But she continued to wish for closeness to and comfort from the very parents who caused her loneliness and terror. These yearnings filled her with guilt. In adolescence, she sought relief in asceticism and in prayer to a patriarchal God. In time, however, she replaced this comforting protector with a new resource of self-forgiveness derived from an identification with women of strength. Today, she often prays to herself—a new, more forgiving self coming to the succor of an older, feebler one needing absolution from the feelings of guilt experienced by so many survivors of trauma.

> In *Mary*'s life, it was an aloof, egocentric, rather than a terrifying, father who troubled the mother-daughter relationship. After a childhood in which she idealized Christian martyrs, she spent years searching for acceptance from others

and yet always felt uneasy about expressing her needs. After a detour through student activism, the women's movement, a failed marriage, attachment to an older female teacher-mentor, addiction to alcohol, and a recovery through AA, she succeeded in giving her membership in a religious community a personal definition, drawing from it a new sense of self-possession and belonging. The lifelong task for her has been to find acceptance without self-abasement.

For *Hannah,* religious engagement means reentry into an ancient heritage from which she had felt excluded by her family. As a youngster, she was kept from active participation in Jewish ritual because she was a girl, whereas her older, less gifted brother was admitted to the study and recital of Holy Scripture. Furthermore, she felt severed from a beloved grandmother by parents who were too secular and assimilated. In her chosen occupation as a teacher in a religious school, she found a way to mend the broken connections with the past—and yet she cannot rid herself of the feeling that she is an interloper and a trespasser.

First, these sketches make clear that religion, quite aside from creedal differences, is appropriated in personally distinctive ways. One sees or stresses in doctrine and practice what one needs to see or stress. Whether any one of these individuals is more or less religious than another is therefore not a sensible question because one cannot array these people along a single continuum as correlational approaches require.

Indeed, it is far from clear that any of the individuals occupies a stable position in the domain of religion. Religious orientation is apt to be a fluctuating attitude. For this reason, too, it seems implausible to seek the statistical association between religious commitment and self-esteem and the like. As Catherine's submission to a fatherlike God began to fail in providing her the forgiveness she sought, she began to look to other sources and eventually returned to a reconfigured relationship with God. Barreto's cases make clear that religious orientation is in a state of continual retuning and repositioning with respect to other commitments and landmarks in the person's life.

By juxtaposing cases in this manner, we stress the particularity of each. Our contrastive apprehension of equivalents impresses us with their distinctive character. Each case is thus situated as one possible configuration among others. Religious solutions to problems in living are evident as more or less coherent for each person and no longer as mere "individual differences" on some imaginary dimension. In this way, the reader's sense of a variegated wholeness may be invigorated. For it is the assembly of cases that makes the religious culture a culture.

Second, our interest in the determining factors constituting such solutions is whetted. We are guided to recognize that a religious orientation is not a ready-made option on a cultural menu, but a commitment-in-process that "would have to be set in series with the rest of the life of the person" (Dollard, 1949, p. 26). As one takes the process view, one is also led to ask why Mary has turned away from one temporary solution to another, how the student movement and AA eventually came to fail in fulfilling her needs. The answers to such questions, however tentative, tend to help readers dwell on the links and chinks within developmental continuity.

Third, the close view of any personal narrative sheds light on transfunctional wholeness and fragmentation. For example, Barbara, who warns against yielding to the devil's temptations and recommends a life of Tolstoyan simplicity, revealed an unsuspected competitive vein to the interviewer. Not only does she compare her modesty somewhat superciliously with the crass ambition of colleagues, friends, and family members, but in a domain seemingly insulated from her daily moderation, she earns a living as a merchandiser of jewelry. In this work, she gets pleasure from demonstrating an effective sales pitch to the sales clerks (Barreto, 1990):

> One time there was this forty year old gal, a chunky little thing walks into the store. She is so concerned that her husband will kill her for buying it. And I knew she wanted it. So I told her, "Buy the necklace; if he doesn't like it bring it back. But when he sees you tonight, let him see it with nothing else on." [She laughs] She [the customer] bought it. She [the clerk] was shocked. That was a pleasurable sale. (p. 14).

To reject Barbara's religious aspirations as hypocritical would be to set one part of her life above another. If our interest is in whether religion can bring peace to a troubled soul, then our question might instead be whether Barbara requires her religious ideals to help her obtain material and sensual satisfactions that she would otherwise find unacceptable.

The developmental and transfunctional whole-making perspectives cannot be strictly separated. For example, Jesse's religious attitudes illustrate his evolved vision of secular authority. As a black man who grew up in the South, he accumulated experiences with protectors who shielded him from harm but who were nevertheless corrupt. As an adult, he practices a form of prayer that, in its ironic and scolding address of God, reflects his mundane social experience over the course of a lifetime. This makes clear that the coherence of a life across its various domains is itself an evolving one.

These excerpts from Barreto's (1990) study illustrate the appreciation readers may acquire for the diversity, the subjective construction, the evolving nature, and the coherence of life across its various domains.

There is, however, another more encompassing perspective on wholeness that cannot be taken up here, one that easily eludes the student of the single case but impresses itself on the attention of the multiple-case researcher. It concerns the manner in which social figures and forces are internalized by each individual studied. A cultural and historical nexus binds these cases together. This means that the juxtaposition of various individual versions of religiosity can place the religious culture as a whole in sharper relief. Paradoxically, the narrative study of lives, far from miring us in the details of so many individual existences, can open a special window on the social panorama not accessible from any other vantage point.

In this chapter, I have deliberately put off a host of technical questions, customarily pursued by mainstream researchers, to open up a long-neglected discussion: Which readers and subjects will benefit from participation in multiple-case life history narratives as regards the conduct of their own lives—and in what ways—is a question that will interest developmental and educational psychologists. For us, such parametric questions are less urgent than the prior issue, much obscured, of the ethical implications of our methodological choices. And yet, even this phrasing minimizes the problem because it suggests that such choices are independent of the goals of knowledge. One purpose of this section has been to show that narrative studies are not a new approach to the mainstream's old goals but represent quite different, even antithetical, goals.

Narrative Contextualization

In this final section, I ask what peculiarities of the narrative approach to lives produce the characteristic images of wholeness taken up here. By their very nature, life narratives contain references to the context of the actions and events they feature. The context need not be brought in by a deliberate maneuver after having been deliberately stripped from the to-be-purified dimensions—by randomizing it, holding it constant, or systematically varying it. As Sarbin (1993) points out, to pay the context of an action its due requires more than taking some additional ("contextual") variables into account, such as class, residence, or culture. This is so for the following reason.

People who tell stories about their lives will, without special prompting, place events in the context of social interaction, general history, personal development, and the totality of their engagements in the world. Even the situation in which a story is told is marked within it. This is the very stuff of telling stories. In this way, narrators naturally irradiate life events with significance. An act appears as meaningful when it is seen, say, as a turning point, a follow-up, a defiance, or a preparation for another act.

A contextualist approach to a life narrative acknowledges the "spread," the "specious present" of each action within it (Pepper, 1948, pp. 239-240). That is, any action points forward and backward in the sequence, engendering a sense of its "pastness" and "futurity."[10] It also reaches out toward and draws into itself related life-historical, cultural, sociostructural, and other relevant items of specification.

What we colloquially call "a very meaningful" act or event is usually one that is densely supplied with such references. What we somewhat arbitrarily refer to as the context of an action sheds significance on that action quite as much as the reverse. In a narrative, the context does not explain the action as much as it specifies its meaning. Even less does the action explain the context; it, too, clarifies and articulates the context as having the peculiar signifying potentialities that were needed to specify the action in the given manner. For example, an act that appears defiant in a specific way throws the background it defies into a sharper light so that we can understand the specific form of defiance that it generated. A discontinuous act clarifies the direction of past trends.

The arbitrariness of the distinction between an act or phenomenon and its context, given that each specifies and informs the other, is one of the defining features of narrative. What this means in interpretive practice—and what makes it so relevant to the creation of larger wholes—is that we do not deal in independent and dependent variables. Barreto's cases in their particularity as well as in their comparability can be satisfactorily grasped only in the frame of contemporary American culture. To go one step further, if we take a contextualist approach, we must regard ourselves as obtuse to this culture until we have discovered how it impinges on individual lives (Dollard, 1949). To assert that act and context inform each other means that, in terms of signification, each is internal to the other, giving it its specific import. (For a helpful discussion of contextualism see Stephen Pepper, 1948.) Nothing aids this process of mutual specification as much as narratives. Indeed, Sarbin (1993) regards "narrative as the most felicitous root metaphor for contextualism" (p. 61).

The effort to comprehend a life story adequately requires that readers stretch their interpretive capacities so as to grasp the reciprocal interiority of context and act or event. The mechanistic conceptions of human behavior and experience fostered by the mainstream social sciences do not prepare readers for this, insofar as all domains of study are usually divided into variables—the "purer" the better—and causes are seen as remaining outside their effects, achieving the latter by the transmission of forces rather than the specification of meaning.[11] But readers of life histories can achieve adeptness in grasping life stories on the training fields of fiction, in which actions are commonly set within the same types of context—life-historical, cultural, and so on—as are considered important in the study of real lives. Systematic work on the problem of stretching imaginative capacities would surely be helpful in understanding how individuals are made whole.

By now, it must be clear that despite the welter of material with which any carefully collected narrative presents us, there is no proportionality between the amount of detail and the number of lives or actions we are led to understand. Context limits as it broadens. It broadens in that it admits—in fact, searches out and draws into its compass—what mainstream psychology seeks to banish. In doing so, it also sets a firm horizon: Precisely because narratives inherently refer to specific contextual configurations—moments, eras, places, fellow human beings—we must renounce any universalizing ambitions.

The lines between the mainstream's and multiple-case narratology's ethical and epistemic goals are now drawn: The mainstream's is a goal of conquest; the multiple-case researcher's is one of restoring human capacities. The mainstream's ethical reticence protects the grandeur of its dream—the classic dream of positive science—to clasp the investigative domain wholly, without residual, in a gigantic embrace of empirical laws, leaving no space unoccupied by the force of theory. The knowledge it dreams of must be valid beyond time and place, the certifying observers impersonal, interchangeable. By contrast, the narratologist, concerned with individuals and groups groping for clarity about themselves within their world rather than with a domain to be brought under theoretical control, makes no claims to eternal verities but gestures toward a few fugitive but luminous exemplars, as though to say, This, too, is what being human can be like.

Notes

1. Narrative approaches are not always aimed at life histories, and the latter may be approached with nonnarrative methods. Neither narrative nor mainstream psychology, featured in this chapter, is deemed internally homogeneous. The necessary qualifications will, I hope, become evident in the course of discussion.

2. Kurt Lewin's proposals of action research are a prominent exception to this rule (Peters & Robinson, 1984).

3. But see Goldstein (1939) for a vigorous critique of this segmentalizing presumption.

4. No one has put this point more lucidly than Bacon (1826). He explicitly drew the parallel between experimentation in the study of nature and the discomfiture of individuals: "For like as a man's disposition is never well known till he be crossed, nor Proteus ever changed shapes till he was straitened and held fast, so the passages and variations of nature cannot appear so fully in the liberty of nature, as in the trials and

vexations of art" (Vol. 1, pp. 78-79). And more poignantly still in the Latin version, *"Natura arte irritata et vexata"* (Vol. 7, p. 110).

5. Janet Landman drew my attention to this point.

6. The fact that some things that were ethically acceptable in the past no longer meet today's standards is often explained by saying that people's sense of dignity has more nearly caught up with their potential wholeness. Even those who are skeptical about the notion of such progress, however, will grant that people do not always have a firm grasp on what is in their interest. But critics may rightly object to a notion of human dignity only partially and precariously represented in a subjective sense of dignity. For if individuals and groups cannot claim to monitor how governing authority interprets their need for integrity, then the door is open to oppression. Unfortunately, this objection to the critique of ideology cannot be taken up within the frame of this article.

7. The term *Unmündigkeit* usually designates the civic condition of minors and legal wards. Here it refers to the psychological and social-psychological characteristics of minority—lack of judgment and discernment, naiveté, obliviousness to obligation and consequence.

8. I have addressed these important questions elsewhere (Rosenwald, 1985, 1992).

9. The five studies in Barreto's work are drawn from people referred by local clergy who knew them to be "experiencing religion as a constant and integral part of their daily lives" (Barreto, 1990, p. 10). The sketches presented by Barreto focus on recurring themes of the participants' subjective experience of religious life culled from the interviews. For further information, see Barreto (1990).

10. This is conveniently illustrated in the study of diaries. Every entry in a diary is constituted by the anticipation of being reread, and this anticipation is represented in the entry's construction. Every entry also points to what preceded it and to what might have occurred. The potential promise of rewriting and rereading are the motive in the keeping of diaries (Wiener & Rosenwald, 1993).

11. As indicated earlier, narrative material is not immune to noncontextualist or anticontextualist treatment. It can be dimensionalized, quantified, and in other ways assimilated to the fragmentation strategies favored by the mainstream. But it need not be. It is my contention in this chapter that if it is not, then it can catalyze ordinary readers into reaching for larger wholes. Whether it will do so in any given case remains to be seen.

References

Akbar, N. (1991). Paradigms of African-American research. In R. L. Jones (Ed.), *Black psychology* (3rd ed.). Berkeley, CA: Cobb & Henry.

American Psychological Association. (1953). *Ethical standards of psychologists.* Washington, DC: Author.

Bacon, F. (1826). *The works of Francis Bacon, Baron of Verulam* (Vols. 1 & 7). London: Rivington.

Barreto, S. (1990). *The psychological function of religion in everyday life.* Unpublished manuscript, University of Michigan, Ann Arbor.

Cassirer, E. (1951). *The philosophy of the Enlightenment.* Boston: Beacon.

Dollard, J. (1949). *Criteria for the life history.* New York: P. Smith.

Erikson, E. H. (1980). *Identity and the life cycle.* New York: Norton.

Goffman, E. (1952). On cooling the mark out. *Psychiatry, 15,* 451-463.

Goldstein, K. (1939). *The organism: A holistic approach to biology derived from pathological data in man.* New York: American Book Company.

Kant, I. (1949). What is Enlightenment? In L. W. Beck (Ed. and Trans.), *The critique of practical reason: And other writings in moral philosophy.* Chicago: University of Chicago Press.

Kornhauser, W. (1959). *The politics of mass society.* Glencoe, IL: Free Press.

Lykes, M. B., & Stewart, A. J. (1986). Evaluating the feminist challenge to research in personality and social psychology, 1963-1983. *Psychology of Women Quarterly, 10,* 393-411.

Marcuse, H. (1969). *Eros and civilization.* London: Penguin.

Milgram, S. (1974). *Obedience to authority: An experimental view.* New York: Harper & Row.

Pepper, S. C. (1948). *World hypotheses.* Berkeley: University of California Press.

Peters, M., & Robinson, V. (1984). The origins and status of action research. *Journal of Applied Behavioral Science, 20*(2), 113-124.

Rosenwald, G. C. (1985). Hypocrisy, self-deception, and perplexity: The subject's enhancement as methodological criterion. *Journal of Personality & Social Psychology, 49*(3), 682-703.

Rosenwald, G. C. (1986). Why operationism doesn't go away. *Philosophy of the Social Sciences, 16,* 303-330.

Rosenwald, G. C. (1988a). Toward a formative psychology. *Journal for the Theory of Social Behaviour, 18*(1), 1-32.

Rosenwald, G. C. (1988b). A theory of multiple-case research. *Journal of Personality, 56*(1), 239-264.

Rosenwald, G. C. (1992). Conclusion: Reflections on narrative self-understanding. In G. Rosenwald & R. Ochberg (Eds.), *Storied lives: The cultural politics of self-understanding* (pp. 265-289). New Haven, CT: Yale University Press.

Sarbin, T. R. (1993). The narrative as the root metaphor for contextualism. In S. C. Hayes, L. J. Hayes, H. Reese, & T. R. Sarbin (Eds.), *Varieties of scientific contextualism* (pp. 51-65). Reno, NV: Context Press.

Scarr, S. (1988). Race and gender as psychological variables: Social and ethical issues. *American Psychologist, 43*(1), 56-59.

Schumaker, J. F. (Ed.). (1992). *Religion and mental health.* New York: Oxford University Press.

Tamney, J. B. (1992). Religion and self-actualization. In J. Schumaker (Ed.), *Religion and mental health* (pp. 132-137). New York: Oxford University Press.

Wiener, W. J., and Rosenwald, G. C. (1993). A moment's monument. In R. Josselson & A. Lieblich (Eds.), *The narrative study of lives* (pp. 30-58). Newbury Park, CA: Sage.

Wulff, D. M. (1991). *Psychology of religion.* New York: Wiley.

❦ 18 ❦

Ethics and Narratives

Guy A. M. Widdershoven
Marie-Josée Smits

*A*t first sight, stories seem to be of little relevance to ethicists. Stories are about concrete events and experiences, whereas ethicists look for universal rules. Moreover, stories are presented in a descriptive way, whereas ethical norms are prescriptive. Of course, ethicists have often shown interest in stories. They have used stories to illustrate the point of general rules or to enlarge their plausibility by giving them a basis in history. In both cases, however, the story was regarded as secondary to the ethical rule that was at stake.

Recently, several ethicists have expressed a more fundamental interest in stories. They claim that ethical issues cannot be dealt with unless one thoroughly knows the situation and focuses on the meaning of the issue for the people involved, a meaning that can be established only through interpretation of the stories they tell. This position, which entails that stories are fundamental for ethics, can be described as a narrative turn in ethics. This narrative turn, however, raises the question as to how stories can help us to make an ethical evaluation. In exactly what way can the experiences of people who are involved in a problematic situation tell us what is the right course of action? How can concrete feelings contribute to a general evaluation?

In this chapter, we will explore the role of stories in ethics in more detail. We will start with an overview of the narrative turn in medical ethics and nursing ethics, which presents itself as an alternative to the abstract and general approaches that are current in the domain of health care. Then we will critically examine the issue of whether a narrative approach is a suitable basis for ethical evaluation. We will contend that stories do not simply describe events but give them meaning by showing how they fit into a practice. By telling stories, people present their actions as aiming at a common good. Next, we will go into the ethical aspects of narrative research. We will argue that the point of narrative research is to make explicit the view of the good life, which is embodied in stories. This involves a process of interpretation in which the perspective of the researcher and that of the story are merged into a new view of how to live. We will also present a story that comes out of our own research, the story of a nurse about his experiences with an elderly patient on a hospital cancer ward. We will show that this story gives insight into ethical aspects of nursing practice if interpreted from a perspective that emphasizes meaning making and care. Finally, we will complement our ethical interpretation of the nurse's story with a description of the role the story plays in the context of nursing practice.

The Narrative Turn in
Medical Ethics and Nursing Ethics

The dominant approach in medical ethics is to apply general normative principles to concrete cases (Beauchamp & Childress, 1994). The relevant principles are *autonomy, beneficence, nonmaleficence,* and *justice.* According to the principle of autonomy, the physician should not overrule the patient but respect the patient's wishes. The principle of beneficence functions as a countervailing power saying that the physician does not have to follow the patient's orders but has to judge what is in the patient's interest. This may lead to a course of action that is against the patient's preferences. The principle of nonmaleficence again emphasizes the physician's responsibilities in stating that he or she should never harm the patient. The principle of justice places the doctor-patient relationship in a wider context by demanding a comparison of treatment opportunities of various patients.

The four principles function as an ethical grid, which structures the presentation of a case and directs the discussion. The emphasis is on preferences, risks, and rational decision making. Ethical reasoning is regarded as following a calculus, which ideally results in one good solution. The procedure is abstract in that it starts from general principles, tries to eliminate emotional issues, and aims at a universally valid conclusion.

From a philosophical perspective, this top-down, general, and rationalistic approach of ethical issues in health care can be criticized. Choice is not a matter of deductive calculation. Every choice is situated (Merleau-Ponty, 1945). Ethics is a part of life in which emotions, reason, and fate are intertwined (Nussbaum, 1986). The emphasis should not be on certainty but on uncertainty. One should not look for rational solutions but be aware of the futility of logical reasoning. Nussbaum stresses the problematic intertwinement of engagement and conflict, the unavoidable interrelation between passion and spite. Moral issues cannot be solved by an act of reason; they require involvement and intuition. This intuition can be sustained, according to Nussbaum, by stories. Nussbaum argues that people should read stories to learn about conflicts and to become engaged in moral practices. Stories tell us more about morality than any philosophical treatise can. Stories show us the tragic character of life and make us aware of subtle tensions within moral practice.

The narrative turn in philosophical ethics, which can be found in the work of Martha Nussbaum, is echoed in texts on medical ethics and nursing ethics. For several ethicists, the principle approach has lost its attraction. Instead, these authors emphasize the ambiguity and complexity of health care practices and focus on doubt, uncertainty, and tragic choices. They also stress the importance of stories. According to Benner (1991), ethics is in need of stories about real communities because stories give room to doubt, anxiety, and hope as elements of concrete human interactions. Stories show intentions and feelings as part of contextual and intersubjective ways of meaning making. They contain knowledge about practical situations and show us patterns in practical life. Cooper (1991) argues that nursing ethics should be built on stories about nursing practice. Stories make us understand ethical issues in nursing because they focus on concrete experiences of uncertainty, fear, hope, and mutuality. Parker (1990) argues similarly:

> Embedded in these too often untold stories are the rudi-
> ments of a nursing ethic that could be truly meaningful to
> nurses. Yet as professionals we are struggling to develop a
> theory of nursing ethics without really listening to what our
> experiences with patients tell us. (p. 34)

The narrative turn in medical ethics and nursing ethics is based on the conviction that we need stories to get a more elaborate view on ethical issues in health care. General normative principles are too abstract and crude to come to grips with practical problems. If we want to understand ethical issues in health care, we should start from the way in which the participants give meaning to the situation by telling stories that express concrete commitments, emotions, and doubts. We can only hope to find adequate ways of dealing with ethical problems if we are prepared to listen to the narratives of the people involved.

Narrativity and Ethical Evaluation

Although narratives may help us to better understand a situation and especially to learn how the situation is experienced by the participants, it is not directly clear that they can help us to make an ethical evaluation of the situation. How can a story about a problematic issue in health care tell us in what way one should deal with this issue from an ethical point of view? How can a story that someone tells about his or her experiences help us to decide whether a specific action is called for? How can a story, which tends to focus on description, lead to an ethical position, which is prescriptive?

Ricoeur (1990) argues that the dichotomy between description and prescription is not useful to characterize a story. According to Ricoeur, stories are in between description and prescription. Stories describe events in a meaningful way. Such descriptions are not just enumerations of facts. A story shows that the events are part of a meaningful pattern. A story relates what people do in such a way that we are invited to see the point of the action. Stories are not about separate actions but about practices. A story shows us what is at stake in the practice. This means that a story presents the activities it describes as part of a larger project that aims at some good. A practice is not something that someone does on his or her own. Practices are shared endeavors, which one has to learn from and perform in interaction with others. The story highlights the interactional dimension of the actions described, their embeddedness in a shared way of life. A story makes explicit the aim (or telos) of a practice as a shared tradition.

According to Ricoeur (1990), the teleological nature of practices is the basis for ethics. A practice has an aim that is ethical in the sense that it is directed toward "the good life with others in just institutions" (p. 202). The teleological character of practices is the foundation for moral obligations. Moral rules (such as the Golden Rule) are based on the concrete reciprocity of practical orientation toward the good life. On the other hand, moral norms express lived reciprocity in a more elaborate way. They make us aware of the need to take into consideration the perspective of all who are involved. Thus principles such as autonomy and justice are important not as elements of a calculus but as expressions of lived solidarity, which grow out of and have to be integrated into concrete practices (Ricoeur, 1990).

Ricoeur (1990) stresses that narrativity is the pivot between theory of action and theory of ethics. Stories elucidate the teleological character of action and prepare the ground for an ethic founded on the notion of practice as an endeavor that is aimed at the good life. Thus stories are not ethically neutral. They invite us to regard actions as part of a larger project that embodies a view of a common good. Still, Ricoeur's approach of the relationship between narrativity and ethics shows a rather limited view of the importance of narratives for ethics. Narrativity serves as an introduction to ethics; it is not regarded as a part of ethics. According to Ricoeur, narratives make us aware of the teleological character of action; Ricoeur's discussion of teleology itself, however, does not refer to stories. Likewise, his treatise on moral obligations does not include a reference to narrativity. In the chapters on teleology and moral norms, stories are remarkably absent.

What seems to be lacking in Ricoeur's (1990) exposition of the relation between narrativity and ethics is the idea that stories are not just literary creations but that they are a central element of life itself (see Widdershoven, 1993). People constantly present themselves and their actions toward others by telling stories. They try to clarify their view of the good life with others in just institutions in stories told to one another. Thus the teleological nature of action is dependent on narratives. Stories do not just make us aware of teleology; they express and realize it. Likewise, stories present us with concrete examples of intersubjectivity and care. In doing so, they have a moral significance (see Tronto, 1993). Last, stories embody normative obligations. Moral norms are first and for all expressed in the stories that people tell about their lives and their interpersonal relations. Stories are essential ingredients of practices: They make explicit their ethical orientation toward the good life, a life that is to be lived with others in social conditions that are just.

We may conclude that a story is not just a collection of data; it creates a unity that makes events part of a larger project aiming at a common good. By telling stories, people interpret their actions and justify them toward each other. Thus storytelling is an ethical endeavor. Every story evaluates the events that it describes; it claims that the actions involved contribute to the common good. A story about a problematic issue in health care not only tells us what one of the participants experiences, but also entails the claim that this experience is relevant for the issue at stake and that the issue can be adequately evaluated only if this experience is taken into account and integrated into a practice that aims to deal with the concrete situation.

Ethics and Narrative Research

Stories give us insight into the nature of practices as ethical endeavors. Consequently, ethicists should not focus on principles but study the narratives that are told by practitioners. Ethicists should assemble stories and interpret them as expressions of what is at stake in practices dealing with ethical issues. In short, ethicists should do narrative research.

Narrative research itself, however, is not ethically neutral. Narratives have to be interpreted to become meaningful. Such an interpretation starts from a preunderstanding (Gadamer, 1960). In listening to a story, we already have some notion of what it is about. Thus in understanding the vision of the good life expressed in a narrative, we already have some idea about the aim of the practice that is presented. Without a notion of health and its importance in life, we would not be able to understand stories about health care practices. The preunderstanding that guides narrative research can be based on general life experiences. It can also be founded on a more profound knowledge of health care practices—for instance, stemming from field research. We will return to the role of this latter form of preunderstanding when we will present the example from our own research.

Of course, preunderstanding is not the same as fully developed understanding. In listening to a story, we may be urged to correct our views about the practice that is presented. The story aims to create a better understanding than we had before. This does not mean, however, that our former ideas are simply given up and replaced by new ones. Rather, understanding results in a new view in which our former perspective and the perspective presented by the story are merged. Understanding can be characterized as a fusion of horizons (Gadamer, 1960). Understanding a story takes the form of a dialogue between interpreter and story. Such a dialogue starts from presuppositions but is also open for new experiences. As Gadamer concludes, "understanding in dialogue is not holding on to one's own point of view, but being transformed into a common position, in which one no longer is the same as one was before" (1960, p. 360).

From this perspective, narrative research is itself an ethical endeavor. It involves engagement of the researcher with the stories and practices that are studied. The vision of the good life that the stories express and the practices that they present have to be regarded as relevant not only to the people involved but also to the researcher and his or her world. This does not mean that the stories are taken at face value. Rather, the stories are evaluated as answers to the question of how to live. A narrative that offers a new view of the good life can enrich our experience and contribute to our understanding of life. A narrative about a problematic issue in health care can give us a new perspective on how to deal with health and disease. This presupposes, however, that we are able to integrate the new perspective into our own notion of the good life. Thus the interpretation of stories starts from an ethical orientation toward the good life and aims at a greater and richer understanding of what the good life might entail in concrete social and historical conditions.

A Nurse's Story Interpreted as an Expression of a Practice of Care

The story we present in this section comes out of a research project on ethical issues in the oncology ward. The study focuses on the place of ethics in the daily work of nurses. The research includes gathering stories from nurses about their own practice. The research is based on ethnographic methods. Ethnography can make us aware of ethical issues in everyday practice (see Jennings, 1989). It provides us with preunderstandings that can guide our interpretation of nurses' stories.

During a morning shift, a male nurse told the other nurses what happened between him and a patient the night before. The patient, Mrs. Rose, was 67 years old. Her husband has died and she has no children. She suffered from bone cancer in a terminal stage. She was in the hospital because she had broken her arm and was unable to take care of herself. She therefore could not return home. Mrs. Rose had agreed that the nurses apply for a place in a nursing home. She has now been 5 weeks on the cancer ward. The nurse told the following story:

> When he entered Mrs. Rose's room, she was crying. He sat
> down. He knew she felt very desperate. Several times she
> had told the nurses she did not want to live any longer. After
> a while, he asked her what was troubling her. She told him
> she was very sad and hated being unable to take care of
> herself. She had always loved to read the newspaper, and
> now she could not even read the headlines. Her head felt
> like it was filled with batting. For some time, the nurse
> talked with Mrs. Rose about her feelings. During this

conversation, he asked her cautiously if there had been a moment in her life at which she had thought about euthanasia. Mrs. Rose was relieved that he brought up the subject. She had wanted to talk about it but had not dared to do so. She said she was afraid that the staff might be shocked by the issue of euthanasia. The nurse asked her whether she wanted him to talk about it to the other nurses and to the physician. Mrs. Rose answered affirmatively. She said that she was glad that someone wanted to help her. The nurse told her that he did not know what the outcome would be but that he would start the discussion.

The story of the nurse clearly has an ethical effect. It presents the conversation as a mutual attempt to clarify the right way for Mrs. Rose to deal with her situation. The story shows how the nurse managed to make Mrs. Rose's experiences more concrete as he mentioned the issue of euthanasia. Thereby, her vague feelings of desperation were turned into a request that could be discussed further. The nurse was rather outspoken in bringing up the issue of euthanasia. The reaction of the patient proved, however, that he was not impressing the idea of euthanasia on her but helping her to express her own feelings. The story presents the nurse's actions as part of a practice: the practice of taking care of the patient (see Tronto, 1993). Taking care, however, does not mean taking over the responsibilities from the patient; it means helping the patient to formulate her needs.

Our interpretation of the nurse's story is influenced by our own ideas about the characteristics of nursing. It is guided by preunderstandings that stem from our participation in nursing activities on the ward. Our interpretation is founded on our preconception of what it is like to be a nurse in the oncology ward, a preconception that we gained through our ethnographic research. Our interpretation includes some doubts about the way in which the nurse brings up the issue of euthanasia. Is he not hurrying the patient? These doubts are also part of our preunderstanding resulting from former experiences. They make us consider the situation more carefully. In the end, however, the story convinces us that the nurse has acted in a responsive and responsible way. Thus the process of interpretation results in a fusion of horizons in which the story's view of the nurse's practice and our own view of it are merged and a new conception of care is formulated—a conception that sees care as enabling.

The Role of the Story in Nursing Practice

Participating in the ward not only enabled us to collect stories and interpret them from our own experiences of nursing practice but also made us aware of the role these stories play in the context of everyday nursing practice. Our ethnographic research made us see how nurses use stories to organize their practice in relation to other nurses, physicians, and patients. Stories not only reflect ethical practice; they also sustain and structure this practice. But to do so, they have to be convincing to others and motivate them to take part in the practice.

Nurses' stories mostly aim to engage other nurses. Thus the story of the nurse about his conversation with Mrs. Rose was directed toward the other nurses present at the morning shift, trying to make them understand Mrs. Rose's situation and urging them to joined action. In this, the story was very successful. The nurses who were present at the shift were impressed by what the nurse told them. They interpreted the story in the light of their own experiences with Mrs. Rose in the past few days. They all felt sorry for her and decided to inform the physician at once.

When the nurse told the story to the physician, his reaction was quite different. He clearly disapproved of the nurse's actions. He said that the issue of euthanasia should be something between patient and doctor. The nurse should not have been the one to take it up. Thus the story did not convince the physician that the nurse's actions had been part of a responsible practice. It did not motivate the physician to join in with the practice presented. Only reluctantly did he agree to arrange a meeting with Mrs. Rose, her brother, a nurse, and himself to discuss the matter further.

At this meeting, which took place some days later, the physician was again very hesitant to join in with the practice envisaged by the nurse. He did not go into the patient's feelings of despair but talked a long time about the history of her illness. He did not discuss the meaning of life, given the present condition of the patient, but stressed that he wanted to know whether her request for euthanasia had been made autonomously. He especially wanted to make sure that she was not suffering from a depression. He finally decided that Mrs. Rose should see a psychiatrist. During the meeting, the issues that were brought up by the nurse were put aside. The themes of care and commitment central to the nurse's story were replaced by the notions of etiology and autonomy stemming from the vocabulary of medicine and principlist medical ethics.

In the end, the nurse's story had little effect on the course of events. After 2 weeks, Mrs. Rose was moved to a nursing home without any mention of the issue of euthanasia to the nursing home staff. The nurse had been able to motivate the other nurses but he had not been able to engage the physician in the process of meaning making and care described in the story. On the contrary, the physician clearly dismissed the ethical claims inherent in the nurse's story and fully relied on the notions of traditional medical ethics. There was no sign of any encounter between the nurse's perspective presented in the story and the physician's perspective presented during the meeting. The perspectives did not meet, let alone merge into a common horizon. Thus to present ethical issues in stories and to make explicit the ethical aspects of stories through narrative research and interpretation does not in itself make narrative ethics a success in health care. As long as stories that focus on care and concern are put aside by physicians as irrelevant rather than becoming part of the discussion, the practices that these stories envisage will not get a prominent role in health care.

Conclusion

A narrative approach to ethical issues in health care focuses on the stories that the participants tell about their experiences. These stories give us insight into motives, expectations, aims, and convictions of the persons involved. A narrative can make us understand how people give meaning to a concrete situation and why they respond to it through a specific action. Narratives are not just descriptions of feelings and actions; they present these feelings and actions as part of a practice. Narratives are ethical in that they express the teleological nature of practices as endeavors that aim at a common good.

Narrative research focuses on the way in which stories express what is at stake in life. Therefore, it highlights the ethical dimension of stories. Narrative research aims to make us aware of the way in which people structure their lives by telling stories that present their actions as part of a practice striving toward a common good. These stories, however, do not speak for themselves. They need to be interpreted. In interpreting stories, we start from preconceptions about the good that is central to the practice the story is about. The process of interpretation that takes place in narrative research results in a fusion of horizons, in which the view of the good life that is expressed in the story merges with the notion of it that started of the interpretation. Thus narrative research is ethical in that it refines our view of the good life.

The story of the nurse about his conversation with Mrs. Rose gives a concrete presentation of nursing practice as an ethical endeavor characterized by care for the patient's well-being. Our interpretation of the story as an expression of a practice of care was guided by ethical preunderstandings, which we acquired through ethnographic research on the ward. The interpretation led to a specification of our conception of care emphasizing the response of the patient. From a nursing ethics perspective, both the story and the effect it had on the daily practice on the oncology ward are significant. The story presents a practice that is guided by an ethic of care. The response of the other nurses makes clear that the practice that is expressed in the story is a common endeavor shared by all of the nurses. The reaction of the physician and the outcome of the meeting, however, show that a practice that is founded on care and concern is not easily integrated into a health care system in which principle-oriented medical ethics is still dominant.

References

Beauchamp, T. L., & Childress, J. F. (1994). *Principles of biomedical ethics.* Oxford, UK: Oxford University Press.

Benner, P. (1991). The role of experience, narrative, and community in skilled ethical comportment. *Advances in Nursing Science, 14*(2), 1-21.

Cooper, M. C. (1991). Principle-oriented ethics and the ethic of care: A creative tension. *Advances in Nursing Science, 14*(2), 22-31.

Gadamer, H.-G. (1960). *Wahrheit und methode* [Truth and method]. Tübingen, Federal Republic of Germany: J. C. B. Mohr.

Jennings, B. (1989). Ethics and ethnography in neonatal intensive care. In G. Weisz (Ed.), *Social science perspectives on medical ethics* (pp. 261-272). Philadelphia: University of Pennsylvania Press.

Merleau-Ponty, M. (1945). *Phénoménologie de la perception* [Phenomenology of perception]. Paris: Gallimard.

Nussbaum, M. C. (1986). *The fragility of goodness: Luck and ethics in Greek tragedy and philosophy.* Cambridge, UK: Cambridge University Press.

Parker, R. S. (1990). Nurses' stories: The search for a relational ethic of care. *Advances in Nursing Science, 13*(1), 31-40.

Ricoeur, P. (1990). *Soi-même comme un autre* [The self as an other]. Paris: Editions du Seuil.

Tronto, J. C. (1993). *Moral boundaries: A political argument for an ethic of care.* New York: Routledge.

Widdershoven, G. A. M. (1993). The story of life: Hermeneutic perspectives on the relation between narrative and life history. In R. Josselson & A. Lieblich (Eds.), *The narrative study of lives* (Vol. 1, pp. 1-20). Newbury Park, CA: Sage.

About the Contributors

Gail Agronick is a doctoral candidate in the Personality Psychology Program at the University of California, Berkeley. Her work on adult development examines the influence of social change on individual lives and the narrative sense of self. She has a long-standing interest in the sociology of science and the ethics of psychological inquiry.

Terri Apter is a Fellow of Clare Hall, University of Cambridge. She received her PhD from the University of Cambridge. She has written extensively on girls' and women's psychological and social development. Her book *Altered Loves: Mothers and Daughters During Adolescence* highlights the way apparently rebellious teenage girls work to maintain relationships with their mothers. Her most recent book is *Secret Paths: Women in the New Midlife.*

David Bakan is Professor of Psychology Emeritus at York University in Toronto. He has written extensively on the history, theory, and methods of research in psychology. His earlier work, *On Method,* contained a critique of statistical and experimental methods. His most recent work is *Maimonides on Prophecy,* exploring Maimonides's notions of ways of knowing—particularly his notions of prophetic and kabbalistic ways of knowing and, most particularly, his notions of the role of both reason and imagination in such knowing.

Dan Bar-On is Professor of Psychology and Chair of the Department of Behavioral Sciences at Ben-Gurion University of the Negev. He received his PhD at the Hebrew University of Jerusalem. His research has included subjective theories of male patients who had had a first heart attack and quality of life issues for high blood pressure patients. His books *Legacy of Silence: Encounters With Children of the Third Reich* and *Fear and Hope: Three Generations of Holocaust Survivors' Families* draw from his pioneering field research in Germany and his ongoing effort to understand the aftermath and transgenerational effects of the Holocaust on both Germans and Jews.

Yoram Bilu has a joint appointment in the Department of Psychology and the Department of Sociology and Anthropology at the Hebrew University of Jerusalem. His publications deal with folk religion, ethnopsychiatry, and dreams and culture, mainly among Moroccan Jews in Israel.

Susan E. Chase is Associate Professor of Sociology and cofounder of the Women's Studies Program at the University of Tulsa, Oklahoma. She is currently studying university students' ways of understanding race, gender, and sexual orientation.

Gwendolyn Etter-Lewis is Associate Professor of English at Western Michigan University. She earned a PhD in linguistics from the University of Michigan and specializes in women's oral narratives. She is the recipient of numerous honors and awards, including a Fulbright research fellowship based at the University of Zambia, Institute for African Studies. She is the author of, among others, *My Soul Is My Own: Oral Narratives of African American Women* and coeditor of *Unrelated Kin: Race and Gender in Women's Personal Narratives*.

Pirkko Lauslahti Graves received her doctorate in psychology from the University of Michigan and her psychoanalytic training from the Washington Psychoanalytic Institute, where she is Supervising and Training Analyst. In addition to her private practice in psychotherapy and psychoanalysis in Baltimore, Maryland, she is also involved in epidemiologic research as Senior Research Psychologist at the Precursors Study, The Johns Hopkins University School of Medicine. She has published extensively in the fields of psychoanalysis and epidemiologic studies.

Emanuela Guano is a doctoral candidate at the Department of Anthropology of the University of Texas at Austin. She is currently investigating the construction of identity in Argentine public culture.

Ravenna Helson is Research Psychologist at the Institute of Personality and Social Research and Adjunct Professor, Department of Psychology, at the University of California, Berkeley. She began the Mills Longitudinal Study in 1957, when the first participants began their senior year in college. She has studied stories of authors of imaginative literature in relation to their lives (e.g., "E. Nesbit's 41st Year: Her Life, Times and Symbolization" in *Imagination, Cognition, and Personality,* 1984) and, with members of her research team, has written several articles using narrative techniques to study women's adult development (e.g., "Lives of Women Who Became Autonomous" in the *Journal of Personality,* 1985).

Ruthellen Josselson is Professor of Psychology at Towson State University. Recipient of the APA Henry A. Murray Award (1994) and a Fulbright Research Fellowship (1989-1990), she has also recently been Visiting Professor at the Harvard Graduate School of Education and Forchheimer Professor of Psychology at the Hebrew University in Jerusalem. She is author of *Finding Herself: Pathways to Identity Development in Women* and *The Space Between Us: Exploring the Dimensions of Human Relationships.*

Amia Lieblich is Professor of Psychology at the Hebrew University of Jerusalem, where she served as chairperson from 1982 to 1985. Her books have presented an oral history of Israeli society, dealing with war and POWs, and military service and the kibbutz. Recently she has published two psychobiographies of female writers: *Embroideries* (about Dvora Baron) and *Towards Lea* (about Lea Goldberg).

Edna Lomsky-Feder completed her PhD in 1994 in the Department of Sociology and Anthropology at the Hebrew University of Jerusalem, where she is now a postdoctoral fellow. Her PhD thesis was about the meaning of the war experience among Israeli veterans. Her current research focuses on the experience of immigration among individuals from the former Soviet Union.

Melvin E. Miller has been interested in philosophy, narrative, and the creation of meaning for most of his life. His longitudinal research on the development of worldviews naturally evolved from such interests. He received the PhD from the University of Pittsburgh. He is Professor of Psychology and Director of Psychological Services at Norwich University. Among his publications is *Transcendence and Mature Thought in Adulthood: The Further Reaches of Adult Development,* coedited with Susanne Cook-Greuter. He has been very active in organizing and promoting the Society for Research in Adult Development.

Richard L. Ochberg is Assistant Professor of Psychology at the University of Massachusetts–Boston. He coedited *Storied Lives: The Cultural Politics of Self-Understanding* (with George Rosenwald) and *Psychology and Life Narratives* (with Dan McAdams), and he is the author of *Middle-Aged Sons and the Meaning of Work.* His interest is in careers and identity. He is currently studying how academic ambition estranges some working-class students from their families.

June Price is a doctoral candidate at New York University, Division of Nursing, and a clinical specialist in child psychiatry at New York Hospital-Cornell Medical Center. From 1981 to 1992, she was Director of Community Services at Manhattan Children's Psychiatric Center, New York City.

George C. Rosenwald received his doctorate from Yale University. He is a Professor of Personality and Clinical Psychology at the University of Michigan and a psychotherapist in private practice. He recently coedited (with Richard Ochberg) *Storied Lives: The Cultural Politics* *of Self-Understanding* as part of a larger interest in the political conditions of individual and social development.

Marie-Josée Smits is a doctoral candidate and researcher at the Department of Health Ethics and Philosophy at the Rijksuniversiteit Limburg in Maastricht, the Netherlands. She is a nurse and has studied nursing sciences and theory of health sciences. She is pursuing ethnographic research on ethics and care for oncology patients, with special emphasis on care ethics.

Scott W. Webster is a Phi Beta Kappa graduate of Gettysburg College. He holds a master's degree in history and is presently pursuing a PhD at the University of Maryland at College Park. A former James A. Finnegan Foundation Fellow who has served as an editorial assistant to the *Pennsylvania History* and *Maryland Historian* journals, he works at the University of Maryland's Center for Political Leadership & Participation where he is assisting James MacGregor Burns and Georgia J. Sorenson on their forthcoming book on leadership in the Clinton White House.

Guy A. M. Widdershoven is Professor and Head of the Department of Health Ethics and Philosophy of the Rijksuniversiteit Limburg in Maastricht, the Netherlands. He has written various articles and edited a number of books on philosophical hermeneutics and its relevance for the humanities. Currently, he is pursuing theoretical and empirical research on the place of ethics in health care.